MW00909975

COMPUTERS

THE PLAIN ENGLISH GUIDE

Almost everything you need to know about computers, even if you don't know ANYTHING about computers.

Phillip A. Covington

ILLUSTRATED EDITION

Computers: The Plain English Guide

Copyright © 1991 By Phillip A. Covington

THIRD EDITION

FIRST EDITION/FIRST PRINTING - 1988

All rights reserved. No part of this work may be reproduced, or transmitted in any form, or by any means, electronic or mechanical, including photocopying and recording, or by any information storage or retrieval system, without prior written permission from the publisher. Request for permission should be addressed in writing to QNS Publishing, P.O. Box 821, Jackson, Michigan 49204-0821.

Library of Congress Catalog Card Number: 88-92376

ISBN 0-942059-01-8

Printed and bound in the United States of America.

This publication may be purchased in bookstores, or directly from QNS Publishing by calling 1-800-QNS-TODAY (767-8632).

Additional copies may also be obtained by sending a check or money order for $19.95 plus $3.00 for shipping and handling (per copy) to QNS Publishing, P.O. Box 821, Jackson, Michigan 49204-0821.

Quantity discounts are available. For more information please call (517) 784-5550 or write to us at the address above.

Credits

Editor—
James M. Ethridge

Illustrations and artwork—
Paul Nelson
Grand Rapids, Michigan

Cover layout—
The Electronic Publishing Center
Grand Rapids, Michigan

Cover artwork—
Village Graphics
Richland, Michigan

Preface

If you have ever wanted simple answers to your questions about computers, this book is for you. **Computers: The Plain English Guide** does not require you to have any knowledge of computers to start. After reading it, however, you will be armed with useful information about almost every aspect of computing you are likely to encounter in your day-to-day conversation or use of computers. Naturally, skill comes only with experience, but the information in this book will put you far ahead of most beginning and intermediate level computer users in understanding how and why computers work the way they do. It covers the how and why of each topic discussed, and in many cases gives an explanation of how certain features of computers came about. No other single book offers as much convenient, basic, and practical information for the uninformed as **Computers: The Plain English Guide**.

This book is ideal for managers, teachers, students, office workers, business owners, and many others. It is adaptable to self-study, corporate training, introductory courses in high school or college, and other uses. Review the table of contents and you will find many topics of interest—each clearly explained. Just the sections on making computer-related purchases can save you many hundreds or even thousands of dollars, not to mention sparing you the headaches of making uninformed decisions.

The author, a computer buff for over 20 years, owned and operated many computers for his own personal or business needs during that time, and experienced first-hand the frustrations that can arise. Especially in the early days of computing, at times it seemed there were more problems than solutions. Salespeople were often untrained and couldn't answer important questions that would help the prospective purchaser. Those "in-the-know" were often at the other end of the extreme, seemingly able to provide answers only understandable by a computer-science engineer with a Ph.D. Virtually all of the computer books on the market seemed to take the same approach, again leaving the uninitiated with few places to turn for help. Many people bought computers only to find that no programs were available to fit their needs. Yet others were greatly disappointed to learn that the system they purchased didn't suit their needs at all. School teachers, managers, and business owners felt equally frustrated because they were often not informed enough to provide answers and solutions for the computer users they were responsible for.

Both then and now an increasing number of people are under pressure to keep up with technology as the work-place computerizes.

As a former consultant the author specialized in introducing computer systems to small and medium-sized organizations. He often worked with people who, like those just described, felt frustrated, intimidated, or had even given up in their attempt to find simple, easy-to-understand answers to their questions about computers. To better serve these and other computer users, he set out to develop a pamphlet that would answer the most commonly asked questions. What was intended to be a small "pamphlet" turned into a major project as it became apparent that people were literally desperate for information about computers that anybody could understand. Not just kindergarten level basics that leave the reader with little more knowledge than how to turn on a computer, but truly useful information that would help them on a daily basis, and for years to come. The end result was a small spiral bound publication with no illustrations.

The response to that first edition was overwhelmingly positive, and confirmed that people were searching for an easy-to-understand and convenient way to learn more about computers. In this new edition we try to do an even better job of helping you accomplish that goal. Large easy-to-understand illustrations and diagrams help give you a clearer picture of many of the topics discussed. New material and a number of new chapters have been added to make sure you'll have up-to-date information on the rapidly changing technology of computers.

There are many good computer publications available, but almost all of them assume that readers already know a lot about computers. Some publications are easy to understand, but cover only one topic—word processing, spreadsheets, etc.—not the wide-ranging kind of information you are likely to need in real day-to-day situations. **Computers: The Plain English Guide** puts it all together in one simple book. We are sure that as thousands of others have, you will find this book to be one of the best investments you've ever made.

This edition of **Computers: The Plain English Guide** has drawn heavily upon comments from readers to make it even more comprehensive and helpful. If you have comments or suggestions we would like to hear from you.

Notes About Reading This Book

Computers: The Plain English Guide is intended to be a first source of information for anyone who wants to begin building computer competence. The book provides general but comprehensive information about the principles upon which all computers operate. Because the IBM-PC and similar microcomputers have established themselves as a virtual standard for small computer systems—and are usually the first equipment you will encounter—this book gives special attention to how computer principles are utilized in such machines. The information in this book is carefully presented so that it will also be useful if you are dealing with other types of equipment, including home computers, mainframes, minicomputers, terminals, workstations, and older computers.

You'll never run into a term that isn't clearly explained, and new information is usually introduced in such a way as to build upon knowledge gained in previous chapters. Those entirely unfamiliar with computers are encouraged to read through the whole book at least once to develop a good understanding of the topics being discussed. More experienced readers will find the book useful as a reference or resource book because its format makes browsing or looking up a single topic equally simple.

The first time a new word or term is explained, or in places where it is being reintroduced in a new context, it appears in **BOLD PRINT** and capital letters. If there are additional references to a subject elsewhere in the book they can easily be located by using the index. Many topics are cross referenced within the text for added convenience. Subchapter titles are bold and large, making it easy to find discussions of specific topics. A brief list of resources also appears at the end of the book to help direct you to useful products and services.

After reading **Computers: The Plain English Guide** you will be able to better understand the more advanced books and publications available about computers, as well as situations you are likely to face in your own work-place or home. Along the way, just remember, "There is nothing mysterious about computers. There are only people or publications that make them seem so!"

Table of Contents

Table of Contents

Chapter 3

A GUIDE TO CLASSIFYING COMPUTERS BY TYPE 45

Chapter 4

COMPUTER HARDWARE 51

Chapter 5

SOFTWARE 81

Chapter 6

Chapter 7

Chapter 8

Chapter 9

Table of Contents

Chapter 1

GETTING STARTED

Many tasks have a way of seeming to overwhelm us at first—almost like the way you may feel when faced with an enormous stack of laundry or dishes to do, or the bathroom needs to be cleaned, or the grass is so high that your lawn is starting to look like the Amazon jungle! Spring cleaning is another chore that tops few people's lists of favorite things to do on a warm sunny afternoon. But these tasks all share two things: You always feel better when they are finally done, and things always seem to go much faster if you break the work down into little pieces that are easier to handle. The same approach applies equally well to learning about computers, and that's what this book is all about.

The brief chapter which follows covers some very basic ground you must travel on your way to becoming an experienced computer user. It will answer some of your questions about computers while providing a little reassurance in the process. Like the first chapter, those which follow break things down into "bite-sized" chunks which are easy to read and digest. Each new section, however, covers new ground and takes you closer to a working knowledge of computers. When you've completed this book and see just how useful computers can be, and how easy it was to learn about them, you'll have that very special feeling of accomplishment that makes it all worthwhile!

WHAT IF YOU FEEL THREATENED BY COMPUTERS?

If one of your reasons for purchasing this book was because you find computers intimidating, this first chapter will help put the subject into better perspective and go a long way toward making the experience of learning about computers a painless one.

Let's start by considering what may seem like a silly question: people have spent a lot of time worrying about computers, but how much time do you think computers have spent worrying about people? The obvious answer, of course, is absolutely none! Computers can't think, at least not the way people do. So while millions of people are worrying about the impact of computers, computers quietly go on doing what they've been doing since they were invented, totally oblivious to the fears people have about using them.

The most important point to keep in mind is that computers are designed to be used by people. They are simply tools—just like screwdrivers, wrenches, adding machines, and typewriters. Computers are more complex than most other tools, but because of this complexity they are infinitely more versatile and useful than any combination of other equipment you could imagine. In the same way that other tools help you in countless ways to do things you could already do yourself, but help you do them faster and better, a computer can take the drudgery out of routine tasks and make life easier for you in the process. Computers still can't help you take out the trash, but then you don't have to worry about waking up tomorrow and finding that one has taken your place, either! Like any other tool, without people like you and me to actually put them to use, computers would be entirely useless.

And just look at some of the advantages people have over computers. People can think independently, develop creative solutions, and head off problems before they arise. A computer is unable to do any of these things because it can only do what it has been instructed (programmed) to do. Let's take a grocery store checkout lane, for example: while computers do a great job of automatically reading prices and totaling sales slips, what happens when you get to an item that lacks the specially coded label the cash register reads to obtain the item's description and price? What if the label is torn, damaged, or smeared with ink, or someone forgets that he or she has a large box of laundry detergent in the bottom of the shopping cart? Even

3

the best of computers are unable to handle situations like these. A store employee, however, can easily deal with these situations and many more like them while keeping the checkout line moving.

It is understandable that you might still feel threatened, however. Computers are invading nearly every area of life, and such phenomena as computer "viruses" that disable entire computer networks serving defense, scientific research, and business give everyone the eerie feeling that "we" aren't really in control any longer.

Certainly, when you are trapped in the maze of an electronic telephone answering system—"If you want this, press 1, if you want that press 2...," and what you really want is something else—or when you want to talk to "a real person" and all your bank provides is a computer voice telling you that you have a negative balance, the intimidation and frustration can be intense. It is important to keep in mind, however, that, on the whole, computers have improved countless areas of life in ways that would have been impossible without these electronic helpers.

Still feeling a little threatened? Well, what else is there to be afraid of? Three of the things people fear most are: loss of life, loss of love, and the unknown. Other than in the unlikely event someone should throw a computer at you, or you drop one on your big toe, we can pretty much eliminate the first fear. As for the second fear, while it is true that some people spend large amounts of time with computers, I've never heard of someone falling in love with one, or a computer stealing someone's boyfriend, girlfriend, husband or wife; of course, there's always a first time for everything! Lastly, we have the fear of the unknown, or of change. Change is unavoidable, since without change there can be no progress. The unknown and change go hand-in-hand because change always brings with it new things to learn, and unknown ground to cover. These two fears probably keep more people from doing more things than all other fears and excuses combined. This really just amounts to a lack of information about what we are afraid of.

As a child, you may have been afraid of the dark because you didn't know what was there when the lights were turned out. And few of us grew up without hearing at least an occasional story that caused bedtime shivers. The only reason you aren't afraid of the dark now is because you're armed with more information. The more you know about something—an unfamiliar subject, using a new gadget, etc.—the more comfortable you become with it. In the same way, by equipping yourself with a greater knowledge and understanding of computers and how you can benefit by

4

using them, you will also eliminate your reasons for feeling threatened. You might still be thinking, "that all sounds good, but a computer could edge me out of my job, and that's a real threat." Granted, if a computer could take your place that would be a real threat. But really, could a computer do all of the many things you do, as well as you do them?

In reality, computerization only helps people do what they've already been doing, in a more efficient way, and it has been brought about through the efforts of people who once knew no more about computers than you do now. The real threat to you is that people who make better use of computers than you do—whether at work, in school, or at home—will probably get ahead faster, and, of course, you can't blame that on a computer. Whether computers are involved or not, as with almost everything else in life, the people who better prepare and equip themselves for the task at hand will always be the ones who excel.

COMPUTERESE

Whether in hobbies or in business, most activities seem to have their own specialized language. For many of us these words can often be unfamiliar, confusing, or even intimidating. At the same time, it would be hard to get along without such words—what else would you call a home run in baseball, for instance? Or, how could you tell a cook to let a mixture simmer if there wasn't a special word for it? Similarly, a variety of unique words and terms have been adopted for describing computers and their related parts. Many of the components which go together to make up a computer system could not be easily described, if at all, unless special terms were used. Fortunately, a relatively small vocabulary of such terms will allow you to learn about, understand, and use computers, as well as carry on a reasonable conversation about them.

Words describing computers are usually acronyms; some are abbreviations. For instance, **RAM** is an acronym for **RANDOM ACCESS MEMORY**, and **Ctrl** is an abbreviation for the **CONTROL KEY** on the keyboard. Some of the easiest terms to learn are those formed by making compound words. You'll have to ignore the fact that some of these words would normally be considered misspelled or improper English. Aside from descriptive terms, another reason compound words are used so often is because of the way most computer files must be named. Unlike a manual filing system on which you can write anything that will fit on the folder, computers all have rules as to how a filename is written. (Notice that before computers were commonplace, "filename" would probably have been written "file name.") Many computer programs do not allow filenames to start with anything but a letter of the alphabet. Most also limit the length of the filename, and prohibit it from containing blank spaces. MS-DOS (an operating system which will be explained shortly), for instance, limits filenames to 8 characters in length. So, with MS-DOS, "PERTAXES," "DIETMEAL," and "MEDREC," would be valid filenames, while "PERSONAL TAXES," "DIET_MEALS," and "MEDICAL RECORDS" would be invalid. As you can see, just a few rules like these could encourage the making of many new words. (Note: Because most software does not allow a filename to contain spaces the underscore "_" is used instead.)

TYPING ABILITY

You should have at least some basic typing skills to use a computer to maximum advantage. This is not to say that if you don't know how to type you should give up on the idea of using a computer. In fact, some computer programs can be operated very effectively with only one finger. A few—like drawing programs—don't require the use of the keyboard at all! However, as it was with most new things you have learned, you'll find that as your typing skill increases so will the ease and satisfaction with which your work on a computer is completed.

If you have never used a computer, but you do know how to type, you're in for a surprise. No matter how fast you type now you will probably be able to increase your typing speed as soon as you start using a computer! Why? Because you will be less concerned about making mistakes. Even if the typewriter you've been using is of the modern electronic variety, mistakes—sometimes even simple ones—can take a lot of time to correct. On the other hand, you will seldom make a typing mistake on a computer that isn't easily, if not instantly, correctable, and this gives you more confidence and freedom to concentrate on doing the job. Most good computer programs include features that help you avoid making mistakes; some even help you correct a mistake after it has been made.

7

If you're using a computer at work where a lot of typing is required, your employer will judge your work based not only upon the job you do, but also on how fast you do it. If you're a student, your teacher will expect the papers you turn in to be neatly and accurately typed. Whatever you use a computer for, you can probably do it better, and faster, if you know how to type. One last thing to consider: handwriting is becoming all but extinct in the modern world. If you don't know how already, you'll find that learning how to type was one of the best investments of time that you've ever made. If you happen to learn how to type on a computer keyboard, then so much the better!

There are many ways you can learn in your spare time. Typing courses are usually available through local school or community education programs; many are free of charge. Software programs that teach you how to type are also available for most computers. Department and toy stores also offer a battery-operated typing instructor that you can use to learn at home. If your need for better typing skills is work related you may wish to check with your employer. Many companies are eager to help employees who want to improve. Some will set up an in-office instruction program or pay your tuition for an outside typing course.

COMPUTER CLASSES AND INSTRUCTION

You may decide that you want to take classes in order to learn more about computers or a specific software program. If so, there is an enormous variety of instruction available— through classes at local schools, computer dealers, and, sometimes, the makers of the equipment and/or programs you will be using.

If you want to learn more about computers—the equipment—an introduction to computers course will probably provide you with the greatest knowledge, in the shortest period of time, for the least money spent. Often such courses are offered free, on a limited basis, by local computer dealers or public schools. Make sure the course offers hands-on experience with computers and software programs. Intro courses allow you to become more comfortable and knowledgeable about computers, but usually do not leave you with a proficiency in operating any given program, such as a word processor, spreadsheet, etc.

Aside from intro-type courses, you may wish to obtain instruction for the specific software program you will be using. Computer stores often offer courses on specific software programs that they sell, and in the case of a hard-to-find or unusual

8

program, they may be the only ones in the area who are familiar with it. Instructional material may also be available directly from the publishers of the software, such as the workbook that accompanies the popular WordPerfect word processing software. If it is an extremely popular program, like WordPerfect, Lotus 1-2-3 (the spreadsheet), etc., you may find that courses are also offered through local schools or colleges. However, it is unlikely you will find such courses for a large variety of software. There are so many thousands of software programs available that it would be impossible for schools, or computer dealers, to offer a course for each one.

For those who are more serious about the study of a specific area, courses in database management, computer-aided drawing (CAD), programming, etc., are almost always available through local colleges and community education programs. People often take these courses because they relate to their use of computers at work. If you take one of these more serious courses just for your personal satisfaction, you should keep in mind that if you don't put to use what you learn—on the job, your own computer at home, etc.—your newly acquired skills may quickly diminish or be forgotten. It can be difficult trying to remember how to use a software program, especially a complex one, that you don't have reason to use very often.

If you are buying a computer, or software, or both, instruction may be offered free with your purchase, although what sometimes appears to be "free" has simply been included in, or added to, the purchase price. In any case, if you feel you will need instruction you can always try to negotiate it into your software purchases. It never hurts to ask, and you may end up getting extra value that would not have been included otherwise. If your need for better computer skills is work related, you may wish to check with your employer; many are eager to help employees who want to improve. Some employers will, or already have, set up in-office computer training programs. If not, your employer may be willing to pay your tuition cost for taking outside instruction.

Just one caution about obtaining instruction: Many people have invested their time and paid tuition to obtain training for themselves or their employees—only to find out afterward that it was either the wrong training, or altogether unnecessary for their application. Some software programs are easy to use or can be learned easily from the instructional materials included with the package, or provided as a part of the purchase. All but the most common and popular programs each contain their own unique features. Thus, training received on how to operate accounting programs, for instance, might prove to be useless with your system because even though it is an accounting program its design could be entirely different than the system that you used in training.

Unless you are certain that the training received will directly apply to the system you will be using, about the only instruction sure to provide you with usable information beforehand is an introduction to computers or a typing course. Once you have actually obtained, or started using, a specific system you will be in a much better position to determine whether additional training might benefit you.

THE LEARNING PROCESS

This is just a gentle reminder that learning to use a computer is not a spectator sport. No matter how much you read, who you talk to, or how many classes you take, you won't begin to learn and fully appreciate the capabilities of computers until you have used one. Whenever possible, the best place to learn is with a computer—and any other necessary hardware or software—available to you so that you can see and do as you learn.

LOOK BEFORE YOU LEAP

When you first start working with a new computer or software product, you will most likely be anxious to use it. Keep in mind, however, that while there is nothing wrong with fast learning—hastily made decisions, or doing something before you are familiar with the steps involved, may backfire. The instruction manuals and training materials provided with most systems can help you avoid frustrating and costly mistakes. It is a good idea to completely familiarize yourself with the instructions (or take any required training) before operating a computer system that is new to you. Since computers first became widely available, great progress has been made in making them easier to use, but they are still far from foolproof. Plugging in the wrong cables—or even plugging the right cables into the wrong place—can damage delicate circuits. A wrong button inadvertently or carelessly pushed may cause something you'll wish you hadn't. By taking things one-step-at-a-time you will not only learn at a much more relaxed pace, but will better understand how to get the most from your computer system along the way.

Chapter 2

HOW COMPUTERS WORK:
THE INSIDE STORY

Did you ever stop to think that magicians have one of the strangest jobs in the world? They actually get paid to confuse people! They entertain their audience by performing many tricks so fast that no one has a chance to see how it is really done. But if they didn't closely guard the "secret" of how each trick is engineered the mystery would be gone. People would know that, as complex and astounding as the tricks appear, they are only a series of steps for the magician to follow.

Like many other things in life, computers seem complex only when looked at as a whole. As you are about to see, many of the parts that together make up a computer system are really not very complex or mysterious after all.

The goal of this chapter and those that follow is to provide you with enough information about the parts of a computer system for you to have a truly usable understanding of computers and how they work. Instead of just giving "stand-alone" definitions like those found in dictionaries or glossaries, wherever possible each term or concept is introduced after previous examples have helped you gain a better understanding of the new topic being discussed. And, when more involved topics are explained, every effort is made not to weigh you down with material you are unlikely to have a use for. This chapter will not only give you the understanding needed for topics covered in later chapters, but, regardless of how much computer technology advances, will provide you with a strong foundation of computer literacy upon which you can build in the years ahead.

11

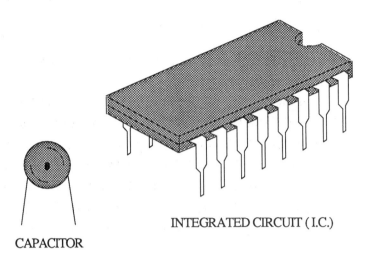

INTEGRATED CIRCUIT (I.C.)

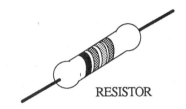

CAPACITOR

RESISTOR

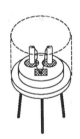

TRANSISTOR

The Evolution of Electronics
From the Vacuum Tube to the modern day I.C.

(Components are not necessarily drawn to scale)

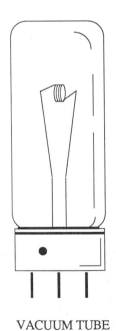

VACUUM TUBE

12

WHERE IT ALL STARTED

In the beginning, there was the vacuum tube—or at least for all practical purposes that's where the modern computer got its start. If you're old enough you've probably had personal experience with these now almost-extinct technological wonders. They look like an odd sort of clear light bulb that glows in the dark. So fascinated were people by vacuum tubes that when they first became common people would often gaze into the backs of their radios, and later, their TV sets, wondering how the softly glowing tubes made them work.

Movie and TV producers cashed in on the public's fascination by making sure plenty of vacuum tubes appeared in the strange contraptions they used in their science fiction productions. Why was there so much fuss over vacuum tubes? Because without them modern technology as it was known then and as it exists today, including the computer, would probably not have been possible. What is now taken for granted, but was not so simple before the vacuum tube, is the ability to control electricity. Not just turning it on and off as a light switch does, but making it behave in special ways, or like flowing in one direction but not the other, or being allowed to flow through one wire or circuit at a different rate than another. The vacuum tube, also known as the electron tube, made many of these things possible because it has the interesting ability to control the way electricity passes through it.

By combining vacuum tubes with other electronic components (resistors, capacitors, etc.) you can assemble almost any device—an amplifier, radio, TV set, even a computer. Many early computers were actually built using vacuum tubes. However, because tubes often burned out they simply weren't reliable enough for a device as demanding as a computer. For some large computers there were people whose only job was to constantly look for and replace tubes that burned out. Even when working, vacuum tubes were bulky and inefficient; they used large amounts of electricity and gave off a lot of heat in the process. Then came the invention of the transistor, which does the same job, better, in less space, and uses less electricity.

In the years following the introduction of the transistor, that remarkable device was multiplied, modified, and miniaturized to produce even more efficient and varied devices, in the form of new generations of **MICROCHIPS** (also called just **CHIPS**); the more specialized **INTEGRATED CIRCUIT** (IC) chips; and the ICs used in computers which are more commonly known as **MICROPROCESSORS**. Today such devices allow almost anything electronic to be made extremely compact, to have a low demand for electricity, and in many cases—including computers—to be efficient enough to be operated on batteries. The low-cost mass production of electronic devices has brought them within the reach of almost any business or home. Despite the decreased size and increased sophistication of modern devices, however, the resistors, transistors, microchips, and other components used in their construction still perform basically the same functions as the vacuum tube, somehow altering or modifying—and thereby controlling—the behavior of electricity. By monitoring and interpreting these controlled patterns of electricity, computers are able to perform complex, almost magical, feats.

You may be surprised to find, therefore, just how simple the world inside a computer really is, for the most powerful of these electrical characteristics on which the computer is based is no more difficult to explain than a household light switch!

ONES AND ZEROS: THE LANGUAGE OF COMPUTERS

Computers perform the many things they do based solely upon whether tiny electrical "switches" are turned on or off, assigning the number 1 to switches that are turned on and the number 0 to those which are off. Computers really are not as smart as most people believe; in fact, they are far dumber than you or I. Internally a computer is incapable of understanding the words and numbers you type into it; it cannot even tell the difference between the letter *A*, and the letter *B*. It cannot think on its own, or do anything unless it is told (programmed or instructed) to do so by someone like you. Even then, when you type instructions into a computer—or watch its response—everything going on inside is still based upon the same simple system of 1s and 0s.

People have many wonderful abilities that we all take for granted, but have you ever stopped to think of all the things that must take place for us to do even something simple like riding a bicycle, driving a car, or reading this book? Your brain has to convert the light it receives from your eyes into images you can understand. It has to calculate the exact distances you should move your arms, legs, feet, and hands to steer the car or bicycle, or to turn a page without tearing it. If you are playing tennis your brain must calculate exactly where you will have to be to hit the ball, how hard, and at what angle. The brain has to do all of these things at the same time, at lightning speed, with accuracy. Yet, while all of this is going on you still have the ability to be thinking about something else, or daydreaming!

Even sophisticated computers cannot do most of these things. But they do have a number of useful advantages, including speed and accuracy. Computers can do many things infinitely faster than people, and make no mistakes in the process. Likewise, the jobs computers do best are those which require a great number of repetitive actions, a great deal of accuracy, or both. No doubt you are still wondering how a computer can do anything at all if it can only recognize the numbers 1 and 0. The answer is that the computer functions using a method known as the **BINARY SYSTEM**.

THE BINARY SYSTEM

The term **BINARY** is derived from the prefix *bi*, meaning two, or composed of two parts. In a rough sense, anything that can only have two states or conditions—such as on or off, and 1 or 0—can probably be considered a binary system. The light switches in your home could be considered a binary system because a light bulb can only be on or off. While the binary system is foreign to many people, a system based only upon 1 and 0 would have to be simple, and that's just what computers have to be on the inside in order to work.

Think about how long it took you to learn the alphabet when you were a child, and how to put those letters together to form words and sentences. A comparable amount of time was probably required to learn about numbers and math. On the other hand, how much easier would it have been if you had had only two things to learn: 1 and 0? The answer, of course, is *MUCH EASIER*! That is why computers were designed to use only 1s and 0s. They can't do the things that people do, but they can use electricity. Computers can also tell whether or not an electrical switch is on or off, and because on and off can also be represented by 1 and 0, it was the easiest possible solution.

1s and 0s are easier to write than many symbols, and take up very little space. Math is greatly simplified—although more time consuming—because you never have to work with more than two numbers. It's all really just a matter of what you are accustomed to. For instance, most of us have heard of the metric system, but in this country people are more familiar with using whole decimal numbers and fractions to represent weights, distances, and to measure. Even so, the metric system works, and is actually a much easier way of representing weights and measures. The same is true of the binary system of 1s and 0s being an easier numbering method to use with computers, even though many people are unfamiliar with it. By the way, you'll find that terms of measurement from the metric system are often used when talking about computers—kilobytes, milliseconds, etc.

Any new system or method of doing things may seem strange until you develop a better understanding of it. We are comfortable with a system based upon 10 numbers only because it is so familiar. If we had one more finger on each hand, the chances are we would instead be comfortable with a number system based upon 12—kind of the same way a foot is 12 inches in length because that was actually the length of someone's foot.

In the 2-based binary system, things are represented differently from what you are used to with the 10-based decimal system. Everything is based upon the number 2, and multiples of the number 2. You will never see, however, a binary number represented as a single digit all by itself; the number 1 in binary, for instance, would actually be expressed as 00000001. The number 1 still means 1, and the same is true of 0, but, in order to make things easier when working with computers, binary numbers are always grouped into 8-digit blocks known as **WORDS**, even though they contain no letters. A binary word is simply a group of so many 1s and 0s. Theoretically, there is no limit to the size of a word, although it must always be based upon the number 2 and multiples of 2: 2, 4, 6, 8, 16, 32, and so on. There is also no such thing as a binary word made up of an odd number of 1s or 0s such as 1, 101, 11101, etc.

As you will soon see, there has to be a way for these groups of 1s and 0s to represent numbers larger than themselves, as well as letters of the alphabet and the other characters and symbols needed to make a computer work. Because 1 and 0 can be used to represent more than just numbers, another name has been given to them. Where the inner workings of computers are concerned, a 1 or a 0 is instead referred to as a **BIT**, short for **BINARY DIGIT**. A bit can be used to make up a binary word, and as mentioned earlier, is better thought of as simply being on or off. The computer looks at a bit no differently than you do a light bulb: either it's on or it's off; it can be in only one of these two **STATES**. The **STATE** of a bit is also referred to as being either **TRUE** or **FALSE**. To summarize, the state of a bit that is represented by the digit 1 is referred to as being *on*, or *true*, while a bit that is represented by the digit 0 is considered to be *off*, or *false*.

Because computer words can, theoretically, be any size (8, 16, or 32 bits long, etc.), another term, **BYTE**, was decided upon to refer to the standard grouping of 8 bits that may be strung together to form a **WORD**; both contain 8 bits. Words larger than 8 bits are always divided into bytes. An 8-bit word can hold 1 byte of information (i.e., 1 character or space), while a 16-bit word holds 2 bytes and a 32-bit word is 4 bytes long. The memory capacity of computer devices is also always described in bytes. It takes 1 byte to store the letter *A*, for instance, while the word *money* takes up 5 bytes—1 byte for each letter or character. To make large amounts of memory easy to describe, thousands of bytes of memory are described as **KILOBYTES**, while millions are referred to as **MEGABYTES**. Kilobytes is usually abbreviated to just the letter *K* following the number of bytes—640,000 bytes would more commonly appear as 640K. Megabytes is usually abbreviated to the letters *Meg*, or occasionally just the letter *M* following the number of bytes—10,000,000 bytes would be written as 10Meg, or 10M. For convenience' sake it is understood that when the K or Meg suffixes are used the number they refer to is being rounded somewhat. Technically, however—because of the binary nature of computer memory—1K actually equals 1,024 bytes, while 1Meg ends up being 1,048,576 bytes. The lack of this knowledge has confused more than a few people when they watch the memory test that runs on-screen when most computers are first turned on, or when they read specifications in product brochures or technical manuals, and a greater than expected number appears. The suffixes **KB** and **MB** are also sometimes used to refer to the number of bytes. You should be aware, however, that these suffixes are more commonly used to describe the number of bits—such as when describing computer communications—rather than the number of bytes (See "Kilobit and megabit," on page 174). This dual use of the suffixes *MB* and *KB* can sometimes lead to confusion.

Unlike the 10-based system where digits appear to the left of the decimal point only if they have a value greater than 0, the same is not true of binary numbers. In an 8-bit word a binary 1 is expressed as 00000001 even though the remaining spaces have a value of 0. In a 16-bit word a binary 1 would be expressed as 0000000000000001, a 32-bit word as 00000000000000000000000000000001, and so on. The positions (bits) in a word that contain 0 are still considered to have a value, it's just that they are referred to as being *off*, or *false*.

Leading Zeros

Even though decimal numbers do not have to be entered using the binary format, the practice of using zeros to fill the spaces before a number is still one you may encounter, even in the day-to-day operation of a computer. When working with computers you will often see decimal numbers written with 0s in front of them. A common example would be in a program that requires you to enter a date. The program might not allow you to enter 1/1/91, for instance, because it is expecting 2 digits to be in the month and day even though the month of January and the first day of the month can be expressed with just the decimal digit 1. Instead, in this case you would have to enter 01/01/91. Because the program knows October through December and the 10th through 31st days of the month require 2 digits, it requires you to fill in 2 spaces whether they are really needed or not. Many programs are not as picky, however, and would even allow you to enter 1/ 1/91. This same format may apply to other numbers as well. For instance, in a check-writing program where you are allowed to write checks up to $999,999.99, if you wanted to write a check for only $9.95, the program might not allow you to enter it that way. Instead, you might have to enter the amount as $000,009.95. The extra 0s are referred to as **LEADING ZEROS** or digits. Thanks to newer, more flexible software it is becoming less necessary to use leading 0s when entering dates and other numbers into computers. Incidentally, because computers are designed to be simple and avoid errors, you will notice that when dealing with computers the number zero almost always has a slash through it (or a dot in the middle). Otherwise, it would be too easy for us humans to accidentally mistake the number *0* for the letter *O*. When a slash or dot are not used on a zero it is usually more slender and oval shaped than the letter *O*.

Examples Of Binary Numbers

As mentioned earlier, bits and bytes are used to represent more than just binary numbers, and are adaptable to working with decimal numbers, letters of the alphabet, and so on. For our purposes it will not be necessary to go into the methods of binary arithmetic. In case you're curious, though, the following example shows the numbers 0 through 10 as they appear in binary. To the right of each number there is an explanation of how each binary place (same meaning as a decimal place) is used and added together to form a complete number. Binary is really not very different from the 10-based decimal system you already use: the columns (places) are simply different, and their value is based upon the powers of 2 instead of the

18

powers of 10. By the way, if you're not familiar with raising a number to a higher power, it is really quite simple. To raise a number to a certain power—the 2nd power for example—multiply the number by itself that many times.

For instance, 2 to the 2nd power is 2 x 2, which equals 4. 2 to the 3rd power is 2 x 2 x 2, which equals 8, and so on.

HOW TO COUNT TO 10 IN BINARY

Decimal Number	Binary Equivalent
0	00000000 (Nothing in the 1s column)
1	00000001 (1 in the 1s column)
2	00000010 (2 to the 1st power)
3	00000011 (2 to the 1st power + 1)
4	00000100 (2 to the 2nd power)
5	00000101 (2 to the 2nd power + 1)
6	00000110 (2 to the 2nd power + 2 to the 1st power)
7	00000111 (2 to the 2nd power + 2 to the 1st power + 1)
8	00001000 (2 to the 3rd power)
9	00001001 (2 to the 3rd power + 1)
10	00001010 (2 to the 3rd power + 2 to the 1st power)

You may have guessed by now that the largest number you can represent with an 8-bit byte is 256, expressed as 11111111; the farthest place to the left (2 to the 7th power) added together with the powers of the remaining 7 places adds up to 256. Because an 8-bit byte contains only 8 places, and because the maximum value a binary place can have is 1, the largest number that can be represented is 256. You can quickly determine the largest number that can be represented with a binary word by simply raising 2 to the power of the number which represents the size of the word. For an 8-bit word (a byte), 2 to the 8th power equals 256. The largest number that can be represented by a 16-bit word is 65,536, and so on.

HOW COMPUTERS APPEAR TO THINK: THE LANGUAGE OF LOGIC

Just as a different system of math applies to binary numbers—called **BINARY ARITHMETIC**—computers use a related binary method for decision making. This method is entirely based upon whether the state of a bit is on (or true), or whether it is off (or false). This is the simple language of logic. Simple because it is based entirely upon just two things, whether something is true, or false. The language of logic is referred to as **BOOLEAN LOGIC**, or **BOOLEAN ALGEBRA**. But don't worry, you won't have to be a whiz at algebra to understand the basic functions of this special language because it is a simple system; that's why computers use it.

The decimal math system you and I are accustomed to has four basic operators: addition, subtraction, multiplication, and division, represented by +, -, *, and / (computers use the asterisk for the multiplication symbol and a slash for division). The language of logic has seven basic operators: **EQUAL TO** represented by =, **NOT EQUAL TO** < >, **GREATER THAN** >, and **LESS THAN** <. The three remaining operators are represented by the terms **AND**, **NOT**, and **OR**. Even though all of these can be used to make logical decisions, technically only the last three are considered Boolean operators. These operators can be combined, using parentheses if needed, to form as complex an equation as the problem requires—much the same way as you combine decimal math operators to solve more complex problems.

To show you how simple—yet powerful—this language of logic can be, let's look at a few examples that might apply to everyday situations. You have seen or may live on a street that uses rural mailboxes. These mailboxes always have a small metal or plastic flag that can be left up to tell the carrier that mail needs to be picked up. For this example, picture a street with only 8 houses on the block—this is the same number of bits as there are in a byte. Imagine for a moment also, that the flag on each mailbox represents a bit. If the flag is up, the bit is **ON** (or **TRUE**), if the flag is down, the bit is **OFF** (or **FALSE**). Now let's add the carrier to the picture. Let's further assume that none of the houses on this block have any mail coming today. So the only reason the carrier is driving down this block is to pick up mail.

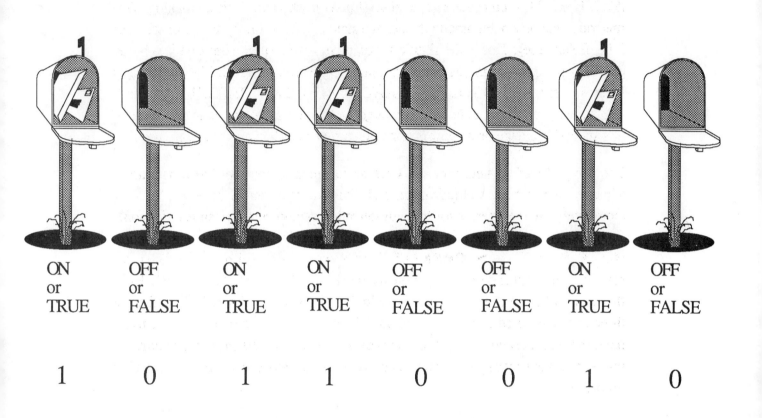

ON or TRUE	OFF or FALSE	ON or TRUE	ON or TRUE	OFF or FALSE	OFF or FALSE	ON or TRUE	OFF or FALSE
1	0	1	1	0	0	1	0

8 pieces of information or BITS equals one BYTE.

The carrier starts driving at one end of the block (or **BYTE**), and continues to the other end. Along the way he or she is checking the **STATE** of each flag (or **BIT**), to see if it is up (**ON** or **TRUE**), or whether it is down (**OFF** or **FALSE**). If it is **TRUE** the carrier knows there is mail waiting and picks it up. If the flag is down (the bit is **FALSE**) the carrier knows there is no mail in the box and continues down the street. Without this simple system of logic think of the time and trouble mail carriers would have to go through to stop at each box and physically look inside to see if there was mail. This is why so many neighborhoods have mailboxes with flags—they save the postal system time and money. But just as important, the system is effective while remaining simple. Computers use a similar method for the same reasons.

Other operators of logic can also be applied to everyday situations like our mailbox example. If you were to sell or trade in your car you probably would do so with some guidelines as to the amount you would accept. You might say that you would give up the car if someone's offer met your asking price or was **EQUAL TO =** it, and that you would not except an offer that was **LESS THAN <** your price. You would probably always accept an offer **GREATER THAN >** the price you were asking. If you felt the car was worth every dollar you were asking—but not more, and not less—you would probably reject offers that were **NOT EQUAL TO < >** your asking price.

As mentioned earlier, logic operators can be combined to solve complex problems. Using the previous example again, you could simplify the conditions of sale by combining the first three logical conditions into one statement. If you would sell the car for your asking price—or for more, but never for less—you could express the same thing using the simple logical statement **> = (GREATER THAN OR EQUAL TO)**. Keep in mind that while for these examples we have spelled out the logical operators *and* shown their corresponding symbol, in actual practice you would only use one or the other, but never both. **EQUAL TO**, for instance, would be expressed as **=**, or **EQUAL TO**, but never as **= EQUAL TO**, or **EQUAL TO = combined**—they both mean the same thing.

Next let's use the three Boolean logic operators **AND**, **NOT**, and **OR**. You might say for instance, that if your alarm clock goes off tomorrow, **AND** the car starts, you will be at work on time. You could also refer to the outcome or **STATE** of that situation—or the solution to the problem—as being **TRUE**. On the other hand, if these things did **NOT** happen the state of the situation—or the solution to the problem—would be **FALSE**, and you might not arrive at work on time. You could go further by saying that if you win a large cash prize, **OR** you inherit a million dollars, you may never arrive at work.

As you can see, logic provides a simple and efficient way of expressing many problems and their solutions. Logic is the only language computers use and understand, and because they rely on it so heavily you will often see it carry over into the operation of equipment or programs that you use. In these cases, you will need to understand what logical statements are, and how to use them to get the results you need.

For instance, you might want to "ask" a program that keeps track of your sales to list everyone whose sales territory is Florida and who had sales between $20,000.00 and $30,000.00 during the months of January or March. While it would be nice if the computer could understand such a request, it's more likely you will have to rephrase your request into a logical statement that the program and computer you are using will be able to understand. To illustrate, let's assume we're using a hypothetical software program called "SALESWARE."

The above request and resulting output might appear as follows:

```
SELECT ALL NAMES
FROM  SALES_FILE
WHERE
STATE = FLORIDA
   AND SALES > = $20,000.00 AND SALES < =$30,000.00
   AND MONTH = JANUARY OR MONTH = MARCH
```
_____

John Doe
Nancy Chaplin
Will Rogers
Mark Twain

_____

End of report...

Using the wrong logic is the same as giving incorrect instructions, so, naturally, you will get the wrong result. The computer didn't make a mistake, but was just doing what you told it to. Computers will do *exactly* what you tell them to even though the result may not be what *you* expected. This most often happens when the information you type into a computer does not follow the proper **SYNTAX**. Syntax is another way of saying that what you type must be spelled right, punctuated properly, and located properly within the line typed. Following are examples of improper syntax (for our SALESWARE example only, since the actual syntax required varies from program to program):

```
SELECT ALL NAME (column name spelled wrong)
FROM SALES FILE (illegal space in filename)
WHERE,          (illegal punctuation ",")
STATE = FLORIDA
   AND SALES > = $20,000.00 SALES  < = $30,000.00
          (missing separator or operator, "AND")
   AND MONTH = 1 OR MONTH = 3
          (numeric date format not allowed)
```

This is where the saying **GARBAGE IN, GARBAGE OUT** came from. The results you get from a computer—the **OUTPUT**—will only be as good and as accurate as the instructions and data—the **INPUT**—that you give it. Because you're already accustomed to using logic in everyday situations without thinking about it, it won't take long for you to become accustomed to organizing that same type of logic into the statements that are often used in computer programs.

Before leaving a discussion which included the term *input*, you may wish to note the following: **INPUT** can come directly from you through a computer keyboard, or from a disk drive, magnetic tape, over the phone line, etc. It can consist of instructions or commands, information or data, or both. **INSTRUCTION(S)** and **COMMAND(S)** have the same meaning, and refer to any input that tells the computer what to do and how to do it. **INFORMATION** and **DATA** also have the same meaning, and are what commands and instructions act upon. For instance, in the SALESWARE example, "SELECT ALL NAMES FROM SALES_FILE WHERE," "STATE =," and "AND SALES =," were examples of commands, while "FLORIDA," "$20,000," and "NANCY CHAPLIN," were examples of the data those commands acted upon. Data can also be included in, or be a part of, commands. If someone wanted to be picky, however, he or she might say that in this example the names—the output—were the only *true* data, and that everything else—the input—consisted of commands.

VARIABLES are unknown numeric or alphabetic values, or values subject to change or variation. The letter **N** (or **n**) is commonly used to represent a numeric variable—2 * N = 10 is the same as saying 2 * (an unknown number) = 10. Alphabetic variables are often represented by the term **STRING**, meaning a *string* of characters. A name more closely resembling the type of string variable is frequently substituted for the term *string*. For instance, an instruction manual might tell you to type **SAVE [FILENAME]**, where the word *FILENAME* is more descriptive and meaningful than would be **SAVE [STRING]**. Brackets ([ ]) are frequently used to indicate where string input should be located within a command. If a numeric or string value is known from the beginning and will never change, it is a **CONSTANT**. If a value is unknown, or if it is known but subject to change as a program runs, it is considered a variable. Input can consist of constants, variables, or both. When using software programs and/or their instruction manuals, you are likely to encounter at least one of the terms just discussed. If you were to look in the SALESWARE instruction manual for directions on formatting the commands used in our example, you would see instructions similar to these:

```
SELECT ALL [column name(s)]
FROM [filename]
WHERE
STATE = [state name]
   AND SALES > = [n] AND SALES < = [n]
   AND MONTH = [month name] OR MONTH = [month name]
```

The binary system, logic, and data input and retrieval are all closely related processes. Some extremely well designed programs totally isolate the user from having to have a knowledge of these underlying processes. This is the exception rather than the rule, however, because most software requires you to *talk* to it in a language that computes easily, rather than the straightforward English you are used to. Information provided in the preceding text and examples will allow you to understand the syntax used in the majority of software and manuals you will use.

THE HEXADECIMAL SYSTEM

You now know that computers use the binary numbering system because it is better suited to their electrical nature. However, while the binary system is easy for computers to use, it is not such a breeze for humans; a person can manipulate decimal numbers in much less time than it would take to assemble them in binary. To make things easier for people who program and service computers another numbering system was put into use, the **HEXADECIMAL** system, **HEX** meaning 6. Since 6 is a multiple of 2, hex is still compatible with binary, but is a much easier system for people to work with.

Hexadecimal closely resembles the decimal system you are already accustomed to. It is, however, a more compact and efficient way of representing numbers. Unlike binary, which is awkward and requires at least 8 places (32 places is not uncommon) to represent numbers, even large numbers can be represented with ease in hex. For instance, the number 2,576,980,377 is 10011001100110011001100110011001 in binary, but can be represented by a shorter number, $99999999, in hex. The dollar sign in front of the number tells you it is expressed in hexadecimal. Hex numbers may also contain letters, because you can only count to 9 before you run out of normal decimal digits. For example, the number 65,536 is 1111111111111111 in binary, but is represented by the all-letter number, $FFFF, in hex.

Like binary, hex is used often by programmers and service technicians who need to work on the inside level of computers. While a knowledge of the way computers use binary logic and methods will help you a great deal in understanding computers, your knowledge of hex will be sufficient if you are able to recognize hex numbers when you see them, and understand what they are. However, for those of you who are curious, the following example shows the numbers 0 through 17 shown as they appear in hex. If you're in the mood for something a little challenging, review the way binary numbers are assembled, and then figure out how to do the same thing with hexadecimal numbers based on 16. Have fun!

DECIMAL AND HEXIDECIMAL
NUMBERING SYSTEMS COMPARED

Decimal

0	1	2	3	4	5	6	7	8	9	10	11	12	13	14	15	16	17
00	01	02	03	04	05	06	07	08	09	0A	0B	0C	0D	0E	0F	10	11

Hexadecimal Equivalent

ASCII: THE ALPHABET OF COMPUTERS

The International Morse Code which has been used by telegraphers and radio operators throughout the world represents the alphabet by assigning a special dot-dash code to each letter. Morse code was developed as a standard and reliable method of communication that would be understandable by all users of the Roman alphabet. A somewhat similar coding system, called **ASCII**, is used with computers; the acronym stands for **AMERICAN STANDARD CODE FOR INFORMATION INTERCHANGE**. (ASCII is pronounced "ask-ee," and is never referred to verbally by pronouncing each initial.) It is an international code which allows electronic devices to use numbers to represent language, graphics, control codes, music, etc.

Computers translate what you type into them into ASCII. These codes are then converted back into letters, numbers, etc., as they appear on a monitor or printout. For example, the ASCII code for the letter A is the number 65, B is 66, C is 67, etc. The number 1 is represented in ASCII by 49, while 50 is the code for the number 2. A dollar sign ($) is represented by 36, a space is represented by the number 32, and so on.

Even though an established set of ASCII codes exist for English, that is by no means the limit of what can be represented. Similar coding systems can be constructed to allow a computer to generate almost any character you can think of. These range from special letters needed for foreign languages to graphics characters for drawing lines and pictures.

CONTROL CODES AND CHARACTERS

There is a special type of ASCII code called a **CONTROL CODE**. As the name implies, these are codes (a group of 1 or more characters) used to actually control and tell computers and other devices what to do. Unlike regular characters which are designed for people to see, control codes are usually directed at the computer and are not visible to users. This is why they are sometimes referred to as **INVISIBLE, HIDDEN**, or **EMBEDDED, CODES**. Embedded codes sometimes take advantage of the fact that a byte can hold more information than a letter or character. This is because not all of the 8 bits in a byte are needed to represent the number code for many characters. For example, ASCII only makes use of the numbers 32 to 127 for commonly used **PRINTABLE** characters, a-z, 0-9, etc. Up to the number 127, which is 01111111 in binary, you will notice that the farthest place to the left is still unused. The extra bit can be used as a special code for something else, even while the remaining bits are being used to represent a character. This technique is used in communications, where the 8th bit is often referred to as a **STOP BIT**, and is used to signal the end of (or stop in) a phase of communication. Word processors use a similar method: the text you type appears normal on screen, but the word processor embeds special codes in or next to some characters so that when the text is printed it carries with it information to control or tell the printer what to do. For instance, you might want one word underlined, while you want another to appear in **bold print**, and yet another in *italics*. Control codes are used extensively by computers and programs, especially for controlling communications between devices attached to the computer.

While *control codes* (a group of one or more characters) are almost always created intentionally by software or the person using it, users often create *invisible*, *hidden*, or *embedded characters* by accident, and are not even aware of what they have done. This sometimes occurs when someone is typing and he or she is unaware they are also depressing a key such as Alt or Ctrl. Just as holding down the shift key will produce an altered variation of the same characters (in this case capital letters), in some programs holding down the Alt or Ctrl key while typing will produce altered variations of characters. To the eye, however, the fact that the character was produced using a nonstandard ASCII code probably won't be detectable. Few software instruction manuals offer advice on locating or correcting problems caused by hidden or altered characters. However, because the problem is most often literally invisible, such characters can present one of the most frustrating problems you will ever run into while using a computer.

For instance, what if the software program you are using required you to type the command "PRINT-TO:LPT1 REPORT1" within a file designed to execute the commands it contains. But when you run the program to execute the instructions contained within the file it stops working and generates an error message when it reaches the above command. According to the software instruction manual the command was typed correctly (See "Syntax," on page 24), but repeated attempts to run the program result only in the same error message. What could possibly be wrong? Well, in this case, you were not aware that you accidentally held down the Ctrl key when you typed the hyphen between "PRINT" and "TO," and even though the hyphen looks perfectly normal to the eye the software sees it as a different character because "Ctrl-" produces a different ASCII code than just pressing the "-" key alone. Modern software is far less susceptible to these kinds of problems than it once was. So holding down the shift key while pressing the space bar, or the ctrl key while pressing the hyphen, isn't likely to get you into too much trouble. But, to be on the safe side, it is a wise practice to avoid holding down unwanted keys while you type, and to retype any characters you are suspicious of. If a command or some other text you have typed looks OK but just doesn't seem to be working properly, try erasing the line in question and retyping it; because, on occasion, an accidentally-typed hidden character may very well be the trouble maker.

The preceding explanations are not intended to give you a complete knowledge of binary logic and math, the hexadecimal system, or ASCII and control codes. However, it is very likely that as you become more involved with computers you will encounter these terms or situations while using programs, in instruction and technical manuals, in specifications marked on certain equipment, and even in sales brochures or other material that you read. Enough information is provided here on these topics so that you won't be totally lost. If you are not able to understand altogether, you will at least be able to comprehend what is being discussed and seek further assistance.

At first you were probably skeptical about what could be done with only the two simple numbers 1 and 0. But by now you've seen that what often seems complex, when looked at a different way, can really be made into something very simple. The possibilities of what you can do with that something—in this case computers—are only as limited as your imagination, and the imagination is limitless. It has been said that the computer is one of the few tools of its kind ever to be invented. That's because most other tools were invented by someone for a purpose. The computer, however, does not exist for any given reason. Instead, it is capable of performing any task which someone can think of and program it to do.

MICROPROCESSORS: THE HEART OF A MODERN COMPUTER

Even though it is perfectly acceptable to refer to the normal collection of components—keyboard, monitor, disk drive(s), case, etc.—as a computer, this is not entirely accurate. The **MICROPROCESSOR** housed inside, also referred to as the **CPU** or **CENTRAL PROCESSING UNIT**, *IS* the computer. This very compact device is a highly miniaturized electronic circuit (**INTEGRATED CIRCUIT** or **IC**) that packs the power of millions of components (transistors, resistors, etc.) into a single computer **CHIP**. The CPU chip does virtually all of the work, but its small size and lack of visibility make this an easy fact to overlook. People tend to think of a modern computer as a complete unit—a **SYSTEM** or **MACHINE**—or, as it is sometimes crudely referred to, a **BOX**. In reality, though, most of what you see is just a collection of components—power supply, cooling fan, etc.—which the CPU needs to function properly and communicate with the outside world. Even the small black casings which enclose the chips are themselves mostly for human convenience. The electronic components inside the casings are actually much smaller. But if the entire chip—including the case—were made that small, people would literally not be able to handle and assemble electronic devices without tweezers and a microscope. These incredibly compact dimensions are what allow the modern computer, as well as many other everyday devices, to be small enough for practical use.

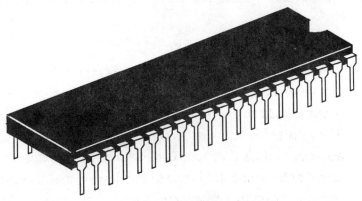

Intel 8088 (CPU)

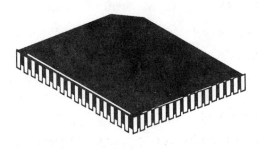

Intel 80286 CPU

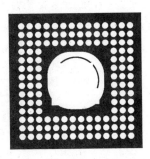

Intel 80386 CPU (Bottom View)

Some of Intel's Microprocessors

Microchip Construction

Most of the internal components in an electronic device, including your TV and stereo, could be reduced to a single small chip (providing you wanted to spend the money to do it). These days, the resulting chip is often much smaller than a postage stamp.

After a device is selected to be reduced to a microchip, electronics engineers design (or redesign) the electronic components—transistors, resistors, etc.—in such a way that they can be assembled or *drafted* onto a huge sheet of drafting paper. The paper has to be huge, for it would be impossible for someone to actually draw a microchip in the miniaturized scale it will eventually be reduced to. After this giant *electronic blueprint* has been carefully checked, the drawing is reduced to a size that will fit inside the black microchip casing like those shown in the illustration. (Some of these miniaturized circuits are so small they can pass through the eye of a sewing needle!) From this tiny drawing is made what amounts to a very sophisticated negative—not totally unlike those you get from a photo store. Using this negative the circuits and components on the drawing are literally *photographed*, or *etched*, onto the chip's surface.

The chip itself is made of silicon, one of the most abundant raw materials available. The silicon used to make chips, however, is highly refined, and infinitely more pure than the silicon found in ordinary beach sand. Because a silicon chip is so small and fragile it would be difficult to handle directly, so very thin—virtually microscopic—wires are attached to the chip's outer edges. This whole arrangement is enclosed in the black microchip casing. (It is acceptable to refer to either the casing itself or the silicon wafer inside the casing as the *chip*, although, technically, the actual chip is inside the casing.) These wires are then connected to the sturdier and easier-to-handle connectors sometimes referred to as **SPIDER LEGS**, or **LEADS**, which you see extending from the edges of a microchip. Some smaller chips—and similar devices such as transistors—have connectors extending from only one edge of the chip.

Computer Power

All microchips are given a number by their manufacturer. When referring to a computer or microprocessor, the number also tells you how powerful it is. Many things determine the power of a microprocessor, but the most important two are word size and the speed of the chip itself. (Please keep in mind that the speed of the microprocessor—the chip itself—and the total system speed of the computer it is installed in, are two related but separate specifications. The microprocessor is just one—although the most important—component that makes up a complete computer.) The larger the word size a computer uses the more information it can process at one time, and the faster it will operate. This is because a word can only hold so much information, and computers must combine them when more capability is needed. The process of combining words can be inefficient and awkward, and is why most modern computers use a 16- or 32-bit word size. 8-bit or smaller microprocessors are typically seen only in home computers, or those for special or limited applications, examples of which are communications terminals, telephones, calculators, and home appliance and automotive controls. Up until the late 1980s 32-bit technology was typically found only in large minicomputers and mainframes. Only very powerful, specialized, or experimental computers currently use word sizes greater than 32 bits in length. (See chart on page 35.)

The Internal Clock: How Computer Speed Is Regulated

Among the factors which determine the power of a computer are how the microprocessor is manufactured and what additional components are included within the system's cabinet (also referred to as the **CHASSIS**, pronounced "chas-ee"). To a large degree, however, speed is determined by the microprocessor's **CLOCK SPEED**. Like many timepieces, these clocks utilize the frequency of the vibrations from a quartz crystal to accurately regulate speed. (Clock speed is unrelated to the calendar-clock most computers also have for providing the date and time.) Unlike a watch and most other timepieces, the clocks in computers maintain time in divisions of millionths of a second, referred to as **MEGAHERTZ**, or simply **MHz**. The faster the clock speed the faster computers work. All of the internal operations of a computer rely on this precision electronic clock to coordinate their operations. Most computers also contain a separate **CLOCK/CALENDAR** and small **ONBOARD BATTERY** which maintains the time of day, and the date.

Some of the more common clock speeds for small computers are 4, 6, 8, 12, 16, 20, and 25 MHz; 4 to 8 MHz is the typical speed range for home computers, while 8 to 16 MHz is common for most small business computers. Faster speeds usually indicate a high performance machine—although as of 1991, with technology improving and prices dropping, clock speeds of 20, 25, and even 33MHz were becoming common on IBM PCs, Macintoshes, and similar small business computers. (By 1991 speeds of 50MHz+ were already being talked about.) Because not all software functions properly at high clock speeds, good computers allow the clock speed to be changed—**STEPPED DOWN** or **STEPPED UP**—through software or hardware to a lower or higher speed. A test which measures the speed of a computer or one of its components (disk drives, RAM, etc.) under actual use is referred to as a **BENCHMARK**.

The CPU

The CPU not only performs all needed calculations and processing, but also coordinates the operation of the other components which together make up a computer system. The memory, screen displays, disk drives, printers, etc., are all under the direct or indirect control of the CPU. Smaller, additional microprocessors are sometimes used inside a computer, as well as in devices connected to it, to take some of the workload off the CPU. These auxiliary microprocessors are known as **COPROCESSORS**—the most common example being the math coprocessor chips used to increase mathematical speed and precision. Some advanced computer designs also use disk and/or video coprocessors to increase the speed and performance of those components.

Devices other than computers—such as terminals, printers, etc.—which contain their own microprocessors are referred to as **SMART** devices, meaning that to some extent they have the ability to function independently of the main computer's CPU. A smart printer that has enough memory, for instance, will still be able to complete a report or printout even if you disconnect or turn off the computer it is connected to. The more smart devices a computer contains or uses the faster and more efficiently it operates. Devices that do not contain their own microprocessors and must use the main computer's CPU for processing capability are referred to as **DUMB** devices. Disconnecting a dumb printer from the computer while it is printing will disrupt the printout because the printer relies on the computer's CPU.

COMPUTER MEMORY

Like the elephant, computers never forget—well, almost never, anyway. Computers accomplish their seemingly prodigious feats of memory and instant recall by making use of a number of standard storage methods which provide either 1) **TEMPORARY** (or **RANDOM ACCESS** or **VOLATILE**) **MEMORY**, or 2) **PERMANENT** (or **NONVOLATILE**) **MEMORY**.

SOME OF THE MORE COMMON CHIPS (CPUs) AND THEIR USES

(speeds vary depending upon version)

Chip Number	Word Size	Clock Speed	Type of Computer
6502	8 bits	2 MHz	Home
6510	8 bits	3 MHz	Home
8080	8 bits	2 MHz	Home/Business
Z-80	8 bits	4 MHz	Home/Business
8086	16 bits	6 MHz	Business
8088	16 bits	6-8 MHz	Business
80286	16 bits	8-16 MHz	Business (high performance)
80386	32 bits	16-33 MHz	Business (very high performance)
80486	32 bits	33+ MHz	Business (ultrahigh performance)
68000	32 bits	8-16 MHz	Business (high performance, multiuser)
68020	32 bits	16-32 MHz	Business (very high performance, multiuser)
68030	32 bits	33+ MHz	Business (ultrahigh performance, graphics, multiuser)

RAM: Temporary, Random Access, Or Volatile Memory

Temporary information and work-in-progress is most commonly stored in what is called **RAM**, or **RANDOM ACCESS MEMORY**, chips. Random access memory chips depend upon the presence of electrical energy to store information. When you turn the power switch off on a computer or device containing RAM, all information in the RAM chips is lost, which is why RAM is also called volatile memory. Why, you might be wondering—if the information stored in RAM is lost when you turn off the power—is this kind of memory used at all? There is one answer to that question, *speed*.

Random access memory can store and retrieve information *very* rapidly. Thousands, and even millions, of pieces of information can be handled in RAM in only one second! In case you're wondering whether you need a computer that fast, don't worry. Even if you don't need a fast computer now, as your knowledge and use of computers increase you will begin using larger and more complex programs, which require greater and greater speed—and tomorrow's programs and applications will demand still more speed. It is highly unlikely that you will ever complain that your computer is too fast, but you could be very sorry if it is too slow.

What is RAM memory used for? Besides the fact that at any given time a computer is using RAM internally to keep track of hundreds, even thousands, of important pieces of information (See "The computer is quicker than the eye," on page 42), all software programs must have access to RAM in order to function. Perhaps it is easiest to think of RAM as a kind of giant scratch pad—although a very precise and orderly one. Just as you sometimes write down part of a calculation you're working on—or store it in a calculator's memory—so does a computer. Computers cannot magically solve problems any differently than you or I. There are no shortcuts; they also have to follow basic rules to solve a problem. In fact, because computers must break down each problem until it is in its simplest form, they have to do a surprisingly large amount of work even to do something as simple as adding 1 + 1. If RAM weren't fast, the large number of calculations computers require for problem solving would take hours instead of seconds. This is also why humans have always been able to outperform computers at certain tasks. You may not have been aware that for years college math whizzes have astonished scientists by their ability to solve many complex problems faster than a calculator or computer can. And, while each year the gap narrows, computers are still not able to beat the world's best chess masters (although they can beat just about anyone else).

RAM is basically a temporary place for the computer to juggle information back and forth, or hold data while it is being used or worked on. The computer and the programs you use require varying amounts of RAM, and many programs run faster when they have more memory to work in. In fact, your software is the biggest determining factor for how much RAM is needed.

RAM used to be one of the most expensive components of computers. Since the more RAM you had the better off you usually were, it was desirable to have large amounts of it. However, even if you could afford to buy it, the technology at the time meant computers were often limited to only 64K of RAM or less. Thanks to growing demand and modern manufacturing RAM is now available in abundant quantities, at prices that are a mere fraction of what they used to be. That is why today, computers—even home computers—with 1Meg of RAM or more are commonplace.

In the 1970s 64K was every microcomputer owner's dream. By the 1980s most business computers and programs required a minimum of 256K to 512K to run. Many of today's business programs have reached a size and level of sophistication where 640K—the former memory limit for MS-DOS-based computers—is just the starting point. Fortunately, however, unless you have a unique application or intend to run multiuser software, 640K is a more than adequate amount of RAM for most programs. On 8-bit computers 640K is usually the maximum amount of memory you can use unless you purchase special hardware; 16- and 32-bit computers can often go beyond 1Meg with ease. Graphics programs and large spreadsheets are examples of software that might require more than 640K or 1Meg of RAM.

Within reason, you can never have too much RAM. Besides buying the minimum amount of RAM your system will require to run, get as much RAM as you think you'll need in the near future, and that you can afford to buy. For an MS-DOS computer it is highly recommended that you get no less than 640K. Not only will your system run more efficiently with more RAM, but you'll be able to run a greater variety of the software you might want to buy in the future. In most cases it is also cheaper to get your system with the amount of RAM you want at the time of purchase than to add it later.

Because information stored in RAM is lost when you turn the power off, you'll also need a permanent method of storing the information you enter into your computer system. These methods of storage are referred to as **PERMANENT STORAGE** or **MASS STORAGE** devices. The most popular way of accomplishing permanent storage on computers is with DISK DRIVES. Disk drives, and the disks they use, retain information even when the power is turned off (See "Mass storage devices," on page 65).

ROM: Permanent, Or Read Only, Memory

ROM stands for **READ ONLY MEMORY**. These are specialized memory chips that have been permanently programmed with instructions, or permanently loaded with data, and retain this information even when the power is turned off. Compared to RAM, ROM memory is extremely slow. This is why it is necessary for a computer to use fast RAM memory as its main temporary storage area and work space. Other than for video games like Nintendo, and some home computers, you see very little software on plug-in ROM cartridges. ROM-based programs simply run too slowly to be practical for serious personal or business use. An additional disadvantage is that, once programmed, the information a traditional ROM chip holds can never be changed or updated. If new features are added to the software you not only incur the expense of buying new ROM chips but you also have to have them installed in your computer. This is why virtually all modern software is sold on floppy disks (See "Floppy-disk drives," on page 66). You will sometimes see a similar type of chip referred to as an **EPROM**, which stands for **ERASABLE PROGRAMMABLE READ ONLY MEMORY**. EPROMs are like ROMs in that they continue to hold information when the computer is turned off, and they are very slow. Unlike ROMs, however, as the name implies, EPROMs can be erased and reprogrammed.

Because of the speed and programmability limitations of ROMs and EPROMs they are primarily used for storing small amounts of information that need to be retained when the power to a computer is turned off. When a computer is first turned on—also referred to as **BOOTING** the machine—and before RAM comes into play, the CPU first has to be programmed with the initial elementary instructions that tell it how to operate. In the first seconds after power-up the CPU accesses special, very small, programs that tell it what to do next. These programs are always stored in ROMs or EPROMs, and represent the major use for these chips. One thing these special programs do is to get the computer ready to be used for running "regular" software. They may also perform certain **DIAGNOSTIC TESTS**—also called **POWER-UP SELF DIAGNOSTIC TESTS**—to make sure all systems are working OK: memory, disk drives, keyboard, etc. Next, the computer tries to find and use yet another special program called the **OPERATING SYSTEM**.

THE OPERATING SYSTEM

The **OPERATING SYSTEM** currently most popular for small computers is called **MS-DOS**, which stands for **MICROSOFT DISK OPERATING SYSTEM**. The operating system can be loaded into the computer from ROM memory or from a floppy disk. More often, however—if the computer has a hard drive onto which the operating system has been installed—the CPU will automatically load the operating system after you turn the machine on. The operating system handles all routine and critical functions of a computer system, such as the drawing the screen display, accepting data from the keyboard, and sending data to and from the disk drives, printers, etc. Software designed to make computer components function properly and operate automatically or with only a little input from a user—such as MS-DOS, Apple DOS, and UNIX—is referred to as **SYSTEMS SOFTWARE**. Once the operating system has been loaded the computer is able to accept input from the keyboard. You may then run software that you have purchased or written yourself.

SYSTEM COMMUNICATIONS

Just as systems software is different than applications software, so are systems communications different than communications programs for users. Communications of various kinds are constantly taking place inside a running computer; this is the case whether an applications program is running or not. These computer-generated communication signals travel within the computer, and to and from outside devices, through special circuits known as the **DATA BUS, COMMUNICATIONS BUS, COMMUNICATIONS PATHWAYS,** or **COMMUNICATIONS CHANNELS**. For instance, when a command is issued that causes information—a letter, report, etc.—to be sent to a printer, the computer first communicates or **TALKS** with the printer to see if it is ready to receive the data. If the printer is not ready—out of paper, off-line, not turned on, jammed, or already busy printing something else—the computer will not transmit its data. Instead, it will either generate an error message telling you what the problem is, or keep checking and send the data when the printer is ready. When the computer receives an OK to transmit its data the information flows from the computer to the printer, where it is processed by the printer's own microprocessor and finally printed on paper. Even while a document is printing there is still constant communication between the printer and computer. If the printer should run out of paper or experience some other interruption the computer will be on the alert for such a signal and take appropriate action. A similar communications process takes place between all other circuits and devices connected to the CPU.

The Communications Highways

Communications between computer devices take place using one of two methods. The first is called **SERIAL COMMUNICATION.** Serial information flows through circuits and pathways in single file, one piece (bit) of data after another. Picture yourself on a single-lane highway with no room to pass on either side—and you're following the car ahead of you. There is also a car behind you, and you all maintain a safe distance from each other. This is about the same way serial communication takes place. It's possible to travel this way, but you can't go faster without bumping into the car ahead of you, and if you slow down you'll be bumped from behind. This is why you probably avoid such roads and take the expressway whenever possible. Serial communication is the most economical method of sending information between computer devices, but it is also the slowest.

The other method, referred to as **PARALLEL COMMUNICATION**, allows more than one piece of data to flow at one time, usually in groups of 8, 16, or 32 bits. Think about a highway with eight lanes, all side by side, one right next to the other. You still aren't allowed to pass, but since everyone has his or her own lane traffic moves along at a much faster pace. This is similar to parallel communication, with 8 or more bits moving through data lines at the same time. Computers use both serial and parallel communication. Because serial communications circuits are easier and cheaper to build, they are used extensively in home computers and other low-cost devices. More expensive personal computers and those used for business—while capable of serial communication—use parallel communication almost exclusively.

Like other internal functions of computers, parallel communication is based upon the powers of 2. As mentioned earlier, the most common word sizes for parallel communications are 8, 16, and 32 bits. Even on more advanced computers with CPUs that use 32-bit words, communications usually take place at either 8 or 16 bits. This is because most devices designed to be connected to a computer were engineered back when the only CPUs available used an 8-bit word-size. Only in the mid-1980s did devices capable of 16- and 32-bit communication start to catch up with the already more advanced CPUs. So, unless you are using components—printers, plug-in circuit boards, etc.— capable of 16- or 32-bit communications,

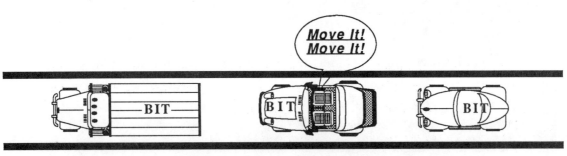

Example of Serial Communications

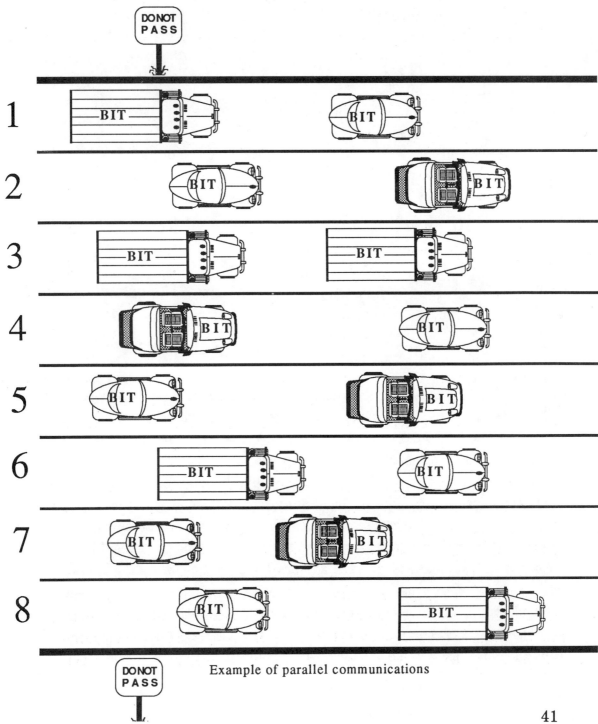

Example of parallel communications

41

your computer must convert its communications signals to 8 bits before talking to these devices. Yes, this conversion process is inefficient, but such is the current state of microcomputer technology. However, more and more devices capable of 16- and 32-bit communication are appearing on the market each year. Regardless of the limitations of attached devices, processing inside the CPU can take place up to its full word size of 8, 16, or 32 bits. The more channels (pathways) there are for data to flow through, the faster the computer will operate.

THE COMPUTER IS QUICKER THAN THE EYE

Having just covered the subject of computer communications, you may wish to make note of an important point. No matter what kind of CPU you have they all share one thing in common, they can only do one thing at a time. It is easy to get the impression that computers do many things at once. After all, you can be typing on the keyboard, watching text appear on the screen, printing out a report, and using the disk drive, all seemingly at the same time. But this is only an illusion. No matter how many data paths a computer system has, all information must eventually flow through the CPU to be processed, and the CPU can process only one instruction at a time.

It is only because computers are so incredibly fast—processing thousands, even **MILLIONS OF INSTRUCTIONS PER SECOND (MIPS)**—that everything appears to happen at once. For instance, most information which appears on a computer screen seems to do so instantly. But the computer is really only *painting* or *drawing* the screen one character at a time. If you could watch things in slow motion you would see characters slowly filling the screen, starting at the upper left-hand corner and continuing character by character, line by line, until all of the information was displayed. Even more incredibly, because the computer can do only one thing at a time—even while printing characters on the screen—it leaves that job and goes to take care of a number of other things. It is constantly running small programs (See "Systems software," on page 39) which are doing things like checking the keyboard to see if a key has been pressed, or seeing if another device—printer, disk drive, etc.—is trying to talk to it, and updating the time on its onboard clock. However, the computer always remembers where it left off and eventually returns to the job of printing the next character on the screen. Obviously, this all takes place in *much* less time than the blink of an eye.

The computer is a master juggler, constantly dividing its processing power between hundreds and even thousands of tasks. But, the fact that everything must eventually be funneled through the CPU—which can only process one instruction at a time—ultimately proves to be the limiting factor on how fast a system will operate. This is referred to as the computer **BOTTLENECK**. The only way to get around this problem is to install additional CPUs so that more information can be processed at one time. Currently, only the most advanced microcomputers are beginning to use such techniques, referred to as **MULTIPROCESSOR** technology. For the most part such sophistication is still limited to mainframes and so-called **SUPER-COMPUTERS**. Fortunately, few of us need such power, and the current 16- and 32-bit machines prove more than adequate for most applications.

IBM AT Computer

Macintosh Computer

Multiuser Computer
or
IBM AT Tower

Several types of computers.

44

Chapter 3

A GUIDE TO CLASSIFYING COMPUTERS BY TYPE

As the computer industry continues to advance at a dizzying pace, and with new designs appearing almost monthly, it is sometimes easy to become confused about which type of computer is which. Devices which qualify as a computer can range from the "black boxes" in late model cars to the toys your children play with to the more traditional home and business computers we are familiar with. This chapter gives a brief introduction to the major computer designs, and then puts them into four easy-to-identify categories for future reference.

Not many years ago most computers were used only by large companies and the government. These systems were usually referred to as **MAINFRAMES**—the name being derived from the nature of their design and construction.

A mainframe computer consisted of a large cabinet—or a group of cabinets—in which the components of the system were housed. Often these systems were so large they required huge rooms all to themselves. The first viable, full-scale computer was completed for the Army in 1946 and was called **ENIAC**, which stood for **ELECTRONIC NUMERICAL INTEGRATOR AND CALCULATOR**. ENIAC occupied 1,800 square feet of space—about the area of an average house—and used approximately 18,000 vacuum tubes in its construction. In comparison, the scientific pocket calculators found in today's department stores for less than $25.00 could easily have outperformed ENIAC! Because early computers generated so much heat, the rooms that housed them almost always had to be air conditioned. Mainframes were designed to offer as much power as the technology at the time would permit. Another distinguishing feature of mainframes—especially modern designs—is the ability to be used by more than one person at the same time.

As time went by and technology improved, a number of companies started manufacturing a new type of system called a **MINICOMPUTER**. **Digital Equipment Corporation**, also known as **DEC**, virtually pioneered the minicomputer industry back in 1959. Minicomputers were smaller and less expensive to purchase, install, maintain, and operate than mainframes, and required less space. Nevertheless, their capabilities often rivaled—and sometimes exceeded—those of mainframes. Many businesses and universities were able to obtain their own computer systems for the first time. This also meant users no longer had to put up with the delays and inconvenience of waiting for access to scarce mainframes.

Similar advances brought about the development of more powerful and still smaller computers, sometimes called **SUPERMINIS**, which were more widely available. Even then, however, computer applications were still limited to about the same groups as before—users in larger institutions and businesses. But the next advance was to increase computer usage explosively.

Major progress was made when vacuum tubes were replaced by transistors, and, later, with the introduction of the **MICROPROCESSOR**, which permitted a **MICROCOMPUTER**. By then microcomputers could easily go into a single cabinet that would fit on a desk, were much lower in cost, and required far less power than even a minicomputer. As more of these new computers were manufactured they became increasingly smaller and cheaper to make. Computers introduced by the mid-1970s—like the **APPLE COMPUTER** by **Apple Computer Company**, and the **TRS-80**, **Tandy Radio Shack-80**—allowed not only businesses and institutions but individuals as well to have practical access to computers for the first time.

By the late 1970s and early 1980s mass production had reduced microcomputers to sizes and price ranges which allowed almost anyone to purchase and use one. So popular and accepted did computers become that they were even available in department and toy stores right along with color TVs, VCRs, and video games. For all practical purposes, however, further development of computers for home use all but stopped shortly afterwards—probably because almost all microcomputers became so economical that they were within reach of the average home user.

Attention focused instead on the **PERSONAL COMPUTER**, or **PC**, which was a more powerful system designed primarily for use by an individual or small business. Many of the people who outgrew the capabilities of their home computers simply moved up to personal computers.

Even with the progress the was made earlier, the development of more advanced microcomputers was still underway. By the mid 1980s this resulted in small computers which despite their size and low cost, could easily outperform earlier minicomputers and mainframes. The term **SUPERMICRO**, was sometimes used to describe microcomputers which were closer in power to the capability of a minicomputer.

A type of computer that has been around for awhile, but is still used primarily for special applications, is the **SUPERCOMPUTER**. As the name implies, these truly are "super" computers. Even today's advanced mainframes cannot match the raw computing power and speed of these machines. This is because supercomputers are built not only using the latest in technology, but lots of it. Cost is set aside in order to achieve the maximum capabilities technology has to offer. The result is a computer which can easily cost tens of millions of dollars or more. For this reason, like the earlier mainframes, supercomputers are currently only used by the government, large companies, universities, and so on. **Cray Research, Inc.,** founded in 1972 by Seymour Cray, sent the first true supercomputer to Los Alamos National Laboratory in 1976, and has remained a world leader in supercomputer technology. The most advanced *normal* microcomputers (PCs) as of 1991 were those based upon the **Intel 486** microprocessor running at 33MHz. Typically these systems contained several megabytes of RAM and were approaching a processing speed of 10 million instructions per second (MIPS). In comparison, supercomputers by that time were running multiple processors at 200MHz, with as much as 2 *billion* bytes (2 gigabytes) of RAM, and were capable of processing in excess of 1 *billion* instructions per second!

Supercomputers are used for applications that require enormous processing power and speed. This includes computers used to track and forecast world weather, graphics and animation computers (such as the one used for the hit movie **Star Wars**), and those for scientific research. Many of the problems supercomputers are used to solve would take years on any other kind of computer—if they could be solved at all. Fortunately, supercomputers appear to be following the same course of increasing sophistication and decreasing cost as earlier computers, and some supercomputers are already on the horizon which will be smaller and more affordable. In the not-too-distant future it is entirely possible that supercomputer technology will become available to small businesses, and possibly even individuals!

As you can see, determining the size and power of a computer system is becoming increasingly difficult as each new design seems to rival the capabilities of those that came before it. Following are some general descriptions (and rough pricing guidelines) which may prove useful and which will be used throughout this book.

Mainframe

A large multiuser system used by major establishments. This type of system requires special installation, is located in an air-conditioned room designed just for it, and can cost in excess of $150,000. Trained personnel are needed to properly operate and maintain a mainframe. Likewise, a service contract is almost mandatory. Virtually all mainframes are 32-bit machines. These units are almost never seen in a small business setting.

Minicomputer

May have capabilities ranging from that of a large microcomputer to that of a low- to mid-range mainframe. A minicomputer usually has multiple users. It may be small enough to fit on a desk, but is usually floor mounted. This type of computer can be installed in most offices without the need for a special air-conditioned computer room, and can cost in excess of $75,000. A trained staff is usually involved in the operation and maintenance of these machines. Service contracts are the norm, but technically capable purchasers sometimes choose to go without them. Minicomputers are always 16- or 32-bit machines. These units are used by large and small businesses alike, and are often found at colleges and universities.

Microcomputer, Personal Computer, Or PC

Will fit on a desk top (or next to a desk), may have multiuser or networking capabilities, and can even be portable. Usually requires no special installation and only minimum maintenance. Some models are as powerful as a minicomputer, but prices are almost always below $30,000 and may be less than $2,000. These computers are also used by large and small businesses, as well as schools all the way down to the elementary level. If a "staff" is involved it usually consists only of one or more trained employees who are not, however, computer specialists. The more complex the system the more likely it is to have a service contract; smaller systems, however, are often not covered. PCs can be 8-, 16-, or 32-bit machines, although by 1990 8-bit machines were becoming much less common. Many PCs are owned by individuals and used at home.

Home Computer

A computer not found in a typical business setting, and almost exclusively purchased by individuals and used at home. Few home computer owners purchase service contracts for their machines because the cost of the contract can easily exceed the cost of the system. Most computers designed for home use are 8-bit machines, with a few of the most sophisticated models offering 16-bit capability. These units are always small enough to fit on a desk top and no installation in the traditional sense is required. Basic system prices are typically under $1,000.

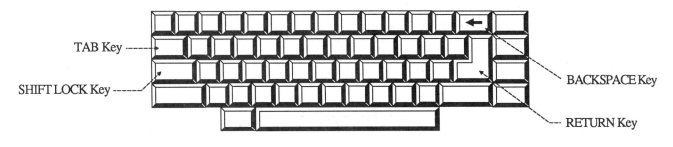

TAB Key -----

SHIFT LOCK Key -----

BACKSPACE Key

RETURN Key

Typewriter Keyboard

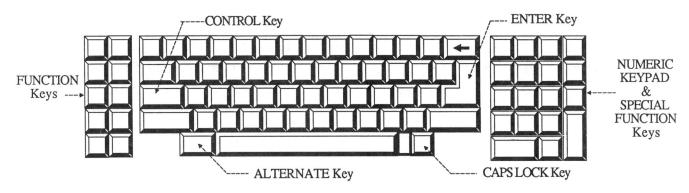

----CONTROL Key

---- ENTER Key

FUNCTION Keys ----

NUMERIC KEYPAD & SPECIAL FUNCTION Keys

----- ALTERNATE Key

---- CAPS LOCK Key

XT Compatible Style Keyboard

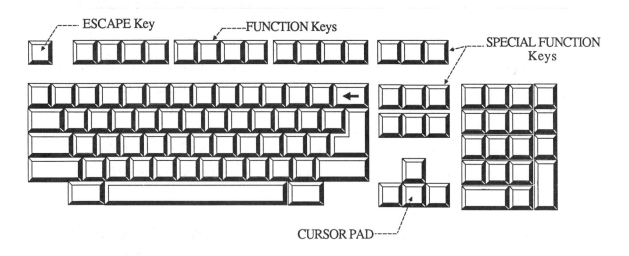

----- ESCAPE Key

-----FUNCTION Keys

SPECIAL FUNCTION Keys

CURSOR PAD-----

Enhanced AT Compatible Keyboard

50

Chapter 4

COMPUTER HARDWARE

The two major ingredients which go together to make up a computer system are **HARDWARE** and **SOFTWARE**. As you will see in later chapters, software is what ultimately makes computers work. But before software (also called *software programs*) can be used you must have a method of interacting with it. Interaction takes place through the use of hardware, and what better place to start a study of hardware than with the discussion of computer keyboards that follows?

KEYBOARDS

Computer keyboards range from a basic layout very similar to that of a typewriter to elaborate arrangements having more than twice as many keys. Some keys function about the same as those found on a typewriter, but many keys are different; some do far more than simply allow the inputting of text.

The alphabetic and numeric keys still perform the same functions, and, as with a typewriter, you still hold down the shift key to access the characters printed at the tops of keys. On a typewriter, certain keys repeat if they are held down. A computer keyboard, however, responds faster than a typewriter and most of the keys will repeat if not released quickly. Until you become accustomed to this feature you may look up to find you have accidentally typed *Missssissssipppiiiii* without realizing it!

Most keyboards also have a **Caps Lock** key which, like the shift lock key on a typewriter, allows you to type continuously in capital letters without shifting for each one. Unlike a typewriter, however, the Caps Lock key allows you to type numbers without having to unshift. On a good keyboard keys like Caps Lock, which can be either on or off, will also have an **INDICATOR LIGHT** to show when the key is on. Indicator lights are usually located either on the tops of the keys themselves or on a separate panel at the upper right-hand corner of the keyboard. Close to this indictor panel, on most keyboards, you will also find a separate 10-key pad to accommodate people working on spreadsheets, bookkeeping, etc.

The key with which you activate commands or cause a carriage return is called the **ENTER** key, often referred to as just **ENTER**. The ENTER key may also be labeled with, or represented in manuals by, a left-pointing arrow. Occasionally, as with a typewriter, the ENTER key is labeled **RETURN**. When referring to computer keyboards, **RETURN** and **ENTER** have the same meaning and may be used interchangeably.

The **BACKSPACE** key is located in the upper right-hand corner above the ENTER key and is usually labeled **BkSp**. The BkSp key is often marked only with a left-pointing arrow. On a typewriter the BkSp key simply moves you back one space, but on a computer keyboard the BkSp key moves back one space while erasing the character that was to the left. It is the left-cursor key which serves the same function as the BkSp key on a typewriter.

The **TAB** key will be found in the same upper left-hand corner location as on a typewriter. It will either be labeled TAB or marked by both a right- and, usually also, a left-pointing arrow. The left-pointing arrow indicates that, unlike on a typewriter, if you hold down the shift key you can tab backwards also.

One new key you will always find will be the **CONTROL** key, often labeled **Ctrl**. This key, like the **SHIFT KEY**, is used by holding it down while at the same time pressing another key. The Ctrl key allows almost every key to have more than one use. For instance, on most computers Control C (or Control Break) will cause software programs to be interrupted, so don't do this unless you're sure it's what you want to do!

A similar key, the **ALTERNATE** key, will also be found on most keyboards. This key will be labeled **Alt** and is most often found below the shift and control keys or next to the space bar. The Alt key functions the same way as the Ctrl key in that it allows other keys to have more than one function when the Alt key is pressed first.

An important group of controls are the **FUNCTION** keys, labeled with a capital F followed by a number. The location and arrangement vary, but they are usually in vertical rows at the left of the keyboard or horizontal rows at the top. When pressed, each key serves a different function according to its number and the software being used. In one program F1 might clear the screen, while in another F1 might cause instructions to appear on the screen. Function keys pressed in combination with Shift, Alt, or Ctrl keys, perform different functions. For instance, F1 and Shift F1 would be considered two different keystrokes. Function keys speed keyboard operations by combining into a single keystroke numerous commands you would otherwise have to key in separately.

A big advantage when using a computer keyboard is the ability to easily see where what you type will appear on the screen. This location is almost always marked on the screen by the **CURSOR**. Occasionally, such as in graphics programs, or when entering a "hidden" password, the cursor does not show on the screen. Cursors come in all shapes and sizes but are usually shown as a blinking square, rectangle, or underline. By using special cursor keys you can move the cursor to any location on the screen before you begin to type. Anything you type will then appear at the point marked by the cursor, which moves one space at a time as you type. The location of the cursor keys varies greatly from keyboard to keyboard, but they are most commonly found on the far right or lower right side of the keyboard. The cursor keys are always marked by arrows showing in which direction the cursor will move when that key is pressed.

On modern computers the four cursor keys (one each for left, right, up, and down) are located in a group by themselves. The less preferable arrangement is one where a cursor function and another function are combined on the same key. If functions are combined in this way there are two ways in which the cursor function is activated. The least popular method requires you to hold down another key, usually Shift or Ctrl, when you also press the key which moves the cursor as one of its functions.

The most common method, however, is this much more convenient one: Above the 10-key pad you will find a key marked **Num Lock**, which allows you to select or "lock" for use either the numbers or the other functions (including cursor control) assigned to the 10-key pad. When the 10-key pad is not locked for numbers, the following functions, besides cursor control, are available on most keyboards: **Home**, **End**, **PgUp**, **PgDn**, **Ins**, and **Del**. The **Home** key, when pressed in most programs, causes the cursor to move either to the beginning of the line or, depending on the program, to the top left-hand corner of the screen. The **End** key causes the cursor to move to either the end of the line or, depending on the program, to the bottom right-hand corner of the screen. The **Page Up** and **Page Down** keys (or **PgUp** and **PgDn**) usually cause the entire screen to move up or down either a page or, again depending on the program, a line or more at a time.

The **INSERT** and **DELETE** keys (**Ins** and **Del**) work either one of two ways, or both, depending upon the program you are using. (Please note that, although it may be located in the same area, the delete key does not serve the same function as the backspace key discussed earlier.) In one method, actually pressing the **Ins** key itself causes all text to the right of the cursor to be "pushed" to the right, and the **Del** key causes text to the right of the cursor to be "pulled" to the left and erased. In the other method, the **Ins** key may be pressed on or off like the Caps Lock key. When this is the case, and the **Ins** key is on, anything you type will cause all text to the right of the cursor to be pushed to the right. When the **Ins** key is off whatever you type simply overwrites the text already on the screen. With rare exceptions (such as a graphics-oriented program like Flight Simulator which is not designed for typed input) the BkSp, Ins, and Del, keys control the insertion or deletion of characters and are frequently used for editing text on the screen.

Other keys sometimes found on the ten key pad are the **ESCAPE**, **BREAK**, and **PRINT SCREEN** keys (**Esc**, **Brk**, and **PrtSc** or **Print Scrn** are also used). The Esc key, as its name implies, allows you to leave or "escape" from whatever it is you happen to be doing at the time. The Break key causes a "break" or interruption in the program or process that is currently running. Lastly, the Print Screen key, if a printer is properly connected, causes whatever is currently on the screen to be printed on paper (not an entire document, just the text showing on the screen).

CAUTION: You should keep in mind that, while the most common keyboard arrangements and functions have been explained, many variations can be found from computer to computer, from program to program, and even from keyboard to keyboard. If you don't know what a certain key does in the application program you are using, check the instruction manual or ask someone. Better to do this than find that by pressing the wrong key you have suddenly caused the interruption of the entire system, or even wiped out hours or weeks of work!

MICE

No, these aren't the kind of mice some people cringe at the thought of! A computer **MOUSE** is a small rectangular or oval box-like device which sits on the work surface next to your computer. It probably got its name because, with its small cord trailing out behind like a tail, it does resemble a mouse. A mouse is another form of input device which you can use along with, or instead of, a keyboard. Most software programs do not require a mouse. More and more, however, software offers you the choice of using a mouse, and many programs (especially graphics-oriented programs) cannot be operated effectively, if at all, without a mouse. Software that works with a mouse makes available choices (such as print, draw, erase, save, etc.) of actions, commands, or functions through on-screen **MENUS** or **WINDOWS**, some of which are referred to as **PULL-DOWN MENUS**. The smallest of these is referred to as an **ITEM** or **ICON**, which is typically in the form of a small square box with a descriptive title below or within it.

You make your selection by moving the mouse over a smooth surface, which in turn moves an indicator or pointer displayed on the screen. When you have positioned the pointer over the selection you want, you push, or **CLICK**, a button on the mouse to execute your instructions; mice typically have two, sometimes three, buttons. Most programs are designed so that clicking once makes available a menu or list of choices or other programs while clicking twice in rapid succession, referred to as a **DOUBLE CLICK**, confirms a selection or executes one of the programs. Continuing to hold down a button while using the mouse is referred to as **DRAGGING**, and is most often used to position or draw an image on the screen. Occasionally, a program may require you to press two buttons at the same time; this is referred to as **CHORDING**.

Graphics and drawing software works extremely well with a mouse since almost all such work consists of moving a pointer around the screen to specify where you want to draw lines, circles, squares, etc. There is little need for a keyboard in graphics work, and the mouse usually allows you to work much faster. However, for non-graphic-oriented applications, such as accounting, a mouse may be much slower than using the keyboard.

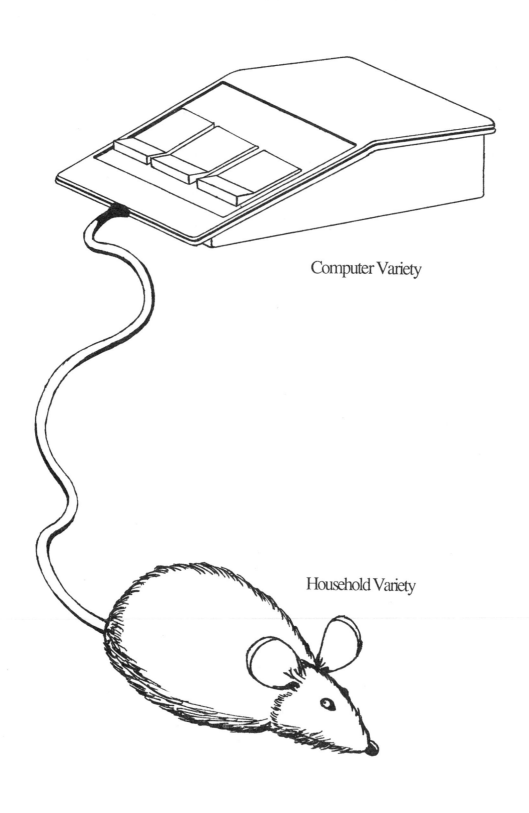

Computer Variety

Household Variety

A Typical Mouse

While you use a mouse by resting your hand on its top, the parts which make it work are located underneath and inside. When you move a mouse, a small exposed ball on the underside rolls across your work surface. Sensors inside detect how far—and how fast—you've moved the mouse and translate this motion into cursor or pointer movement on your computer screen. This is the most common, and least expensive, design, and is referred to as a **MECHANICAL MOUSE**. Mechanical mice are highly reliable, but, because the rolling ball picks up dust and dirt from the work surface, they require periodic cleaning and may occasionally fail. A **MOUSE PAD** is a fabric-covered mat which can be placed on your work surface. Mouse pads not only keep mice cleaner, but, if you have an extremely shiny or smooth desk, they can also increase accuracy by keeping the ball from slipping as it rolls. A more accurate type of mouse which has no moving parts, and is thus far less likely to fail or need cleaning, is the **OPTICAL MOUSE**. Optical mice will work only with a specially designed pad that comes with the mouse, the surface of which contains an optically readable grid pattern (like that of a checkerboard, but much more intricate). An optical sensor underneath the mouse detects movement over the grid on the mouse pad and positions the on-screen pointer.

Trackballs

An alternative to the traditional mouse is the **TRACKBALL**, or **TRACKBALL MOUSE**. While relatively new to personal computers the trackball has been around for quite some time as a screen-control device, both in arcade-style video games and for use with computer engineering and graphics workstations. A trackball for computer use generally resembles a mouse, although its design is often more boxy. It is essentially an upside-down mouse with the **ROLLER BALL** located on top rather than underneath. Instead of moving a trackball across your work surface, as with a regular mouse, you use your fingers to roll the exposed ball on top. Like a mouse, selections are made by clicking buttons located on the top of the trackball. However, there is one important difference: Since a trackball is operated entirely with your fingers, at times it may be awkward to roll the ball *and* still use the buttons for dragging. To solve this problem all good trackball designs incorporate a feature called drag lock, which, when on, has the effect of continuously holding one of the buttons down (electronically) until you turn drag lock off.

Even though millions of mice had been sold by 1991, more and more people were choosing trackballs because of these advantages: Trackballs require very little desk space because they don't have to be moved during operation. More precise control is possible because the ball is larger and because you control it with your fingertips rather than moving your entire wrist and arm, helping avoid the fatigue associated with using a mouse. Trackballs rarely require cleaning or maintenance because the ball does not come into contact with, or pick up dirt from, the work surface. It is also easy for a mouse to move when you don't want it to, either by itself or because your hand moves a little, causing unwanted movement of the cursor on screen, called **CURSOR CREEP**. For these reasons, and more, the popularity of trackballs is steadily increasing. But don't expect to see trackballs totally replace mice, because even though trackballs offer many advantages, there are still some things they cannot do as well as mice. For instance, with a mouse, because it can precisely match your hand movements, you can draw almost perfectly straight lines or even write your signature. On a trackball, however, motions such as these prove to be too awkward for most people. Some people gain the best of both worlds by using a trackball for routine pointing, cursor movement, and selection, and occasionally using a mouse for fine detail while drawing or creating artwork.

LIGHT PENS

While less common than either the mouse or trackball, the **LIGHT PEN** and **TOUCH-SENSITIVE SCREEN** are also devices designed to allow you to interact with a computer. Of the two methods, light pens have been in practical use longer, and are so named because most of them actually do look like a large pen. Instead of lead or ink, however, the tip of a light pen contains a sensor that can detect light. The patterns of light displayed on the screen are translated by software into usable signals, which, like a mouse, are used to choose from selections offered on the screen—you simply point the light pen at the selection you want. Light pens offer some of the same advantages of a mouse, but are generally not as easy to use or as versatile—and holding your arm in the air all day to use a light pen can be tiring.

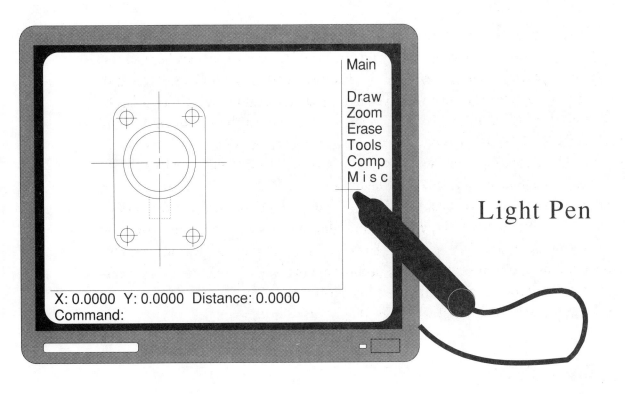

Light Pen

Touch Sensitive
Screen

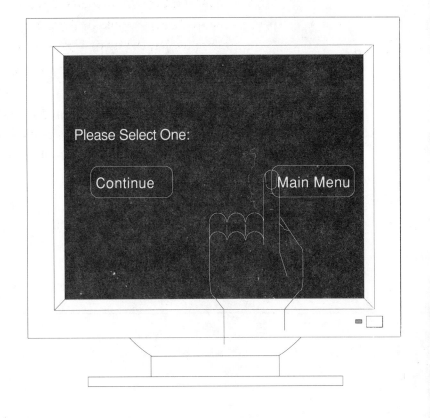

TOUCH-SENSITIVE SCREENS

Some monitors have specially designed screens which allow you to simply touch the screen with your finger to make a selection. The surfaces of most **TOUCH-SENSITIVE SCREENS** are the same as any other monitor, and are not actually sensitive to touch. Instead, the screen is criss-crossed by tiny beams of light that overlay a displayed menu of possible actions. The beams of light come from the inner edges of the monitor's screen housing. When your finger breaks the beams a signal is sent to the software you are using, which then determines your selected action by calculating the intersect point of the two beams of light which have been broken. Touch-sensitive screens are extremely useful for non-computer users, since (in some applications) every necessary selection, or other action, can be made without the need for a keyboard and typing skills. Library card-catalog files and shopping center directories are examples of current uses for touch-sensitive screens.

MONITORS

Computer monitors, the TV-like devices that display computer text and graphics, have a variety of other names, all meaning essentially the same thing—**MONITOR, SCREEN, CRT** (**C**ATHODE **R**AY **T**UBE), **V**IDEO **D**ISPLAY **T**ERMINAL (**VDT**), and sometimes, although somewhat crudely, just **TUBE**. Major advances in the 1980s also produced the flat, thin screen used for laptop computers known as the **LCD** (**L**IQUID **C**RYSTAL **D**ISPLAY); a more sophisticated version of the displays used in wrist watches. The **GAS PLASMA DISPLAY**, while not as thin or energy efficient as an LCD, was also adopted for use in laptop and portable computers. (Incidentally, monitors should not be confused with **TERMINALS**. In combination with a keyboard a monitor is one of the components used in the construction of, or along with, terminals. However, a monitor does not by itself qualify as a terminal [See "Terminals," on page 193].)

Despite the different names, monitors operate almost the same way as a television set. The biggest difference is in the **RESOLUTION** (sharpness or quality) of the picture. Computer monitors must have higher resolution than TV sets so that the text displayed is sharp, clear, and easy to see and read. The text should always stand out from the screen, and the background of the screen should not be so bright that it makes the text hard to read. It is important to take picture quality into consideration when selecting a monitor. Monitors with poor resolution will have clearly visible lines running through each character and/or the characters will be fuzzy and have poorly defined edges. This can be very distracting and can cause eye strain, fatigue, and even headaches. Remember that, as explained below, if you look at *any* monitor closely enough the picture becomes fuzzy. Fifteen inches is considered the minimum distance for proper viewing, with two feet, or arm's length, being ideal.

An easy way to understand how the resolution of a monitor is measured is to look closely at the screen of a TV set or the pictures in a newspaper. (A magnifying glass will help.) You will see that the pictures are actually not solid, but instead are composed of very tiny dots. When viewed at a distance, these dots visually merge to form the characters and pictures that you see as a whole. This technique of combining dots can be used not only to form images on monitors but is also the same one used to form images on paper, photographs, and the film used for motion pictures.

Resolution is determined by the number of dots, also called **PIXELS (PIX** [picture] **ELEMENTS)**, that extend from the left to right edge of the screen, called **VERTICAL RESOLUTION**, and the number of dots that extend from the top to bottom edge of the screen, called **HORIZONTAL RESOLUTION**. A row of dots is often referred to as a **LINE OF RESOLUTION** since each row of dots forms a line across the screen. On a screen with **640 x 400** resolution you would count 640 dots, *or lines*, as you went across the screen, and 400 as you went down the screen. The first number always indicates the vertical resolution (which is usually greater than the horizontal resolution), while the second number gives the horizontal resolution. As with a TV, the actual screen size of all monitors is measured diagonally.

Occasionally, you may run across the terms **40-COLUMN** or **80-COLUMN**, which refer to the number of characters a monitor can display across its width. On a screen with an 80 x 25 character display you would count 80 characters as you went across the screen and 25 characters as you went down the screen. A horizontal line of characters is referred to as a **ROW**, while a vertical line of characters is called a **COLUMN**, so 80 x 25 could also be stated as 80 columns by 25 rows. An 80 x 25 screen is considered standard for a personal or business computer. Other than for home computers, mainly older ones, or for specialized uses, such as the screens on modern cash registers, a smaller screen is impractical for today's applications. Even if your text should extend off the screen, such as a letter longer than 25 rows in length, software allows you to move or **SCROLL** the text up and down so that you may see the entire image. Moving the image left or right is referred to as **HORIZONTAL SCROLLING**, while moving and image up or down is referred to as **VERTICAL SCROLLING**.

While some computers already contain the circuitry needed to make a monitor function, most require the installation of an additional plug-in circuit board, referred to as a **GRAPHICS CARD**. (Many computers come with a graphics card already installed.) In addition, a special software program, called a **GRAPHICS DRIVER**, may need to be installed and run before the monitor will properly display images. Even if your computer comes with a graphics card installed, as you are about to learn, there are many graphics standards, and, if possible, you may wish to specify a different card.

The most common type of monitor, and the one used most often for text, is the **MONOCHROME MONITOR**, sometimes referred to as a **GREEN SCREEN** (the image color most common when this type of monitor was introduced). Monochrome monitors are also available with an amber image color which many people find easier on their eyes. The monochrome monitor is an excellent choice for most applications such as word processing and other text-intensive programs, and, because of the high image quality, is easy to work at for long periods of time.

If you are considering color you should be aware that, currently, there is no such thing as a cheap, high-quality color monitor. This is one reason why the majority of monitors in use for text-based applications are monochrome. On the other hand, because of the way it must create the image displayed on the screen, only a color monitor of the highest quality will be easy to read—and such monitors are expensive. Studies have shown that well-designed software can be operated more effectively by using color to draw the user's attention to the correct area on the screen. You should keep in mind, however, that in a large number of programs color is not used well and may just be a selling point to "jazz up" the program.

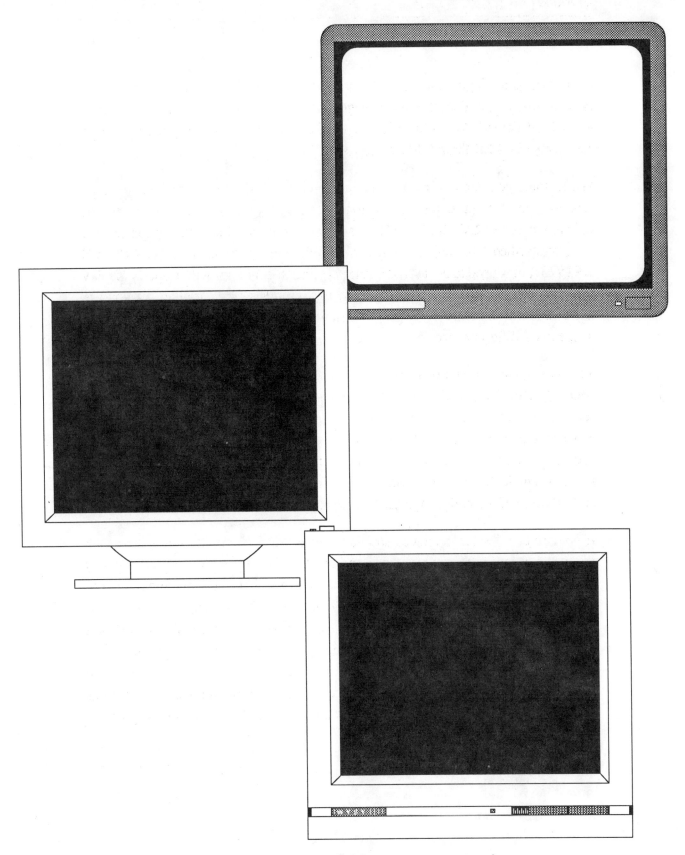

Examples of different monitors.

There are two basic types of color monitors. The most economical one is the **COMPOSITE MONITOR**, in which all colors are combined into one signal (as in your TV set at home) and displayed on the screen. The other, which offers the best resolution, is the **RGB (RED-GREEN-BLUE)** monitor, in which each color is processed as a separate signal. Either kind can be expensive, ranging from several hundred dollars on the low end, to almost a thousand dollars, or more, for the best. The cost of lab-quality RGB monitors, for medical, engineering, or graphics use, can easily exceed $2,000.

While at one time the generic term RGB was used to describe all color monitors, with new technological standards came new names. The first, and now outdated, standard was CGA, which stands for **COLOR GRAPHICS ADAPTER** and offers a maximum resolution of 640 x 200. Next came **EGA (ENHANCED GRAPHICS ADAPTER)**, which has a maximum resolution of 640 x 350, and, while still the most common, seems to be becoming outdated also. Some manufacturers created versions of EGA called **ENHANCED EGA** or **SUPER-EGA**, which offer even higher resolution. Then **VGA (VIDEO GRAPHICS ARRAY)**, which offers a maximum resolution of 640 x 480, came along when IBM introduced its new PS/2 series of computers. Here also, some manufacturers created **ENHANCED VGA** and **SUPER-VGA** versions that can increase the resolution to 800 x 600, and even 1,024 x 768. Yet another video technology, called **PGA (PROFESSIONAL GRAPHICS ADAPTER)**, was introduced by IBM around the same time, but, unlike the others, PGA did not see widespread use. In late 1990, and early 1991, IBM introduced a VGA-like technology called **XGA (EXTENDED GRAPHICS ARRAY)**, which has a standard resolution of 1,024 x 768 and offers far more colors than does VGA. However, XGA is not really compatible with VGA and previous standards, so its popularity remains to be seen. Among the best of these displays, and most expensive, is the **AUTOSYNC MONITOR**, which automatically makes itself compatible with virtually all popular standards, including TV (if you should want to hook up a VCR, etc.). Autosync monitors can offer a hedge against future obsolescence because if a new standard is introduced there is a good chance they will automatically be compatible. All color monitors will display monochrome images, and, while not compatible with a higher standard, are compatible with the standards below it. An EGA monitor, for instance, is compatible with monochrome and CGA, but cannot display VGA images, while a VGA monitor can display monochrome, CGA, EGA, and VGA.

For extensive graphics or design work you may need a monitor that offers even more than those just mentioned. Monitors used for graphics, engineering, drafting, and/or typesetting are often referred to as **WHITE SCREENS, PAGE-WHITE SCREENS,** or **PAGE-WHITE DISPLAYS**; they display black text on a screen with a white background designed to simulate working on a sheet of paper. These monitors are available in extra-large sizes to accommodate more on the screen at one time, are usually monochrome, and offer noticeably superior image quality. Few monitors of this kind cost less than $1,000 and many exceed $2,000. Before running out to buy one, though, you should check to see if your software requires such a monitor, and if your computer system will accommodate it. There are many graphics and design programs that work well with standard monochrome, EGA, or VGA monitors.

Just some final food for thought before leaving the subject of monitors: Perhaps no other part of a computer system can increase or impair your productivity as subtly as a monitor. Almost all modern, full-size keyboards are now comfortable to type on, and if one is poorly designed it is immediately obvious when you start to type; the same applies to mice, trackballs, etc. However, a monitor with inadequate picture quality can sometimes reduce your efficiency, or cause fatigue, without your knowing the monitor is causing the problem. If you will be working with monitors on a regular basis for any length of time, do not overlook the important role they play. A poor monitor—or a good one with the wrong colors selected—*can* prevent you from working effectively, and *can* cause eyestrain and/or headaches that may last for hours after you've finished working.

MASS STORAGE DEVICES

A **MASS STORAGE DEVICE** is any device: 1) that allows your computer to hold more data than what is stored in RAM, and 2) that—unlike RAM—also retains programs and data even when the power is switched off. The most popular mass storage devices are disk drives, and with few exceptions your computer will need to have at least one disk drive in order to operate. Naming conventions for disk drives—on computers both large and small—are well established and easy to learn. Each drive is named using a different letter of the alphabet (referred to as the **DRIVE LETTER**), and naming starts with the letter *"A."* On most computers the first 3 letters of the alphabet are reserved as follows: Drives A and B are used for either one or two floppy-disk drives, drive C is used for the main hard-disk drive, and drive-letters D and up are used for additional hard-disk drives. The removable disks used in some of these drives are referred to by their names rather than the broad term *mass storage devices*. Those names, and many other terms, are described in the following sections.

Floppy-Disk Drives

As the name implies, a **FLOPPY-DISK DRIVE** utilizes a flexible mylar plastic disk—hence the name **FLOPPY DISK**—which rotates within a sealed square envelope of heavy plastic called the **DISK JACKET** or **DISK SLEEVE**. As detailed below, the disk jacket has a round 1.5" opening in the center of the front and back which exposes a slightly smaller hole in the diskette and allows the drive mechanism to grasp the disk and spin it rapidly. A small oblong window in the front and back of the jacket gives access to the drive's read-write head which both reads information from and transfers information to the disk, which is coated with a magnetic recording material very similar to that found on cassette tapes. For many years the 5.25" floppy disk was the standard, but in recent years the 3.5" **MICROFLOPPY DISK** has become increasingly popular (See "Microfloppy," on page 76).

If you have ever listened to a blank cassette tape you are familiar with the hissing sound, or *background noise*, they make. Occasionally, a loud crack or a pop may come through the speakers. Much of what you are hearing is caused by imperfections on the tape; the higher the quality of the tape, the fewer imperfections there will be. On an audio tape these imperfections—called **ERRORS** when found on a floppy disk—seldom affect the final recording in a way that disturbs your listening. With floppy disks, however, *any* **GLITCH,** no matter how small, can cause disastrous results. For this reason, all disks used with a computer should be **CERTIFIED 100 PERCENT ERROR-FREE**; you're taking a big chance if you use disks that do not state this on the package. Most floppy disk manufacturers guarantee their disks to be error-free, and, although they won't be responsible for any losses you suffer as the result of defective disks, they will offer to replace them at no charge.

Typical Disk Directory "Tree Structure."

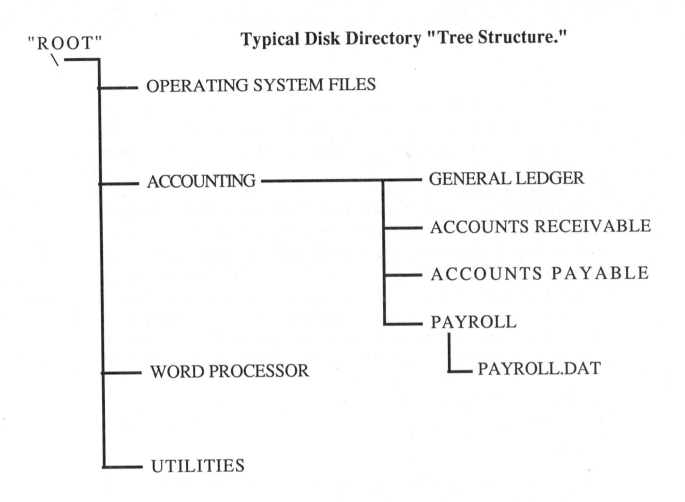

"ROOT"

— OPERATING SYSTEM FILES

— ACCOUNTING —— GENERAL LEDGER

—— ACCOUNTS RECEIVABLE

—— ACCOUNTS PAYABLE

—— PAYROLL

—— PAYROLL.DAT

— WORD PROCESSOR

— UTILITIES

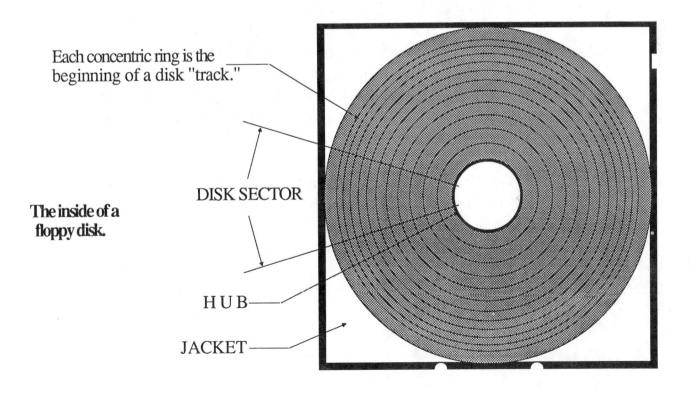

Each concentric ring is the beginning of a disk "track."

DISK SECTOR

The inside of a floppy disk.

H U B

JACKET

Unlike a phono-record, where the grooves spiral in towards the center, the **TRACKS** on a floppy disk form concentric circles (like the rings on a dartboard target). When you close the door of a floppy-disk drive the drive spindle actually "grabs" the disk by the edge of the hole, or **HUB**, located at its center. While on some drives the disk spins continuously, most drives only spin the disk when they need to access information. **READ** and **WRITE** heads—also very similar to those found on a cassette deck—are used to record information on, and retrieve it from, the disk. A precision **STEPPING MOTOR** allows the read/write heads to be accurately positioned over any track, thus allowing random access to any piece of information located anywhere on the disk. The time it takes to do this is known as the **ACCESS TIME** of the drive, and is measured in **MILLISECONDS** (usually abbreviated to just "ms"). When the read/write heads have reached the correct location on the disk the computer can then retrieve the information stored there, performing what is called a **READ**, or it can record information, called a **WRITE**. Whenever the drive is looking for a certain location on the disk it is said to be **SEEKING** that location or information, and the time it takes to find it is referred to as the **SEEK TIME**, or **TRACK-TO-TRACK SEEK TIME**.

Almost all floppy disks currently being used for personal or business computers are of the **DOUBLE-SIDED (DS)** variety, meaning that a disk drive can read and write information on both sides of the disk. Likewise, only one side of a **SINGLE-SIDED (SS)** disk is usable and, therefore, can store only half as much information as a double-sided disk. A double-sided disk drive can use either single- or double-sided disks; however, a single-sided drive can use only single-sided disks. Because most systems need the added storage capacity and speed offered by double-sided disk drives, single-sided drives are usually found only on some home computers. In addition to being single- or double-sided, disks are also available in a variety of formats, the most common being **DOUBLE-SIDED DOUBLE-DEN-SITY (DSDD)**, meaning that twice as much information can be stored as on a **SINGLE-DENSITY (SD)** disk. Computers and disk drives usually divide DSDD disks into 35 tracks to store the information on, which, on an MS-DOS machine, usually amounts to around 360,000 characters (360K). The next most common disk, on MS-DOS machines, is the 5.25" **DOUBLE-SIDED QUAD-DENSITY** disk (**HD** or **HIGH-DENSITY**), which can hold four times the amount of information as double-sided double-density disks—about 1,200,000 characters

(1.2Meg). These HD disks can be divided into as few as 77 tracks and as many as 96. Regardless of type, when a disk has reached its storage limit—when no more data can be written to it—you will receive a DISK FULL error message.

The type of disk required will be specified in the computer's or disk drive's operating manual. Using the wrong type of disks in a drive is not a good idea, and can lead to data loss, so be sure to use only the type of disks specified for use with your computer. When purchasing a new computer you will usually have the option of specifying which type of drive will be installed. Even though DSDD disks hold less information than HDs, because DSDD was the first format and still outnumbers computers with HD drives you may be better off using the DSDD format if you plan to share or swap disks between a number of different computers and offices.

One question that may come up, that doesn't need to be explained here in detail, is whether or not a disk is in the **SOFT-SECTOR** or **HARD-SECTOR** format. Most computers you are likely to use will require soft-sector disks. Packages of disks that are hard-sector will always be marked that way. Soft-sector disks are usually marked also; however, if the box is not labeled it means the disks are soft-sector. Again, use the type specified for your computer. If you use computers with different disk formats be careful not to mix them. However, there is one exception: while a double-sided double-density drive will not read or write to a HD (1.2Meg) disk, a HD drive can *read* a DSDD disk. Many HD drives—especially earlier ones—claim they can also write to DSDD disks, and that those disks can then be used in standard DSDD drives, but this has often proved unreliable. To give you the ability to keep someone (yourself included) from accidentally erasing information, all floppy disks have a **WRITE PROTECT** notch. Blank disks come unprotected, i.e., with the notch exposed, which means it is possible to both read and write to them. If you cover the notch with the little adhesive stickers (**WRITE PROTECT TABS**) that come with the disks the information on the disk is protected from being erased. Unfortunately, this also means that more data cannot be stored on the disk while the tab is in place. If the program you're using operates by continually updating or storing information on the disk, the write protect tab cannot be left in place. Instead, you will have to protect your information by making sure to **BACK UP** your data often (See "Backups," on page 139).

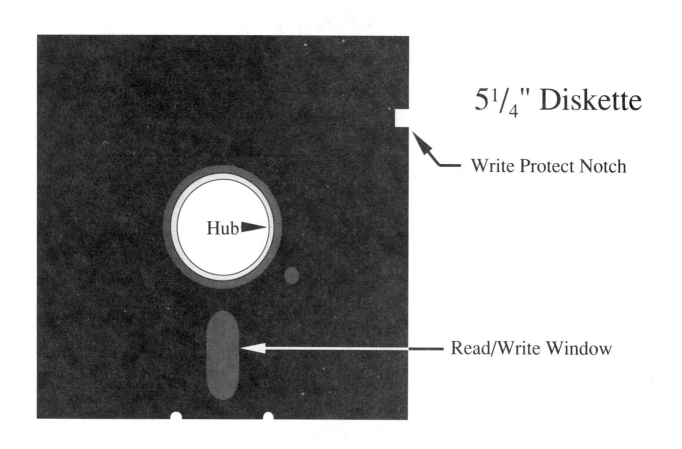

5$\frac{1}{4}$" Diskette

Write Protect Notch

Hub

Read/Write Window

3$\frac{1}{2}$" Micro Diskette

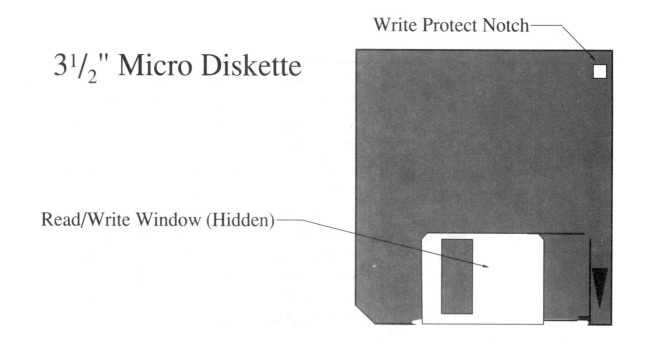

Write Protect Notch

Read/Write Window (Hidden)

Floppy Disk Care And Handling

Floppy disks do require reasonable care and handling. They should never be bent or dropped. If they are, even if no data is lost at the time, it could cause the recording material which coats the disk's surface to flake off, leading to possible data loss in the future. You should never write with a ballpoint pen on a label that has already been affixed to the disk jacket, since the pressure of a pen can gouge the surface of the disk within. Instead, use a felt-tip pen, or, better yet, write on the label before affixing it to the disk. Floppy disks should always be kept away from magnets or sources of magnetism, such as TVs, telephone ringers, adding machines, etc. The disk's surface—exposed through the oval window—should never be touched by anything, for even a fingerprint can damage a floppy disk and cause a loss of data.

If the plastic envelope itself, but not the disk inside, is spattered with a liquid, it can be wiped dry without a problem. If the exposed portion of the disk is spattered with only water, simply let the disk dry (which may take several hours), then copy your data to a new disk, just to be on the safe side. If considerable water or any other liquid gets inside the plastic envelope all is not lost, necessarily, but you've definitely got a problem. Talk as soon as possible with a computer technician or a data recovery service (See "Resource list," on page 273).

Hard-Disk Drives

A more sophisticated relative of the floppy-disk drive is the **HARD-DISK DRIVE** or **FIXED-DISK DRIVE**, both often called just a **HARD DRIVE**. A hard-disk drive operates on principles similar to those of a floppy drive, but there are a number of important differences which give the hard-disk drive dramatically increased performance. The major difference is that the disks of a hard drive are permanently sealed inside the drive's case, thus allowing for greater precision of operation, higher operating speeds, and more storage capacity. You not only cannot remove the disks, but they can't be touched or seen, either. This is because hard-disk drives must operate in a near clean-room environment due to their precision nature. Even particles of dust or smoke can cause unreliable results or the loss of data. A single hard drive may contain as many as six disks or more—even though the entire unit is still considered one disk drive. The disks themselves are referred to as **PLATTERS**.

Unlike floppy disks, which are flexible, hard-disk platters are made of rigid metal with a precision coating of magnetic recording material which is polished to a mirror-like finish. A set of read/write heads is located over both sides of each platter; in other words, a 6-platter hard disk has 12 read/write heads. The platters share the same spindle, and are stacked one on top of the other much the same way as records in a jukebox. This stacking of disks allows the hard drive to be small in size, as opposed to a drive containing a single platter large enough to hold the same amount of data. Earlier hard disk technology was bulky and sometimes required an external housing. However, all but the largest of modern hard-disk drives are small enough to fit inside the computer, and occupy about the same space as a floppy-disk drive.

Hard-disk drives operate by spinning these platters at very high speeds, more than ten times faster than a floppy. When you first turn on a hard drive it takes a little while for the disks to reach their operating speed of 3,600 revolutions per minute (RPM). Until the drive reaches this speed the computer cannot access information on the disks. At this point, a rather high tech feature comes into play: Unlike the read/write heads found in a floppy disk or cassette recorder, etc., the heads of a hard drive do not actually come into contact with the recording material. Instead, the heads remain suspended just millionths of an inch above the surfaces of the platters. This is necessary because if the heads were to come into contact with the very delicate (and rapidly moving) surface of the platter, both heads and platters would be damaged and the data would be lost—this is known as a **HEAD CRASH**.

Hard-disk drives have so many advantages over floppies that they are almost a must for any important computer application. Four of the major advantages are: 1) Because the magnetic coating on the platters is much denser than a floppy's, they can store more information. It would take almost 60 DSDD floppies to store as much information as will fit on a single 20Meg hard disk. 2) Data transfer rates are fast because of the high speed at which the platters rotate. This means programs run faster, which in turn saves you valuable time. 3) Hard disks are highly reliable, secure, and convenient ways to store information. 4) A computer with a hard disk is ready for use almost as soon as you turn it on, since all programs and data it needs to operate can be stored on the drive.

Because they are more complex, hard-disk drives cost more than floppy drives. However, like most computer components, hard disks have become very afford-able, and their use is now the rule rather than the exception. Usually, the instruction manuals even for programs that will run on a floppy recommend installation on a hard disk for anything more than casual use. Most modern software—with the exception of games, personal checkbook and finance programs, etc.—is designed to be used on a hard disk. Other examples of software that requires a hard disk are programs that store large amounts of data (databases, accounting programs, etc.) and (because there would be no one around to change floppy disks) programs that are designed to run unattended.

Even on systems with a hard disk a floppy drive is still needed to transfer new software into the system. Once your software has been installed, however, the floppies can be stored and won't be needed again unless the information on the hard disk is lost. Additional floppy disks will be needed to back up the information stored on the hard disk, unless you have another backup device.

The surface a computer rests upon should be as stable and as motion- and vibration-free as possible. Hard-disk drives are the components most easily affected by motion and sudden movement. Care should be taken to avoid moving or bumping a computer which contains a hard disk—or the desk it sits on. If a hard disk is bumped hard enough while it is running the heads might **CRASH** into the platters. **HEAD CRASHES** are rare with today's modern drives if reasonable care is taken during their operation. If a head crash should occur, some or all of the data may be lost, and the drive will no doubt need repair—which can be very expensive. To be certain no data will be lost, always perform a complete backup before moving your computer, and then make sure the drive is turned off and has stopped spinning; this can take 15 seconds or more. Look in your instruction manuals to find out what command, if any, is used to prepare the drive for moving. These commands will **PARK** the read/write heads in such a way that they will not damage usable portions of the platters when the drive is moved. Different systems use different commands, but a few of the most common are: PARK, SHIP, SHIPTRACK, and SIT. Many systems automatically park the heads of the hard disk after so many seconds, or minutes, of keyboard inactivity, or when the system is turned off.

Now that hard disks are relatively inexpensive, a 20Meg drive is about the smallest you're likely to run across, and is probably the smallest you should buy, and 30Meg and 40Meg are also common small drive sizes. Your software will specify the minimum amount of hard disk space needed; totaling the requirements of all of your software will tell you how much **PROGRAM SPACE** will be needed. Your additional requirement is determined by how much information you are likely to store on the disk at any one time. An individual might only need a 20Meg drive, while a small business might need 40Megs. Some businesses wipe out all information at the end of each year, others maintain past information for years to have ready access when they need it.

One way to get an approximate idea of **STORAGE CAPACITY** is to picture a one-page typewritten letter. Few letters use an entire sheet of paper, so let's assume the average letter occupies 2K of disk space. This would mean an entirely blank 20Meg hard disk could hold 10,000 letters. Remember, though, that a hard disk will never be entirely blank. The operating system of the computer will take up a certain amount of space, as well as the space needed by the software you will be running and the data it (you) will produce. Also keep in mind that you will probably need to purchase additional software later. Even if you think you know what your hard disk needs will be it is always better to add in a little extra margin for future expansion—then round up to the next largest drive—than to find you've purchased a hard disk that's too small. Following is an example of how to calculate hard disk storage requirements:

1. Operating system	1Meg
2. Word processor	4Meg
3. Spreadsheet	2Meg
4. Accounting	3Meg
5. You expect to produce 7-10Meg of additional miscellaneous data in the next one to two years.	10Meg
Total	20Meg

With a 50% safety margin your
minimum disk space requirement is 30Meg

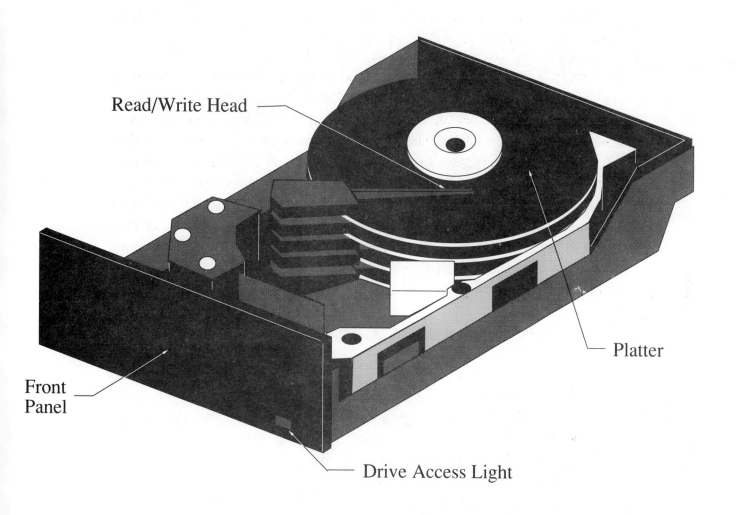

Read/Write Head

Platter

Front
Panel

Drive Access Light

Example of a Hard Disk Drive

Microfloppy Disk

A third type of disk format is the 3.5" **MICROFLOPPY DISK (MFD)**, which may also be referred to simply as a **FLOPPY DISK**. The microfloppy is a compromise between the portability—and vulnerability—of the larger 5.25" floppy disks and the higher storage capabilities and reliability of hard disks. Currently, standard microfloppies hold 720K and HD microfloppies hold 1.44Meg. A microfloppy contains the same type of rotatable disk as a floppy, but the jacket is a rigid case which totally encloses and protects the disk. Instead of having a permanently open read/write window as the floppy does, the microfloppy read/write window is covered by a protective **SHUTTER** which exposes the disk surface only when it is safely inside the disk drive. Because the microfloppy doesn't bend or flex easily like a floppy, and the disk surface is never exposed while outside the drive, it is much less susceptible to damage than a floppy. These features combined with its small size make it easy to store and to transport from computer to computer; you can even carry one around safely in your shirt pocket.

Because the 3.5" disk offers so many advantages over the older 5.25" floppies it has become the format of choice for most new computer purchasers, and is well on the way to replacing 5.25" disks, just as 5.25" disks replaced 8" disks. In the meantime, however, a lot of software still comes on 5.25" disks. This means you will probably need a 5.25" floppy drive to transfer programs to and from your hard disk, or to exchange data with others who still use the 5.25" format. There are also a number of excellent programs on the market that solve this problem by allowing you to transfer data by cabling two computers together directly.

Disk Drive Considerations

Now that you have a good idea of what disk drives are and how they differ from each other, here are some common features and qualities they all share: At least one light appears on a disk drive. If a drive has only one light, when the light is on it indicates that the disk is being accessed—being read from or written to. When there are two lights, one will be on anytime the drive is on—basically as a power indicator light which lets you know the drive is operating. On some larger computer systems there is sometimes a third light (on hard drives only) which indicates whether or not the drive itself is locked. Like a floppy disk with its write-protect tab in place, a drive that is locked cannot be written to. Most MS-DOS computers are now being manufactured with a key which can be used to lock the drive (and/or the keyboard) and prevent someone from tampering with it when left unattended.

Unless a program you are using tells you to do so, be careful never to remove a disk from a floppy drive while the light is on. To do so could interrupt the program, result in the loss of data, and cause damage to the disk drive.

A new disk—floppy or hard disk—must go through the **FORMAT** process and be **FORMATTED** before it can be used to store or retrieve information. The formatting process works by recording permanent—unless you **REFORMAT**—tracks and other information on the disk which allow the drive to organize and locate data. The process can take from less than a minute for a floppy to as much as several hours for a large hard disk. Trying to use an unformatted disk will result in an error. Just a word of caution: Many instruction manuals say that a disk only needs to be formatted once—when it is new. While this proves true for some, as a disk ages wear and tear, static electricity, etc., can damage both the existing format as well as data on the disk. In fact, some manufacturers of hard disks are now saying it is a wise precaution to back up hard disks periodically—every six months to a year—and to reformat them as a way of preventing this problem. This is even more true of floppies since they are often carried around and are more exposed to the environment. New floppy disks that fail to format should be returned for an exchange, and any disk that starts generating read/write problems should be backed up and reformatted or replaced.

What To Do If You Accidentally Erase Something

When you erase a cassette tape you are erasing everything stored on it and making it blank again. Fortunately, when you erase information on a computer disk the information is not really erased. Remember the information the computer places on the disk when it's formatted? Well, when you issue a command to erase data on a disk the computer really only deletes the **DIRECTORY** entries for that data (the internal records of where the data is/was located on the disk). Little, if any, of the old data is actually erased in the process. It is only when the space is needed later by another file that the old data that was "erased" is written over.

If you should erase important information on a disk that you don't have a backup for, don't continue to use the disk to store more information. Writing more information to the disk might cause the new data to be written to the same space occupied by the information you want to recover. It's still there, but once it's written over it will be permanently lost. There are a number of good data and file recovery programs available to save people from situations like these, but to use one of these recovery programs yourself you will have to have at least a basic working knowledge of your operating system and the files your program uses to store information. If you have not yet become familiar with the programs and system you are using there are a number of data recovery services that will try to recover the lost information for you (See "Resource list," on page 273). Success of data recovery programs and services should not be taken for granted, however, for they are not always able to recover your information. Think of data recovery programs only as an option available when an accident or emergency occurs. Don't be lulled into the false idea that your data can be handled casually because a data recovery program can save you from any mistake that might be made. You should also keep mind that, unlike the erase operations just described, formatting a disk *does* erase *all* information stored there, and *extreme caution* should be exercised when using format commands. The *best protection* you have against all disk and data loss problems is to make sure you *backup regularly!* (See "Backups," on page 139.)

How Disk Drives Store Information

People often think of disk drives as being rather mysterious. Information goes in and comes out, but they have no idea of how it's done. The answer is both simple and familiar: Computers store information in **DISK FILES**. There is little difference between the way a computer program stores files on disk and the way information is typically filed in an office. Every file on the disk has its own name—assigned to it by you, the program you are using, or the computer itself. When you, or a program, needs the information in a file, it is accessed, or **OPENED**; the information inside is then accessible. When you, or the program, have finished, the file is **CLOSED**. Leaving a file open may cause data loss or the destruction of the file; in most cases, though, the job of opening and closing files will automatically be taken care of for you by the operating system and software you are using.

A record of the files on all systems is organized and kept in a **DIRECTORY** or **SUBDIRECTORY**. As mentioned earlier, a directory is the method used by programs (including the operating system) to allow files to be easily categorized and managed. A subdirectory is any directory which exists within another, and each is given a **DIRECTORY NAME**. If you picture a tree trunk as being the main or **ROOT DIRECTORY**, with branches being represented by subdirectories, you will be using the classic example used to explain disk drive organization (See illustration on page 67). All files and directories must begin at the root directory and branch out.

Using a four-drawer office filing cabinet as an example, the entire cabinet could be considered the *root*, the main filing structure, with drawers further dividing files into subdirectories. The first drawer (subdirectory) might be named "customer information," the second "employee information," etc. Inside, each drawer could then be further divided into additional subdirectories: Cash-paying customers, customers on account, and delinquent customers, and active employees and employees no longer with the company. Within each drawer (subdirectory) are the actual files. Without directories and subdirectories you might have to wade through thousands of random files before stumbling upon the one you are looking for.

As an example, let's use a database file called "payroll." Each file is further organized and divided into individual **RECORDS**. Remember to also keep in mind that while the files used by many programs are further divided into records, especially database programs, some programs—such as word processors—store *all* data in one large contiguous file. In this example, however, we are assuming that a database is being used, and that there is a different record for each employee. Each record contains all of the information for one employee. This file structure is the same no matter what the name of the file or the information stored in it. Some files are simple, and contain only one record, a letter for instance. Others, such as the payroll example above, contain many different records and large amounts of separate information. The major advantage to storing information in disk files is that, regardless of how it was entered, it can be retrieved in many other useful formats. Not only can a computer quickly retrieve data from any portion of a file, but, with appropriate software, it can reorganize the information using almost any criteria you specify—alphabetical order, zip code, etc. Compare this to the time it would take to go through and rearrange a filing cabinet full of files and records.

This page intentionally left blank.

Chapter 5

SOFTWARE

SOFTWARE—the actual instructions and programs that make computers do what they do—is often a confusing subject because there are so many varieties. Probably the easiest way to determine what is software and what isn't is the "see and touch test." If when a product is installed in, or being used on, a computer, it is something that you can't physically see or touch, even if you took the computer apart, then it's safe to assume it's software. Software may also be correctly referred to as a **PROGRAM**—although *software* is both singular and plural and can refer to one or more software packages, but *program* refers to only one piece of software. For this reason, the terms *software* and *program(s)* are interchangeable, and the term *software program(s)* is equally proper. Specific programs—such as WordPerfect, Lotus 1-2-3, etc.—are often referred to as **APPLICATIONS PROGRAMS** or **APPLICATIONS SOFTWARE**. The various other components that go together to make up a computer system: the CPU, disk drives, printers, plug-in circuit boards, etc., are all considered HARDWARE.

Without software computers would be useless. Like the microwave oven example in the chapter on programming (See page 265), when you first turn on a computer its RAM memory contains no data and no job-related instructions. It sits quietly, doing nothing, until you "program" it and one of the cooking cycles starts. Many instruction manuals for microwave and other appliances actually use the word *programming* when referring to their operation and use. Computers can be programmed in a similar fashion; the major difference is in a computer's vastly greater power and storage capacity compared to the very limited capabilities of calculators, microwaves, and similar devices.

Computers can store and process hundreds, thousands, and even millions of instructions—but only with the aid of software, which falls generally into one of these three categories: **OPERATING SYSTEMS**; **APPLICATIONS PRO-GRAMS** (programs for applying the computer to any kind of job—word processing, inventory, analysis, etc.); and **DEVELOPMENT AND SUPPORT PROGRAMS**.

OPERATING SYSTEMS

Without an operating system the computer itself, and all other types of software programs, could not function. When a computer is first turned on it waits for the operating system to give it instructions on what to do next. The operating system is usually transferred, or **LOADED**, into the computer from either a floppy or hard disk. On some computers—home and portable computers and the controls in electronic appliances being the most notable examples—the operating system is instead stored in, and loaded from, permanently installed ROM chips. Just as a computer system's CPU relies on other electronic components in order to function, the computer as a whole, as well as the software programs you run, require an operating system. As you might have gathered, there have been, and are, several kinds of operating systems, because operating systems have been developed on different kinds of computers, and for different purposes. The first major operating systems were designed for mainframes because they were the first practical computers to see widespread use. When this changed, and the smaller microcomputers were introduced, operating systems had to change also. They had to be designed to fit within the memory constraints and reduced capabilities of the smaller systems.

Each manufacturer of small computers designed its own operating system, partly because there were few standards at the time and also because, in most cases, early computers would operate only with software designed specifically for each model. This gave computer manufacturers a double advantage: If you wanted a program that ran only on their computer you had no choice but to buy their system. Once you owned it, your choices of software were often limited to what that same company made available.

CP/M

The growing demand for software interchangeability among computers led to the development of standard operating systems that would run on different machines. This, in turn, also meant computers could run a greater number of software packages offered by different publishers. The first such operating system designed for small computers to gain popularity and maintain it was one called **CP/M** (**C**ONTROL **P**ROGRAM FOR **M**ICROPROCESSORS) by Digital Research Corporation. For the first time, different computers were able to run a much wider variety of software, even if it had originally been programmed on another model of computer. As time went by, however, CP/M seemed to lose its original focus—and along with it, its compatibility. Ideally, CP/M-compatible software would run on any computer using the CP/M operating system. Computer manufacturers, however, began to use versions of CP/M especially tailored to their systems, effectively restoring the former variety of operating systems and again limiting the choice of software. The response again showed the desire by the industry, as well as consumers, for an acceptable operating system standard. This eventually came about with the introduction of IBM's line of personal computers, the IBM PCs. As had been the case with most computers that came before it, this machine used its own operating system—predictably enough called **PC-DOS**, from which MS-DOS was later spun off as a close cousin.

Because there were so many different kinds of computers, a large number of programs were written for the CP/M operating system. For this reason, one of the intended advantages of CP/M was that it could often make programs written to run on machines of different sizes compatible. What might have once been written for a business computer may be available in a version that will run on a home computer using CP/M, and vice versa. Despite the fact that MS-DOS is today's popular favorite there are still programs floating around for CP/M. Fortunately, if you have an MS-DOS-based machine chances are a CP/M operating system is available for it, so you get the best of both worlds. Keep in mind, though, that the reverse is not necessarily true. Most CP/M-based machines are not able to run MS-DOS, and are best avoided altogether.

DOS

DOS stands for **D**ISK **O**PERATING **S**YSTEM and provides a clue as to its own meaning. *DOS* and *Operating System* are, for all practical purposes, the same thing. The two slightly different terms come from the way operating systems have been used in the past. Although disk drives (for floppies, hard disks, or both) are a standard feature on today's computers, this was not always the case. Early computers had no disk drives, and used punched cards, paper tape, or magnetic tape to store and retrieve information. Early disk drives were often expensive, and, for many models of computers, not available at all. Operating systems, therefore, often did not include provisions for the use of a disk drive. However, disk drives eventually became more widely available, and because of their advantages they also became very popular. If you added a disk drive to your computer system, or purchased a computer that already had one, an operating system which handled disk drives—a DISK OPERATING SYSTEM—was also needed. Virtually all modern operating systems contain the functions needed to handle disk drives, and can be properly referred to simply as "DOS."

Despite the different names, all operating systems serve basically the same function. They handle the internal and routine functions a computer system requires to operate. There are a number of reasons an operating system is essential. For one thing, without being constantly told what to do—"constantly" meaning many times a second—a computer is virtually helpless. Like a baby, computers require help with even the most basic and necessary functions—storing information and display-ing it on the screen; accepting what you type on the keyboard; managing a disk drive; etc. These and many other functions must be started, maintained, and controlled by some kind of instructions; fortunately, however, these functions are common to all kinds of application programs, so they need to be programmed only once. Operating systems programming is extremely complex, however, and relatively few programmers have this specialized knowledge.

As mentioned earlier, another reason for using an operating system is to increase compatibility. Because different manufacturers use different electronic parts and components to make their computers, it is unlikely that a program written on one model of computer would run on another. This is because software is **HARD-WARE-DEPENDENT**. To greatly oversimplify: Computers are arranged on the inside according to what literally amounts to a map (See memory maps under "Software portability," on page 263). These "maps" tell the computer, as well as the software, where to access all of the functions and components needed to operate the computer. Just as a road map for a particular city would be useless somewhere else, a program is not able to "find its way" unless everything in the hardware is where the program expects it to be. For example, the memory location reserved for handling keyboard input on one computer might, on another, be used to control the screen display, and so on.

An operating system can be designed for any computer, regardless of how the machine is put together, that will direct a program to the resources it needs. For instance, a program that uses screen displays, but that does not contain the instructions that send information to the screen, sends the information instead to the operating system. The operating system in turn gives the information the proper "directions" needed for it to be displayed on the screen. Almost any program you are likely to use will work this way: by going through the operating system to utilize the resources of the computer. This is why programs written using a standard operating system, such as MS-DOS, are not restricted to running on only the same brand or model of computer they were written on.

MS-DOS

Even though, like most other computers, the IBM PC required its own version of an operating system, the rapid acceptance of the PC increased the popularity of its operating system as well, so much so that other manufacturers wanted to use a compatible system. They couldn't use IBM's identical system, of course, but they could use a close equivalent, and virtually every one of these manufacturers approached Microsoft (which wrote the original PC-DOS) to provide that equivalent. Microsoft would then design a version of DOS for that manufacturer's model of computer. In some cases these early versions of DOS were not totally compatible from one computer to the next. Most versions, however, were only incompatible in that they contained enhancements not found in a standard version of DOS. (Examples of such enhancements can still be found in today's modern computers. For instance, to save electricity the lighted screens of many laptop computers automatically turn off after so many minutes of keyboard inactivity; when a key is pressed, they light up again. Even though such a feature would serve no purpose on a regular desktop computer, all of the other DOS functions still remain and would have no affect on compatibility.) Eventually, the systems were standardized. Thereafter, the program was—and is—known as MS-DOS (short for Microsoft DOS). Obviously, since MS-DOS was designed to work like the PC-DOS available directly from IBM, for all practical purposes they were identical. So popular were the IBM PC, PC-DOS, and, later, MS-DOS, that manufacturers began building their computers to work almost exactly the same way as the IBM PC. These were, and still are, called IBM PC *compatibles*. Unlike CP/M, however, MS-DOS has remained as standard, from machine to machine, as it is popular. This means that most PC users can use software with reasonable certainty that it will run on any other MS-DOS computer. What are the exceptions? Even when using MS-DOS you will occasionally run across programs that may not operate properly on anything but an authentic IBM—although this is happening less and less often. Also, if you are using a small computer that is not a PC or compatible it will likely use a different type of operating system.

ROM-Based Operating Systems

As mentioned earlier, instead of being loaded from a floppy or hard disk, the operating system for some computers is permanently stored in permanently installed ROM chips. The advantage is that there are no awkward disks to deal with, and that a computer with a ROM-based operating system is ready to use virtually the instant you turn it on. However, a more critical disadvantage is that you can't change or improve its software without literally taking the computer apart—and systems on ROM chips tend to run slower, as well. Therefore, almost all computers designed for business use are designed to have their operating systems loaded from disk. If a computer has only floppy-disk drives, you must always insert the DOS disk after the computer has been turned on. Computers with hard-disk drives can be set up to load DOS automatically from the hard drive when the power is switched on.

UPWARD COMPATIBILITY

UPWARD COMPATIBILITY refers to software or hardware that has been designed so that it will work not only with previous versions or models but also with future or larger versions. With this flexibility you are not left sitting with software that will not run on the newest equipment, but you can also expand into a larger system as your needs grow.

USER FRIENDLY PRODUCTS

The term **USER FRIENDLY** simply refers to software or hardware that has been designed with ease of use in mind—a characteristic nearly every software publisher claims to be true of its programs these days. (After all, are they going to admit it may be *un*friendly?) However, just because a program is user friendly does not automatically mean that it was designed for the first-time computer user. Many excellent software programs which are considered user friendly are designed with the experienced computer user in mind, so that the sometimes minimal documentation and complex commands, while entirely comprehensible to an experienced user, are Greek to a beginner.

Most people simply want to use a computer to get whatever work needs to be done finished as soon as possible, without being inconvenienced in the process. For this to happen, users must organize their information, which is in English, into a form that can easily be processed by a computer. The computer, in turn, must accept this information, convert it into its own internal language, perform whatever processing is needed, and then, finally, convert the results back into a form which can be easily understood by the user. The go-between which allows this interaction to take place between you and the computer is the software you buy.

Software performs many functions, but perhaps the most important one is to convert the information you want the computer to act upon into a format the computer can accept, and then display and/or store the results in a form you can understand. In the same way some of the meaning is often lost when you translate what you want to say into a foreign language, there may be a compromise in trying to get information into or out of a computer in a way which is best for both the computer and the user.

Selecting a program with the best blend of convenience and efficiency involves trade-offs. A major set of trade-offs—**MENU-DRIVEN PROGRAMS**, convenient and easy to learn, and **COMMAND-DRIVEN PROGRAMS**, faster and more productive but requiring more advance training—will be compared in more detail in the following sections.

While nearly all types of programs are available in extremely user friendly or **MULTICOMMAND MODE** versions (software that allows the user to adapt the program's commands, menus, and help screens to their level of experience) you should evaluate your needs carefully before committing to one. Even though user friendly features make learning very easy in the beginning, after becoming experienced you will find it burdensome to have to go through several menus, commands, or instructions each time you want to do something. (Some programs, however, both menu driven and command driven, allow you to select the degree of user friendliness you want at any moment, letting you combine ease of learning with the increased productivity of unassisted operation.)

ON-LINE HELP AND HELP SCREENS

Virtually all software comes with some form of printed instruction manual that you can read to become familiar with it. Even so, however, it can be extremely helpful if the software you are using has the ability to provide at least some assistance while you are operating the program. Such assistance is most often in the form of **ON-LINE HELP**, meaning that by pressing the appropriate key—such as F1—instructions for the operation you are currently performing will appear on-screen. **HELP SCREENS** may actually occupy the entire screen, or appear in the form of a window that overlaps what is already on the screen. In either case, when you have finished using the help feature the screen is returned to normal.

There are many programs where you would want the utmost in user friendliness to at least be available, even if you didn't always use it. Large programs might be one example. Because of their complexity, you might not use any one part of the program often enough to remember all the details of its operation. For instance, while an employee might be well trained in the use of an accounting program, some procedures—such as backing out an incorrect entry, closing the year, etc.—are performed so infrequently that even an experienced operator might not remember the required sequence of events and commands. In cases like these, an abundance of user-friendly features, designed to help the user every step of the way, can prove to be invaluable. You would also want user-friendly features in a program that will be used by employees who may receive little or no formal training in the program's use—such as is often the case with a computerized cash register. In programs like these it is usually best to have as many menus, help screens, instructions, and other user-friendly features as possible.

MENU-DRIVEN SOFTWARE

Just as most good books have a table of contents, most good software programs have menus; they are known as **MENU-DRIVEN PROGRAMS** and use simple methods to help you find and execute the program features you need to use. A computer menu consists of what amounts to a table of contents of the software program being used. The "contents" in this case are the various options, commands, and functions which you will need to use in your program. The first menu you encounter in a program is referred to as the **MASTER MENU**, or **MAIN MENU**. One example might be in the use of an accounting program. The main menu might offer you the choice of routines for working in General Ledger, Accounts

Receivable, Accounts Payable, or Payroll. If, for instance, you chose Accounts Payable, there might be another menu which offered you the choices of subroutines to: Update Supplier Information, Print Aged Accounts Report, Process Checks, etc. Menus come in many varieties, shapes, and sizes that will vary from program to program, often even within the same program.

The most common type of menu lists the options you have to choose from and arranges them in columns on the screen. Each selection will be marked by a letter or number which you enter to tell the program which choice you've made. In a very few programs—mainly those for mainframes and large computers—instead of using letters or numbers to mark each selection on the menu, each selection is marked by an abbreviation, or word, which describes the selection it stands for. With menus like these, you must enter the entire abbreviation or word in order to make a selection. This method is less popular because it is more time-consuming.

Through the use of menus you have a convenient and relatively fast way to find and execute the features you need to use. This type of menu is also called a **USER INTERFACE** because it acts as the interface between you, the user, and the computer (See also "GUI," on page 225). In very small or simple programs there may be only one menu, from which you can access all of the available options. More often, however—especially in larger programs—there are many different menus to guide you to the information you need. In these programs, just as looking up one reference in a book may refer you to yet another reference on the way to finding the information you need, one menu will often lead you to a second or third menu and so on—until you come to the menu which offers the selection you are looking for. Database management programs, and custom programs—such as those found in most large businesses—are among the best examples of software where numerous menus and instructional aids are desirable. It would be undesirable, however, to have to go through numerous menus while typing in a word processing program. If such a program were too user friendly, if every time you wanted to make a change or correction you had to first go through a menu or instructional guides, it would slow you down and interrupt your train of thought.

```
ACCOUNTING        | ACCOUNTS PAYABLE
1. General Ledger  |
                   | 1. Update Supplier
2. Accounts        |    Information
   Recievable      |
                   | 2. Print Aged Accounts
3. Accounts Payable|    Report
                   |
4. Payroll         | 3. Process Checks
                   |
Select (1-4):3     | Select (1-3):_
Press CTRL-M to return to main menu
```

Traditional Menu

"Pull Down Menus"

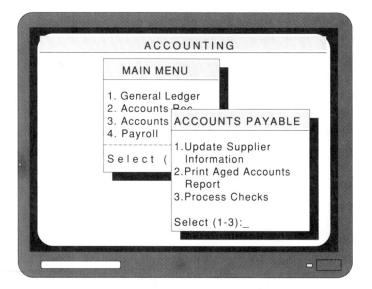

Macintosh Style
Desktop Menus

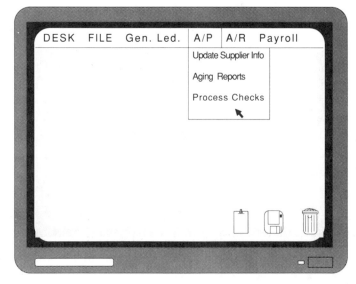

To summarize: User friendliness is typical of MENU-DRIVEN PROGRAMS, and the more user friendly a program is, the less you will have to refer to an instruction manual or other training aid. The program will be designed so that through the use of menus, and other on-screen instructional aids and guides, you should be able to operate it with relative ease, only occasionally having to consult the manual or get outside help. The more time you spend using menus and on-screen aids, however, the less productive time you have. (Going from one menu to another can be time-consuming in some programs. The alternative is described in the next section, "Command-Driven Software".)

In almost all programs, **EXITING**, or **QUITTING**, the menu or screen you are currently using will return you to the menu or screen you were using previously.

COMMAND-DRIVEN SOFTWARE

COMMAND-DRIVEN PROGRAMS require you to learn a command or instruction for each corresponding function you wish to use. While commands to the program are sometimes typed in using abbreviations or very brief phrases, a single key or control key sequence is more commonly used. The advantage of a command-driven program lies in its greater speed of operation. Instead of having to go through one or more menus or instructions to obtain the desired results, your command is executed immediately as soon as you press the appropriate keys. The trade-off is that before you can use a command-driven program efficiently you must first learn each of the needed command sequences and the functions they perform, and that both before and while using such software you will need to make more frequent references to the instruction manual or on-line help.

If you are evaluating a program for frequent, long-term use and cannot find one that allows you to switch from menu-driven to command-driven modes, it would be sensible to compare the long-term efficiency of a command-driven program (with a relatively short learning time and good productivity thereafter) to the immediate advantages of a menu-driven program (with little or no learning time and somewhat slow operation that may never speed up very much).

Among the programs which operate most effectively when command driven are graphics and screen-oriented applications. For example, in a word processing program the key sequence "F2" might move the entire screen up one page, while pressing "control L" might move the cursor to the last word on the line. In a computer-aided design (CAD) program "F2" might allow you to specify the starting point for drawing a line on the screen, while "control Z" might allow you to zoom in on a portion of the drawing. In programs such as these, not only would menus decrease your operating speed and productivity but they would probably also take up valuable space on the screen, blocking a portion of your work and reducing the amount of work that could be viewed on the screen at one time.

THE MAJOR TYPES OF SOFTWARE

Software packages on the market today already number in the thousands, and new software is being developed every day. These packages are constantly changing—being revised and improved, and, sometimes, discontinued. Therefore, no attempt will be made to describe even a fraction of the available *individual* programs. Instead, the *types* of software you are most likely to use will be discussed. These also happen to be the three types of programs you are most likely to encounter in conversation or actual use. Armed with this and other information presented in the book, you will be better prepared to understand, look for, and purchase software.

Word Processing

A simplified definition of word processing could be: doing on a computer what you've been using a typewriter for, only doing it more easily, faster, and better.

The ability to easily correct typing errors is perhaps the most important among the many features that make word processing preferable to using a typewriter. On a typewriter, if you type a letter only to find a large mistake somewhere in the middle, it means having to retype a page or perhaps the entire letter. With a **WORD PROCESSOR** (which refers here to a word processing software program but may also refer to a **DEDICATED WORD PROCESSOR**, a small computer performing word processing functions only) you can correct such a problem without affecting the rest of the letter, and, most importantly, without having to retype it. If there is a letter you use often—a thank-you letter to customers, for instance—you only have to type it once and store it as a file in the computer. Then, the next time you want to send out a personalized thank-you letter, you have only to fill in the customer's name and address and any other nonstandard information.

Many word processors have a specific **FORM LETTER** capability which allows a coded list of customers, or other people you need to contact often, to be kept in a disk file and linked to text stored in another file. If a letter needs to go to one, or all, of them, you call the standing text from the file or type—once only—new text into a new file. The word processor then will automatically type each letter, adding the name, address, and other variable information for each person.

A word processor, sometimes referred to simply as **WP**, displays the text you type on the screen of the computer instead of on paper. If you type more than will fit on the screen it **SCROLLS** to let you see the rest of the letter or text (a feature available in most software). Because the text is on screen, you can make sure it's exactly the way you want it before printing it out on paper. You can also copy text in one part of a document and insert it elsewhere—a process sometimes called **CUT AND PASTE**.

Word processors also have many other valuable features. Have you ever wanted to find a certain word in a long document for some reason, but didn't want to read the whole thing to find it? With a word processor you can use the **FIND** feature to instantly locate any word or phrase (actually, any series of characters, numbers, or symbols) the document contains. If you wish, you can also use a feature called **SEARCH AND REPLACE** to have the word automatically replaced with another one wherever it is found in the text. This can save a great deal of time when you have used an incorrect word throughout the document or find another word you think will work better. If you type a letter on a word processor and find it would look better with a different margin, you can simply change the margin and the letter will adjust to the new setting automatically. Many word processors contain a **SPELLING CHECKER** that will point out misspelled words; some even correct spelling as you type. An electronic **THESAURUS** in many programs finds synonyms (rather slowly, sometimes). There are even programs, which can be purchased separately, that will analyze a document and make suggestions on grammar and content. In short, a word processor not only allows you to type documents but is also a valuable tool that offers many convenient, time-saving features.

You won't get a true appreciation for the capabilities of a good word processor until you see one demonstrated. Once you have seen and used one, the advantages will probably be so evident you may never want to use a typewriter again. But don't throw your typewriter away. For small jobs, such as filling in occasional forms, a typewriter is much more convenient than trying to program a computer to do it, and typewriters are still the only practical way to address envelopes for correspondence where window envelopes or adhesive labels aren't acceptable. Because word processing is based upon typing, it is one of the easiest computer skills for many people to learn. For this reason, and because WP software benefits virtually any operation, it is frequently one of the first programs people purchase.

Database Managers

A **DATABASE MANAGER**, also called a **DBM**, is a program which allows you to store, manipulate, and retrieve information. The information can be as simple as names and addresses, like those stored on a Rolodex, or as complex as a complete inventory system. While it is true that almost all software programs store and retrieve information, the DBM-like functions they contain can seldom be adapted to another application. For example, you would not want to use the vendor-name section of an inventory program to store customer information. A DBM, however, is a general program; it may be adapted to almost any application that requires the storage of information.

The most basic kind of DBM is called a **FILE MANAGER**. As its name implies, it allows you to organize and manage the information stored in a file. You determine the names of the files, as well as the kinds of information they will contain. What would be called file folders in a manual filing cabinet are referred to as **RECORDS** in a computerized system, and the "spaces" within each record—for name, address, etc.—are each referred to as a **FIELD**. Once entered in a DBM the information is much easier to find and use than it would be in a manual filing system. For one thing, you can base your search upon the data contained in any of the fields you have set up. For instance, if your customer database were set up according to customer number, and you needed to find a record but didn't know the number, you could still find the record by searching other fields. You might search for the record by using the name field, or by basing your search on the phone number. In a manual system you might have to literally go through every folder before finding the needed file.

DBMs also allow you to specify and easily retrieve only the kinds of information you need. Unlike a manual system, which could take hours to organize, a DBM can quickly arrange information alphabetically, numerically, and in any number of other arrangements. You can easily retrieve information by last name, zip code, pay rate, social security number—or any other fields in the DBM. Reports can be prepared in a fraction of the time it would otherwise take. The more sophisticated the DBM software, the more ways you can store and retrieve information.

94

There is also a type of DBM known as a **PROGRAMMABLE DATABASE**; these are the ultimate DBMs. Unlike file managers and simple DBMs, a programmable DBM—such as dBASE, FoxBase, Paradox, etc.—also known as an **APPLICA-TIONS DEVELOPMENT ENVIRONMENT (ADE),** is designed to provide a complete applications program. You can actually write a program for one of these DBMs that combines the information storage and handling capabilities of a DBM with the flexibility of a program custom-designed to suit your needs. Programmable DBMs usually offer more advanced database capabilities than other types of DBMs. Some programmable DBMs contain their own built-in programming language, varying from DBM to DBM, but most conform to some style of structured programming, so that programmers familiar with C, Pascal, or some other business-oriented language (See page 260) can easily adapt to the language used by the DBM. While the languages built into many DBMs are convenient and powerful enough for many applications, they usually do not offer the virtually unlimited capabilities of a formal programming language. This is why some of the most advanced DBMs have no built-in programming language at all—instead giving programmers the freedom to work with popular, and more powerful, languages like those mentioned above.

As long as the capabilities of the DBM itself are adequate, with an experienced programmer there are few limitations on what can be done with such a system. Just as a computer's operating system saves a programmer, and a user, a great deal of time and trouble by handling routine functions, a programmable DBM provides all the resources needed for storing and retrieving information. The programmer is then free to concentrate on the details of designing and writing a program that suits the needs of the business.

Many programmable DBMs advertise that they are easy enough to be learned by nonprogrammers and new users, yet provide features that will satisfy experienced programmers as well. Opinions seem to be mixed on this point, but surveys have shown that only a relatively small percentage of buyers without programming experience actually learn how to program after buying a programmable DBM. The reasons for this are fairly obvious: people all tend to do what they do best. Just as most programmers don't have the time, or desire, to enter another occupation, it may not be practical for someone already busy with a career in another field to also learn programming. If your needs are relatively straightforward you may find it takes little time to learn the database and programming commands that will be needed for your application. On the other hand, in the more likely event that you purchased such a DBM for its power and capability in the first place, you probably won't want to invest the time it will require to learn how to develop and program a more sophisticated application.

If your needs are like those of most people, or businesses, few software products will have as great an impact on your operations as a database manager. Therefore, selecting a database manager should be one of your most carefully thought-out and executed decisions. Remember to refer to the sections on buying software and hardware for additional information that will be helpful in making a selection. In addition, following are some *simplified* guidelines that you may find helpful.

FILE MANAGERS—sometimes called **PERSONAL INFORMATION MANAGERS (PIMs)** or **FLAT FILE** databases—are best suited for personal and simple business use, or for personal use by individuals within an organization that has a more sophisticated system for company-wide use. Somewhere between a file manager and the more sophisticated DBMs seem to be the products that will satisfy the DBM needs of most small businesses. As you move through the more advanced programmable systems you eventually reach a point where, for all practical purposes, there is no limit to what can be done—provided you want to spend the time and money. There are a number of DBM systems for mainframes—such as ORACLE—that are also available for microcomputers. While usually much more expensive than their strictly PC-based counterparts, PC versions of mainframe software make it easier to share data with a mainframe. And, unlike what your situation would be with PC-oriented DBMs, if you should grow into a larger system you can take your entire system along with you—since a mainframe version of the software is probably available, also.

While you will be able to determine beforehand the capacity your DBM software will need to have, it can sometimes be difficult to determine how well it will actually operate once you have it up and running on your computer. You also want to be sure that it operates efficiently when being used under maximum load because almost all DBMs slow down as more information is stored in them and as usage increases. Some DBMs can become so slow with increased usage that they are no longer practical to operate. (Have you ever called a company and had to wait for many minutes while they accessed your information, and the operator probably said: "The system is running extremely slow today?") If you are planning to have a custom application programmed around a DBM, arrange for a demonstration beforehand that will show how it operates under a full workload. This can be done by filling the DBM with test, or **DUMMY** information, and then seeing how much longer critical operations, such as finding a record, will take. Many publishers will have test data to show you, but their figures may be biased in their favor. More objective data is often available from the major computer magazines in the form of the periodic reviews and tests they do on database programs. However you may do it, and even if you are planning on buying only a simple file manager, it is a good idea to first find out how it performs when loaded with a large amount of data.

Especially if are looking for a capable DBM to handle a small to medium-sized business, look for one with as few "built-in" limitations as possible. Consider, for instance, a DBM with the following specifications:

Maximum Field Length...................: 80 characters
Maximum number of fields...............: 40
Maximum Record Size...................: 1,024 bytes
Maximum Number of Records Per File: 32,768

Such a system would be utterly impractical for business use, and could easily prove to be limiting even for personal users. At first glance, however, the specifications may seem adequate. After all, the maximum **FIELD LENGTH** of 80 characters would seem to be more than ample for even the longest name or street address, especially since a normal monitor can only display 80 characters across its screen anyway. But keep in mind that, depending on the DBM, it is possible to "wrap" fields longer than 80 characters from one line of the screen to the next—much as a word processor does—so fields longer than 80 characters are often used to store notes and other lengthy information. The maximum **RECORD SIZE** of 1,024 bytes might also seem adequate, in that you could easily store a person's name, company name, phone number, and address, and still have many bytes left before the record is full. But let's create a few sample records and scenarios to help us with our example. Just for our example, next to each field and at the bottom of each record we will add a note to remind us of how much space is being used.

11 bytes	Name.............: John H. Doe
38 bytes	Company Name: Database Software Makers International
14 bytes	Phone#...........: (101) 123-4567
20 bytes	Address..........: 1000 Database Avenue
29 bytes	City, State, Zip: All American, Any State 11111
39 bytes	Note..............: Publishers of database software for PCs

Total number of fields = 6

Total record size (all fields added together) = 151 bytes

If the above record represented your average usage of a data base, things still look pretty good. After all, according to the database specifications you could store over 30,000 records like this before you would run out of space. But, what if your records needed to expand? Consider this situation: You are in the cardboard box business and Mr. Doe said he wanted you to contact him in October about ordering 5,000 of the boxes they sell their product in. This information is too important to leave out, and to file it on paper is to risk losing or forgetting it—and would defeat your purpose of having a database in the first place. Since your DBM limits fields to 80 characters you decide to solve your problem by adding additional fields to give yourself more room for notes. Let's see how the new record layout might look.

11 bytes	Name............: John H. Doe
38 bytes	Company Name: Database Software Makers International
14 bytes	Phone#..........: (101) 123-4567
20 bytes	Address.........: 1000 Database Avenue
29 bytes	City, State, Zip: All American, Any State 11111
39 bytes	Notes, Line 1...: Publishers of database software for PCs
43 bytes	Notes, Line 2...: Talked to Mr. Doe on September 17, 1990. He
40 bytes	Notes, Line 3...: will need to order 5,000 boxes for their
46 bytes	Notes, Line 4...: software product sometime around October 22nd,
35 bytes	Notes, Line 5...: and would like me to call him then.

Total number of fields = 10
Total record size (all fields added together) = 317 bytes

The total record size has now grown to 317 bytes (even punctuation marks and blank spaces are counted by computers). But, even so, you've found a very practical solution to what seemed like a problem—entering long notes—and you still have plenty of capacity left. Well, maybe. Let's go further. It is now March of the following year, and not only did Mr. Doe order as he said he would in October, but his company is growing by leaps and bounds and he needs you to supply his company with more paper products. They have expanded to 3 locations—all of which he wants you to supply—and, because Mr. Doe is now so busy, he wants you to work through the buyer at each office. In addition, the growth at your own company has surpassed even your best expectations. Your company now serves over 12,000 customers, and expects to add over 15,000 customers within the next year and a half. You need to again change your database to keep up. Let's take a look at how it might be done.

11 bytes	Contact 1........:	John H. Doe
26 bytes	Location.........:	Headquarters, All American
23 bytes	Phone............:	(101) 123-4567 Ext: 123
11 bytes	Contact 1........:	Jane M. Doe
33 bytes	Location.........:	Headquarters (Mr. Doe's secretary)
23 bytes	Phone............:	(101) 123-4567 Ext: 124
09 bytes	Contact 1........:	Bob Smith
25 bytes	Location.........:	California office (buyer)
23 bytes	Phone............:	(714) 123-4567 Ext: 213
13 bytes	Contact 1.......:	Richard Jones
20 bytes	Location.........:	Texas office (buyer)
23 bytes	Phone............:	(713) 123-4567 Ext: 323
38 bytes	Company Name:	Database Software Makers International
14 bytes	Main Phone#...:	(101) 123-4567
20 bytes	Address 1.......:	1000 Database Avenue
29 bytes	City, State, Zip:	All American, Any State 11111
14 bytes	Address 2.......:	2200 Word Lane
21 bytes	City, State, Zip:	Los Angeles, CA 90101
20 bytes	Address 3.......:	1000 Spreadsheet Way
16 bytes	City, State, Zip:	Dallas, TX 75200
39 bytes	Notes, Line 1..:	Publishers of database software for PCs
43 bytes	Notes, Line 2..:	Talked to Mr. Doe on September 17, 1990. He
40 bytes	Notes, Line 3..:	will need to order 5,000 boxes for their
46 bytes	Notes, Line 4..:	software product sometime around October 22nd,
43 bytes	Notes, Line 5..:	Purchased 7,000 boxes in October. Called in
43 bytes	Notes, Line 6..:	March and wants me to contact the buyers at
47 bytes	Notes, Line 7..:	their new locations. Bob wants 10,000 boxes, to
46 bytes	Notes, Line 8..:	ship ASAP. Mr. Jones wants 8,000 boxes to ship
47 bytes	Notes, Line 9..:	by April 28th. Remember to call Mr. Doe in May.
46 bytes	Notes, Line 10:	He wants a quote then for a box on a new prod.

Total number of fields = 30
Total record size (all fields added together) = 865

Everything seems to be have gone fine. You've made the necessary changes to your customer database, and entered the new information. But you soon begin to notice that the database is responding slowly. In the past it seemed to take only a few seconds to retrieve a record from the database. Now, however, because the database contains thousands of records, and because your record size has also grown in size from an average of 154 bytes to almost 900, you're finding that it may take 30 seconds or more for a record to appear on screen. And even though you've just finished making some good improvements to the database, you can already see that many more changes will be needed. For one thing, you would like to add an additional address line to accommodate place names like: Professional Plaza, Airport Industrial Park, The Century Building, etc. You would also like to be able to enter a separate note for each person rather than being forced to enter all notes in one place. However, as you go over the proposed changes it becomes apparent that you will have soon reached the maximum capacity of the database. The DBM specifications, that seemed more than ample when you purchased it, are now proving to be very limiting.

Worse yet, as you shop for a new database that will offer the power and capacity you need, you learn that you will be unable to transfer the information electronically from your old database to the new one.

The above scenario is unfortunately all too common. In fact, it was taken from the actual experience of a small family-operated Michigan-based company whose computerized mailing list grew to contain over 30,000 customers (the limit of the DBM). When it happened, not wanting to make the same mistake twice, they sought the advice of a consultant to help them choose new database software. However, because their old database did not have the ability to **EXPORT** data—convert it from its native format to that of another software product, or to ASCII—they were faced with the expensive proposition of having to retype the information into the new database, or have a programmer attempt to write a custom export routine to do it. In the meantime their business was further inconvenienced because they could no longer add customer records to, or modify, their existing DBM.

Even people who carefully plan the purchase of a DBM may fail to take into account the fact that, as more experience is gained on a DBM, the more ways people will find to use it. Unless the planners are experienced with anticipating and handling the growth of successful DBMs, this can be all too easy to do. It is best avoided by carefully assessing your current and future needs, and/or seeking the assistance of someone *experienced* in the design, setup, and use of a DBM system. The time and money you spend are likely to be far less than what would be required if you quickly outgrew the system. Always try to look for a DBM that is limited in capacity *only* by the amount of disk-storage space on your computer. If such a program isn't feasible for some reason, look for specifications that are as generous as possible. Few good DBMs currently offer less than a maximum field length of 128 characters, a maximum number of fields less than 100, a maximum record size less than 4,000 bytes, or a maximum number of records less than 1,000,000. Increased record and field capacity, more DBM manipulation commands, and faster operating speeds are just a few of the things you should notice on higher performance DBMs.

Lastly, since no one can predict the future, and even the best made plans sometimes go awry, make sure the DBM you buy has the ability to export, and import, data—at least in the ASCII format if not others. Most DBMs that offer this feature can read and write dBase and other popular file formats. By making sure your DBM has the ability to export data you will have an "out" should you ever need to transfer your data to another DBM system.

Spreadsheets

In the same way word processing is an offshoot of typing, and DBMs are offshoots of manual filing systems, computerized spreadsheets are based upon their paper counterparts. In fact, there is little difference between the appearance of most computerized spreadsheets and one handwritten on ledger paper. The appearance is where the similarity ends, however, because computerized spreadsheets do the hard work for you. You set up titles, columns, headings, totals, and other information just the same as you would enter them into a ledger. Then you define any calculations that need to be performed on the entries. Once this has been done, all of the entries can be computed and totaled with the stroke of a key or two.

Depending on the complexity of your application, the time saved by a computerized spreadsheet can range from a little to a great deal indeed. This is because not only do spreadsheets have the ability to automatically perform different operations—addition, subtraction, multiplication, division, etc.—on different entries on a spreadsheet, but they do so without error. This eliminates the awkward adding machine tape and rechecking that is needed to make sure entries in a ledger are accurate (although you may occasionally wish to double check the final results). Another big advantage is that, once set up, the same calculations and formulas can be used over and over again. If you change entries the spreadsheet will automatically recalculate the figures. This can make child's play out of running projections and evaluating hypothetical situations. Projections and analysis that would take days, weeks, or months to do by hand can instead be done in hours or minutes.

You can use a spreadsheet for something as simple as keeping track of your checking account and business and travel expenses, or something as complex as job costing or earnings projections. In addition to doing the same things manual spreadsheets are used for, computerized systems offer many new possibilities because of their speed and convenience. They are ideal for estimating because you can set up a basic format for all of the elements, including sales proposals, job costing, and cost breakdowns, and then simply modify the entries to make each new estimate.

The spaces into which you make entries in a spreadsheet are called **CELLS**. The number of columns, rows, and cells available will vary from spreadsheet to spreadsheet. All spreadsheets allow you to scroll to see more than the limited number of cells which can be displayed by a monitor. The more sophisticated the program, the more capabilities and features it will offer. Some spreadsheets offer easier formula definition, while others allow you to define and save often-used keystrokes so they can be executed by pressing only one key; the small program which captures these actions for recall by a single keystroke is referred to as a **MACRO** (a word which has other meanings in different areas of computing and programming). This process is referred to as **MACRO DEFINITION** and can save you a great deal of time. Some spreadsheets allow you to display information in the form of a graph or chart. The ability to sort and use information alphabetically and numerically is also usually available. Many of the newer, or so-called **SECOND GENERATION**, spreadsheets also have the same kinds of abilities to store and retrieve information as a basic DBM. Few spreadsheets, however, see much practical use as database managers.

It may be appropriate in this section to mention a curious point about the accuracy of financial information generated by computer. Many people seem to think that anything generated by a computer "*has* to be right." Unfortunately, however, this is not always the case. Let's say you are using an amortization table/spreadsheet program to generate a report showing the interest and principal payments and remaining balances on a 15-year loan. The annual interest rate is 11 percent and the program required it to be entered as a monthly figure (although, outside of our example, most programs would do this for you automatically). This requires you to divide the annual rate by 12 to determine the monthly interest rate ($11 / 12 =$

.0092). If you inadvertently omitted this step by entering annual rate of 11 percent, or put the decimal point in the wrong place, the resulting figures would be wrong and might go unnoticed for a while, even if the error was large, because "computers don't make mistakes." The same could apply to any other type of software program. Other types of errors may also occasionally be caused by equipment malfunction.

In short, it is often a good idea to check the results generated by a program the first few times you use it or any time you make major programming, formula, setup, or other changes. Thereafter, don't hesitate to check with a calculator, or otherwise verify, any results which seem suspicious or out of line with the general data. Your income statement, for instance, might make it appear that sales were up by $9,000 when, actually, someone had turned a $1,000 deposit into a $10,000 deposit by entering too many zeros.

Integrated Software

The term **INTEGRATED SOFTWARE** has two meanings. In one sense it refers to software which combines—or integrates—two or more applications programs (database managers, word processors, etc.) so that they can be used together and information can be exchanged between the programs and the files they create. In the other sense, the term *integrated* usually refers to a software package, or modules of a software package, that are designed to reduce the number of entries required by automatically transferring data to other sections of the software. For instance, in an integrated accounting package all of the **MODULES** of the program communicate with each other. A sale recorded in the sales register might automatically update inventory and accounts receivable, issue an invoice, and update the general ledger, all in one operation. While the separate modules of most modern accounting packages are always integrated, this was not always the case. It was not uncommon to purchase an accounts receivable module, for instance, and only later find out that you could not transfer the transactions to the general ledger module which you purchased later.

Because word processors, databases, and spreadsheets are among the most popular software packages on the market, a number of publishers have combined these three types of programs into one, in which the three functions work together. You can pull (access or retrieve) the figures or graphs from a spreadsheet and place them into a letter or report you are typing, rather than having to reenter the information by hand. Likewise, the spreadsheet can access information stored in the DBM. The more sophisticated the package, the fewer limitations there are on how the various portions of the program can work together.

SOFTWARE UPGRADES

Just as automobiles and other products are changed and presumably improved more or less constantly, so it is with software. Seldom does a year go by in which a new **VERSION** of a popular software package with new features is not introduced. These **UPGRADES** or **UPDATES**, as they are called, are also used to correct any errors or bugs which have been found since the last version. Each new version has a new **VERSION NUMBER**, usually numbered in a decimal series. For example, when Version 3.0 of a program gets its third upgrade it is called Version 3.3, and this number appears on the program disk and the first display screen as well as on manuals and other materials. When major overhauls of a program are made the numbering goes to the next highest full number; the major revision of Version 3.3 becomes Version 4.0, etc.

Upgrades are often made available to customers free of charge (along with descriptions of program changes and new features) if they have purchased the program quite recently or if the publisher has corrected or **FIXED** a bug in the program that was considered major. If you want to upgrade one of your programs simply to take advantage of additional features in the newest version there is usually a cost involved, but it is lower than the price of the original program. While prices vary greatly, you can expect to pay between $15 and $60 to upgrade software that originally cost between $50 and $250. You may have to pay more to upgrade more expensive software, although only in unusual cases will the cost of an upgrade exceed 30 percent of the cost of the original software package. You should also keep in mind that normal upgrades cover only the original package as used on the original operating system. You may have to pay considerably more if, for instance, you wished to upgrade from an MS-DOS version of a program to a version that runs under the Unix operating system.

COPY PROTECTION

Attempts by software publishers to prevent their software from being used by people who didn't pay for it is known as **COPY PROTECTION**. This is one of those many cases where a few bad apples managed to make things difficult for the rest of us. Originally, software was almost never copy protected. Most of the software in use had been developed by the same organizations that owned the computers it ran on, making copy protection, as it is known today, almost unheard of. Even today, for these same reasons, and because of the different nature of large computers, copy protection is not used on many programs for minicomputers and mainframes. As systems grew smaller, both in size as well as price, and as the number of systems and users grew enormously, many software publishers began to see a need for protection against new users who copied programs already in use rather than buy new copies of programs from the publishers.

Because there are likely to be a few thieves in any large group, as the group of computer users grew larger so did the number of thieves who decided to help themselves to the software that was available. Some people copied because they wanted to avoid paying for their software. Others copied simply for the thrill of **BREAKING** or **CRACKING** the latest **COPY PROTECTION SCHEME. A** never-ending game of cat-and-mouse developed, as software publishers invented increasingly complex and sophisticated copy protection methods which were broken by **SOFTWARE PIRATES** soon after the program hit the market. In some cases, **PIRATED** copies were distributed even before the legitimate software arrived in stores. By the late 1970s and into the early 1980s it was not uncommon for there to be more pirated copies of a program in circulation than copies purchased legally. Widespread violations of this sort are, as the copiers know, almost impossible to police at the level of individual violators. Even so, it is still hard to understand the appeal of getting the program itself for nothing when saving a few dollars means having no tech support for programs by the publisher and no—or a very inadequate—user's manual.

HACKERS—people who simply enjoy spending large amounts of time working on computers—began getting a bad name. Before long, anyone considered to be a hacker was often mistakenly assumed to be a software pirate, or a computer criminal. About this time, software protection itself sprang up as a rapidly booming business, along with firms specializing in computer security. Rather than the exception, copy protection became the ruling standard. Almost every program manufactured for small computer systems, whether for business or home, had some form of copy protection. During this time, the pirates, and people specializing in copy protection and computer security, had a field day. Publishers and the consumers who wished to purchase software legitimately ended up being the losers. Software publishers started spending more money on copy protection in an attempt to reduce losses, and the cost was passed on to honest customers in the form of increased software prices.

But increased prices were not the only thing passed on to customers. Placing copy protection in programs can make them more difficult to install and use, and the customer is also often prevented from making legitimate backup copies. Because this situation so inconvenienced the business users of software most software publishers have already dropped, or are in the process of discontinuing, the use of copy protection schemes. They have instead turned to aggressive and tough legal measures to find and prosecute people who pirate their software. You can help by informing software companies of any pirated copies of their programs you might run across. Reporting piracy will help ensure that you will continue to enjoy the ease of use of unprotected software and the ability to make backup copies of it.

You should be aware, however, that what may be seen as copying by a software publisher may in good faith be seen as legitimate use by a purchaser. For example, is it piracy if someone makes a copy of a program for business use at home? Or are users pirates who place one copy of a program on their main PC for use at their desks, and another copy on their laptop computers for use when they are away?

BUYING SOFTWARE

Your software will most likely fall into one of four categories: 1) Ready-to-use or **OFF-THE-SHELF SOFTWARE**. 2) Off-the-shelf software that is **MODIFI-ABLE** or **CUSTOMIZABLE**. 3) **CUSTOM SOFTWARE** designed specifically for your needs and applications. 4) **FREE SOFTWARE**, more often called **PUBLIC DOMAIN SOFTWARE**.

Off-The-Shelf Software

By far the favorite choice, and usually the best one, for most users is **OFF-THE-SHELF SOFTWARE**. There is such a wide variety of off-the-shelf software, made for so many different machines, that you can almost always find a package that will come acceptably close to meeting your requirements. Some of the advantages of an off-the-shelf program are: little delay between the time you select the software and can have it up and running on your system; reasonable costs; and possibly the opportunity to talk with another user of the same program for a similar purpose to see how well it might work for you. As already hinted, however, while you are likely to find something that comes acceptably close it will almost never be *exactly* what you are looking for. It may be able to accomplish only 90, even 95, percent of the job you would like it to do, the way you would like it done, but, even so, this solution proves adequate for most applications.

Off-the-shelf software is also likely to be the most cost-effective solution—considering the probable cost of a custom-written program that is exactly what you want. But, at the same time, do not underestimate the hidden costs to your business or damage to the morale of employees that can occur from compromising on inadequate software. If those things the software will not allow you to do would severely hamper your operation, or would prove extremely inconvenient or irritating to those using it, look for something more acceptable—or look at alternatives such as modifiable software, custom software, etc. One of the best places to start your search for a software package is at your local computer or software dealer. Not only may they have a package in stock that will satisfy your needs, but you can probably arrange a demonstration. Even if they do not have what you are looking for in stock they will be able to tap a number of resources to help you find it.

Keep in mind that, because of the many different packages available, it is impossible for a store's staff to be familiar with every software package you might want to see. In fairness to the salespeople, as well as yourself, give them time to prepare an adequate demonstration. This way you won't, unknowingly, impose on a salesperson to demonstrate something he or she is not yet fully familiar with—and you will receive a more informative presentation. Naturally, stores should have salespeople already familiar with the most popular packages currently on the market—including word processors, databases, spreadsheets, accounting applications, and so on.

If a local computer dealer isn't able to help you, there are a number of publications available which do nothing but list available software, hardware, or both. These directories and catalogs will often be available from your dealer, bookstore, or library. In addition, you can try searching through computer magazines and journals; some are published specifically for individual industries and professions. If you can't find what you are looking for right away, don't be discouraged. Finding a software package you will be happy with can take time, but the results of a smooth-running system will be well worth it.

A sometimes delicate point that should be kept in mind when looking for off-the-shelf software: if you are unable to find a program that does "exactly" what you want it to, it may be because the manual systems you currently have in place just aren't the right way of doing things. The fact that one's business practices are inefficient can be hard to face, but it is not uncommon for an office system or procedure which has been in use for many years to be the "wrong way" of doing things. Maybe that was the way "Aunt Anne" always filed things for the family business. Or, perhaps Mr. Beetle has been handling your bookkeeping for over thirty years, but that doesn't mean there isn't a better way. Computerization has a way of virtually forcing you to do things in a more organized and efficient manner. Good software is usually designed to prevent users from taking short cuts, makes sure important information is not omitted, and, in many cases, checks to make sure entries are accurate.

In a parts store, for instance, there may be nothing to stop an employee from using a part for store use, or selling a part, and then not bothering to update the inventory records. With a computerized system, however, recording a sale—to a customer or to the store at cost—would automatically cause it to be subtracted from inventory and the necessary general ledger accounts to be updated. This greatly reduces the chance of running out of a certain inventory item, losing track of parts, or having inaccurate records. If there is a defect in your way of doing things now it doesn't make sense to try to find a software package to accommodate the defect. Instead, try to determine if the software packages you are looking at can help you improve things. Ask yourself: "Is it really a matter of not being able to find a package that will do what I am doing now, or do the packages I've rejected actually offer a better way of doing things?"

Modifying Off-The-Shelf Software

If you find some programs that are close to your needs, but none that are just right, find out if they can be modified. A number of software publishers make available what is called the **SOURCE CODE** of a software package—the actual program printed out on paper and documented (See "Source code," on page 256). If you can obtain it, you will be able to hire a programmer to make changes that will adapt the program to your needs. Before you buy software that needs modification get an opinion from an experienced programmer as to whether the software can be adapted to your needs, and whether or not the publisher provides adequate documentation for a programmer to use.

Some software is sold directly by the publisher (and sometimes through stores as well), though it can still be considered off-the-shelf. Often these publishers also sell complete computer systems to go along with their software. If their computer system is a good one, and more than suits your needs, this may be a very convenient way for you to assemble everything needed to computerize your application. If you would rather purchase the hardware from someone else, or if it would prove more economical to do so, these publishers usually allow you to buy just the software portion of their systems. You will find programs like these advertised in the same places that were mentioned for off-the-shelf software.

Public Domain Software

You may have heard of free software. Aside from software you might receive through a promotional offer, this most likely refers to **PUBLIC DOMAIN SOFTWARE**. This term describes software to which no one claims ownership (technically, software that is not copyrighted); therefore, it can be freely copied and shared among users, the general public, without violating any of the copyright laws that apply to commercial software. A wide variety of public domain software for many applications is primarily distributed, or "shared," by people doing just that—copying and sharing it without cost and encouraging others to do the same. Public domain software is also available through some computer and software stores (which charge you only for the floppy disks it comes on or allow you to bring your own disks); through catalogs which list thousands of programs and tell how to get them; from mail-order companies specializing in public domain software that advertise in computer magazines; and computer bulletin boards.

There are a number of things you should keep in mind if you decide to use public domain software. First is reliability: you may have little idea of who wrote the program, or how well it works. As the saying goes: "You don't know where it's been." Because the software may have been copied many times, and perhaps altered or even tampered with, you can seldom be sure of what you are getting and may therefore suffer losses of data and time in using it. In fact, public domain software has often been a prime vehicle for planting viruses (See "Virus," on page 213) or other software "bombs."

This is also why it may not be advisable to "browse through" unknown public domain programs by actually running them on your computer to see what they are. (Despite this fact, many people call computer bulletin boards and download all of the free public domain software they can make fit on their disks. Later, they go through to try to figure out what all of the programs do, and how they operate.) Unless you know specifically what program you are looking for, and what the filename is, and that the program is from a legitimate and reputable source, it might be best to avoid it. Other negatives associated with public domain software are that good instruction manuals are seldom available and that they are usually not as well designed as the commercial software programs sold through stores.

Despite their various drawbacks, however, good public domain software can obviously prove to be a bargain. Many excellent programs have been written and made available this way. The publishers of computer magazines and software and computer manufacturers themselves are often excellent sources of quality public domain software. They usually make their software available through company-operated bulletin boards, and, sometimes, for a small fee the software is available on disk. Online information services provide similar access to public domain software.

Keep in mind, however, that public domain programs are usually small utility programs designed for specific purposes, such as searching for a lost file on your hard drive or changing the color of your screen.

Some word processors, database managers, and other major programs are available as public domain software, but for business use it is advisable to stick with name-brand software. Businesses require only the best software offering industry-standard features; the ability to upgrade to newer versions; good instruction manuals and training materials; and readily available technical support—none of which can be counted on when public domain programs are used.

Shareware

There are a number of companies and individuals which use the same methods as public domain software distributors to market their own software, called **SHARE-WARE**; they also sell directly to users, but, unlike public domain software publishers, shareware companies also normally provide upgrades and technical support. They release a free or low-cost copyrighted version of their program as a demonstration of what their software can do—holding back, however, some vital program element or instructions that would enable the public to make full use of the program without paying for it. If you like it, you purchase the complete software, along with the regular instruction manuals and other documentation, directly from the publisher. Shareware suffers from far fewer image problems than does public domain software. In fact, there may be little noticeable difference, if any, between a good shareware program and a similar commercial program that is sold through stores. The first edition of this book was almost completely written using **PC-Write**, an excellent word processor that's made by a shareware company called **Quicksoft**.

Custom Software

The last, and most complex, way for you to obtain precisely the software you need is to have it custom designed and programmed, but because this route is time-consuming, costly, and demanding, you should first exhaust all other means of finding the software you need—with the exceptions mentioned below. If, however, your needs are unique, and you simply cannot find a ready-made program that will satisfy your requirements, or one that can be modified to do so, then custom software is the only remaining alternative.

Before investigating any custom services you should be aware of the fact that you will pay significantly more than you would for the same software if it were available off-the-shelf. This is due to the fact that, while publishers of off-the-shelf software spend a great deal of money on research and development, they can still make a program available at a relatively low cost because they are expecting to sell that package in large quantities. A custom program, however, is created especially for you. The software house you hire will, in turn, have to charge you for all related research and development costs in order to make a profit—since they cannot sell the program to other customers.

There are a number of exceptions to the guidelines mentioned above for considering custom software. In fact, there are a number of situations where custom software should be one of the first things you look into.

One example would be system setup. When your system is first installed, programming of the software, hardware, or both, may be required before the system will operate properly. If the programming required is too complex for your skills, you will obviously need help. Another example would be where communications are involved. Communications often require special changes to be made to hardware, software, or both, so that your system can talk to another computer using the correct **PROTOCOL**. (*Protocol* is the word used to describe the hardware and software settings needed for each computer to communicate properly with the other.) Often, such changes are referred to as **PATCHES**, meaning they correct or patch over whatever is keeping the software or hardware from working properly, and, because they are so commonly required, they may already be available for your particular system. If so, the cost will be considerably less than having all of the work done from scratch, although you still may have to pay for the patch to be installed. If your need for custom services does fall into one of these so-called standard areas, you will almost always be able to get the work done through your computer dealer, or someone they recommend. These are simple, routine, custom-programming-oriented kinds of tasks that a person trained on your hardware and software should have no problem doing.

While the actual work done in these situations will vary greatly in nature, they will usually have some things in common that will make them relatively inexpensive and fast: 1) The amount of programming needed will almost always be small, perhaps ranging from as little as one hour to no more than eight or ten hours. 2) The cost should be relatively low compared to a full-blown custom application. 3) More or less the same custom work you need done will most likely have been supplied to numerous other customers with the same needs. Remember, though, that the above examples are exceptions, and that, as a rule, custom programming projects are usually time-consuming and expensive.

Where To Go For Custom Software

If you have exhausted all other possibilities and determined that custom software is the best solution for your application, you'll need to find someone who can provide the services needed—as well as to prepare yourself to assist them in doing their job. Your computer dealer, hardware manufacturer, or software publisher, should be one of the first places to look for custom programming services. If they are not in the business of providing such services, they should be able to recommend someone who is. Next, check with people in your business or profession who you think may have had similar work done. There should also be a number of businesses listed in the computer section of your local phone book, or larger cities nearby, that provide custom programming services. If you do use the phone book—because you'll have no clue as to the quality of the services provided, as you would with the other sources just mentioned—be especially sure to ask for, *and check*, references. As a rule, look for the firm closest to you that can provide the best service.

You may be asking: "But how do I know what to look for?" The best way to answer that question is by first giving you a better idea of just what a custom program is, and who the people are that create them. Programming is one of many activities that can fall under the category of a "creative profession." The easiest way to define a creative profession is to say that it is one in which no two people, working on the same problem, will achieve the same result in the same way.

Architecture is an excellent example because, even though all architects are required to be licensed as such, each has his own style and his own way of doing things. So, if two different architects were chosen to build an office building to the same general specifications the two buildings might be as different as night and day in their use of space, light, materials, and so on. The only two things the architects may share is a common interest in the field and the use of the same basic methods and tools.

The same is true of programming. Two programmers may write two programs to perform the same job but it is very unlikely the results would be identical. One programmer might use the programming language COBOL while the other instead chooses to use Pascal or C (See page 260), and one might like to use regular menus while the other designs his or her programs to use pull-down menus and a mouse. One programmer might use numerous help screens in place of a large instruction manual, while the other might prefer to provide a manual. Because approaches can differ so greatly it is important that you help the programmer understand *as fully as possible* what you want and need. One way you can do this is by having as much *written* information available as possible about what you do, how you are currently doing it, and what you would like the computer to do for you (See guidelines under "Buying software," on page 107). Another way is by trying to become as familiar as possible with programs similar to the one you want written so you can say "I like so-and-so in program X" and "I don't want anything like this-or-that in program Y." Finally, ask the programmer to let you know as you discuss your needs and wishes whether you are asking for features which will be very difficult—which means very expensive and time-consuming. As with other types of contracted services, you will find you can get almost any kind of program you want provided you are willing to invest the time and money required to engage skilled people.

You might find the help you need at several kinds of businesses. A **SOFTWARE HOUSE** is primarily in business for the purpose of providing custom software—and sometimes sells off-the-shelf software also. It should have an experienced staff and should be able to provide almost anything needed in the way of custom programming. One advantage to using a software house is that they may have done a program similar to yours for someone else. If so, you may be able to save considerable time and money because they can adapt what they have already designed to your needs, rather than starting from scratch. A **COMPUTER SERVICES** firm is similar to a software house except that they often provide hardware and other services as well. This type of company may be able to supply you with all the components you will need for a computer system—software, hardware, installation, etc. Some of these companies do not have programmers or other specialized people on staff but instead subcontract the work. If you become aware that this is the case, you may want to make sure that a better price wouldn't be available if you dealt directly with a company whose own staff creates custom software.

Software Warranties

Be prepared for software warranties to be *very* different from the warranties you are familiar with for other products. You may enjoy a 5-year, 50,000-mile warranty on your car. You may be accustomed to your local department store allowing a return for any reason within so many days. Warranties that last for months or even years are not uncommon with other products you buy. However, such is not the case when it comes to computer software. Believe it or not, the standard warranty is the virtual equivalent of having no warranty, because you will probably receive only a 30- to 120-day warranty that the media—diskettes or tapes—used to deliver your new program to you are free from defects, period. In today's age of aggressive lawsuits, direct or indirect providers of services are taking every available measure to avoid being hit with an unfair action, and firms in the computer industry are no exception.

Next we enter the vast world of what software warranties *do not* cover, known as the **DISCLAIMER**, in which the publisher of the software disclaims responsibility for whatever is not covered in the warranty. Software disclaimers are often a full page long, sometimes more, and go to great lengths to attempt to free the publisher from any and all responsibility or blame someone might wish to bestow upon it. Most reputable publishers of software have good intentions and have usually shown an interest in helping resolve problems to the satisfaction of both parties—despite the fact that by the terms of their warranty they are not obligated to do so. Software publishers are, however, trying to protect themselves from someone who, for instance, experiences difficulty with his software and then sues the publisher for millions of dollars in lost sales, regardless of the cause. Naturally, software firms do not wish to be held liable for the result of someone else's misuse of their product.

Software Licensing And Ownership

In the case of off-the-shelf software you sometimes own the software once you have purchased it—and sometimes you don't. In many cases you are just paying for a *license to use* the software for a specified period of time. The time span of such agreements is almost always longer than you could ever expect to be using the software. Software is licensed instead of being sold outright because software publishers want to protect their programs from being unfairly used, distributed, or copied, and, while they have little control over software someone buys outright, they can revoke the license of someone illegally copying or using a licensed program.

The rights to custom software usually end up belonging to the person or business paying for its design. This can be a touchy subject, however, because in the design of a program programmers often use code they have already developed—and to which they own full rights. Using existing code reduces both the time it takes to write a custom program as well as the final cost. However, if large amounts of existing code owned by the programmer are used, and under certain other conditions, the programmer may want to maintain the rights to the entire finished program.

No matter who claims ownership, however, at the very least you must be supplied with all portions of the written program (**SOURCE CODE**), and any explanatory notes (**PROGRAM DOCUMENTATION** or **SOURCE CODE DOCUMENTA-TION**), so that if the original programmer becomes unavailable you can still hire another programmer in the future, if needed. This documentation is different from, and not to be confused with, documentation such as manuals, which are provided to help a user operate the finished program.

Any rights you will have to a custom program once it is completed—whether you can package and sell it to others, for instance—should be clearly spelled out in the contract you negotiate with the programmers. If you do not understand, or disagree with, the terms of a contract someone wants you to sign, get a second opinion from someone else in the computer field or from an attorney *experienced in such matters*, who will be able to help you clarify things and avoid trouble spots.

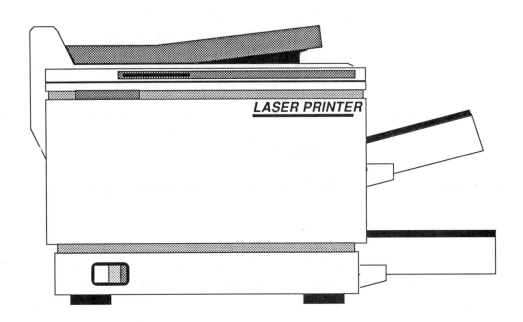

LASER PRINTER

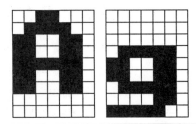

Two letters showing an example of a 9 x 7 print matrix

DOT MATRIX

Examples of different printers

Chapter 6

PRINTERS

Computer printers are simply an efficient way to get the information you have stored in a computer onto paper. This chapter starts with the type of printer that is still the most common, then goes on to explain in detail how printers work, and further on provides information on more modern types of printers—such as the laser printer and the ink-jet printer.

HOW MODERN PRINTERS PRINT

As explained in the chapter on monitors (See "Resolution," on page 60), text and graphics images are not actually solid but are formed by a pattern of tiny dots. With the exception of daisy wheel-type printers, all other printers work by creating a pattern of dots to form each character. Like monitors, **RESOLUTION**, or sharpness, is measured by counting the number of dots running across and down the pattern which forms each character. This dot pattern is referred to as the **MATRIX** of the character. The matrix can be measured by counting the number of dots that form a vertical line through the pattern, and the number that are horizontal, as in 9 X 7 (9 dots high by 7 across), or as the total number of dots contained within a square inch, such as in 300 **DOTS PER INCH (DPI)**.

The Dot-Matrix Printer

The computer printer in most widespread use is the **DOT-MATRIX PRINTER**, which prints the dots required to make up each individual character as described above. Dot creation is accomplished by tiny **HAMMERS** or **PINS** which strike the ribbon against the paper to create each character. Dot-matrix printers provide the greatest versatility and speed for the money spent, with good printers having speeds starting at around 120 **CHARACTERS PER SECOND (CPS)** and some models ranging as high as 300 to 400 CPS or more. The output of high-speed printers is often rated by the number of **LINES PER MINUTE (LPM)** they are able to print. Regardless of the method used, the actual rate at which a printer is capable of operating is known as its **THROUGHPUT**. Unfortunately, many—if not most—printer manufacturers overstate the speed ratings of their printers. It is not uncommon for a printer advertised at 250 CPS to actually print at a speed of about 180 CPS, or less, when operating under a normal workload.

There are two basic types of dot-matrix printers: those designed for high-speed, high-volume, and less than letter-quality, printing, and those designed for letter-quality output which are not as fast. High-speed printers are routinely used for data processing, accounting, and report-generating applications. They are usually very reliable, and some are designed for extremely heavy-duty continuous use. The disadvantage to this kind of printer is that while the print is very readable the characters are too ragged and/or faint for use in outside correspondence—simply because convention calls for business letters to have a sharp, contrasty look. On the other hand, if a dot-matrix printer has a matrix of less than 9x7 (9 dots x 7 dots), chances are you will not be satisfied with the print quality even for reports, invoices, etc. High-speed, high-volume dot-matrix printers are usually installed where letter quality is not important, or where a letter-quality printer will also be available to handle correspondence.

LETTER-QUALITY DOT-MATRIX PRINTERS offer the best of both worlds for most users, both acceptable speed and clean, well-formed characters. In their low-quality, or **DRAFT**, mode these printers typically deliver speeds ranging from 100 to 250 CPS, and 55 to 120 CPS in the letter-quality, or **WORD PROCESSING (WP)**, mode. The best of these printers can indeed print a letter that looks like it was typed on a typewriter. A printer with less than a 24-pin print head will not be able to produce these results as well, or as fast, but can come very close. Good dot-matrix printers are reliable and relatively quiet, with prices starting at about $300 and ranging to $2,000 or more. However, few applications for microcomputers require a dot-matrix printer that costs more than $1,000.

Laser Printers

LASER PRINTERS are currently the most advanced printers available for microcomputers. As the name implies, laser printers actually use a laser to form characters. The laser does not, however, actually burn or print the images on the paper. Instead, the laser beam charges a special metal drum which in turn transfers the charged pattern to the paper passing over it. Finally, toner "sticks" to these charged areas on the paper and heat causes it to form a permanent impression. Some laser-type printers don't actually use a laser beam to charge the drum, even though they use the word *laser* in their name. Even though computer laser printers are a recent development (mid-1980s), the technology is virtually identical to that used in copying machines. In fact, some of the earlier laser printers could actually be used as both an office printer and copying machine. Laser printers are fast—some extremely so—and they are jacks-of-all-trades, being able to print anything from a page of simple text, like a letter, to a drawing or photograph.

The first laser printer to gain widespread use and popularity was the **Hewlett-Packard LASERJET** introduced in 1984. The next advance came with the introduction of the **LASERWRITER** by **Apple Computer** in 1985. All laser printers use some form of **PAGE DESCRIPTION LANGUAGE (PDL)**—a specialized programming language for defining printer output, text, graphics, etc. Unlike the LaserJet, which used its own PDL developed by Hewlett-Packard, the Apple LaserWriter used a PDL called **POSTSCRIPT**, by the **Adobe Corporation**. Because PostScript offered advanced features, and, because it was adopted by many other printer manufacturers, by the end of the 1980s it had become the PDL of choice for those in the graphics arts and desktop publishing fields. Because of the high cost of PostScript printers, Hewlett-Packard and Hewlett-Packard-based machines are still a popular choice for users with less demanding needs. It is for this reason that most software that supports a laser printer supports both of these PDLs—with the exception of some graphics and desktop publishing programs. Most laser printers have a resolution of 300 DPI, although newer models are starting to offer 400 x 400, 400 x 600, 600 x 600, and even higher resolution. The speed of a laser printer is measured in **PAGES PER MINUTE (PPM)**, with the average printer producing 8 to 10 pages per minute. Laser printers can easily cost several thousand dollars or more, but prices are constantly dropping, with basic units costing as little as $1,000 to $1,500.

Ink-Jet Printers

INK-JET PRINTERS work by literally spray-painting each separate character—at incredible speed—directly onto the paper, using jets of ink. These printers are very fast, extremely quiet, and have few limitations as to the type of character they can print, but they sometimes have problems with the ink jets getting clogged up with drying ink. Most good ink jet printers start at around $1,000, and color models are available.

The Letter-Quality Or Daisy-Wheel Printer

Up until the early 1980s all **LETTER-QUALITY** printers were of the **DAISY WHEEL** type. A daisy wheel is simply a disc of metal or plastic which is divided into slim, flexible arms, or "petals"— thus the name "daisy wheel." Each petal makes the imprint of a different character—just like type bars on a traditional typewriter. The wheel is positioned over the ribbon and paper and rotates very quickly to whichever character is about to be printed, at which time a small hammer presses the imprint onto the paper—still about the same way the original electric typewriters worked, but a much more efficient method. Most modern typewriters also use this more advanced electronic method.

The advantage of a daisy-wheel printer is that because it works like a typewriter it prints letters that look exactly like they have been typed. This provides the advantage of a computerized office while still maintaining the personal touch of hand-typed correspondence. However, these printers are generally slow in operation when compared with other types of printers (usually less than 60 **CHARACTERS PER SECOND [CPS]**), most are noisy, and many vibrate a great deal when running. In addition, you have to change the print wheel each time you need a different typeface. A good daisy-wheel printer costs at least several hundred dollars, and can easily run over a thousand dollars. Because more advanced dot-matrix printers are now available which can produce near-letter quality images—and are more economical and reliable as well—such as those just described, the daisy-wheel printer is rapidly going the way of the wagon train.

Line Printers

A **LINE PRINTER**, as the name implies, works by printing much or all of an entire line of characters at one time. Line printers are designed for high-speed, heavy-duty use, and are used almost exclusively for printing continuous forms and reports. These printers place characters on paper using a pattern of dots very similar to—although higher in resolution than—those produced by dot-matrix printers. A number of methods may be used to transfer the characters to paper, including a spinning metal band, chain, or drum, which runs the width of the paper. Line printers are often referred to according to the type of print head they have, and may also be called **BAND**, **CHAIN**, or **DRUM** printers. Speeds typically range from about 150 LPM to as many as several thousand LPM or more, depending upon the model. Because of the greater size and weight of most line printers—in comparison to those mentioned above—their higher cost, and relatively specialized application, they have traditionally been used with mainframes and minicomputers. However, as the capacity and processing power of microcomputers continues to grow, the use of line printers with PCs is becoming more common.

PRINTER TECHNOLOGY: SOME IMPORTANT FEATURES

Serial Versus Parallel Printers

You connect a printer to your computer using a **PRINTER CABLE**. In addition, **PARALLEL PRINTERS** require that a card with a **PARALLEL PRINTER PORT** be installed in your computer before they will operate. As explained in the chapter on serial and parallel communications (See "The communications highways," on page 40) parallel is the faster of the two methods used to allow computer devices to communicate. Parallel printers offer the best performance and the highest printer speeds. **SERIAL PRINTERS** require that a card with a **SERIAL PORT** be installed (See "Bit-by-bit communications," on page 174). Serial printers look and act exactly like parallel printers; the only real difference is that they cannot accept data from the computer as fast. However, because it can be easier to connect serial printers to multiuser and networked systems, they may offer advantages in such applications. For the average system, and the average user, a parallel printer is by far the most popular choice. Most printers come equipped for parallel connection, and some offer the versatility of being able to use both parallel and serial connections. Unless your system requires it, there is probably no good reason to purchase a serial printer.

Print Buffers

Among other things, a **PRINT BUFFER** can free you from having to wait for your computer to print something. Instead of information going directly to the printer it goes into the print buffer, which consists of a RAM storage area inside the printer. Once there, the data is considered **BUFFERED** and the printer completes the operation by printing the information stored in the buffer. When more room is available in the buffer, the computer will send more data. If the buffer is large enough to hold all of the information being sent from the computer, the printer's own microprocessor can continue the job unaided by the CPU of the sending computer. You can tell if the buffer on your printer is this large by printing a sample letter or other output. If after issuing the print command from within your software you are able to continue working—or exit the program—and the document continues to print, you know that your print buffer is at least large enough to hold a document of that size. Having a large buffer can be a big advantage because some programs will not let you continue working if you have sent something to the printer and it is still being printed.

While most printers contain their own print buffers, you can also purchase external stand-alone units that allow you to have as much RAM as you need. External print buffers not only make operations more efficient, but allow for easier unattended operation of the printer and greater versatility. For example, if you have sent a letter to your printer through a print buffer you can continue to make copies by printing them directly from the buffer's memory and, at the same time, be doing something entirely different on the computer. You could, for example, use your word processor to type a letter you need 100 copies of, send it to the buffer, instruct the buffer to send its contents to the printer 100 times, exit your word processor, and then start working in your accounting program. Without a buffer that contained a copy feature you would have to stay in the word processing program—for perhaps an hour or more—and wait until the 100 letters finished printing. Not all buffers allow this kind of versatile use. Those that do usually have a **REPEAT** and/or **COPIES** button for printing the contents of the buffer, as well as a **CLEAR** button to erase anything still in memory. If you frequently spend too much time waiting for your printer to free up the computer a print buffer could be a good investment. If all you need is a regular buffer without the copy feature remember that most printers contain an internal buffer. Some printers allow you to increase the amount of buffer memory available by resetting dip switches (and/or purchasing additional memory). If, however, you have to make an additional purchase anyway, you might as well have the versatility of an external print buffer.

Print Spooling

Similar to the print buffer is a software program called a **PRINT SPOOLER**, which first sends print jobs to a disk file (or files) rather than directly to the printer (or print buffer). The term **SPOOLING** is used to describe the actual process of transferring the information to a disk file. Once the information has been **SPOOLED** the computer is free for other uses. The spooling software then retrieves the information from disk and sends it to the printer in the order received. A disk file used for this purpose is often referred to as the **PRINT QUEUE**. The number of files that can be sent to the print queue before it is full is usually adjustable. Most systems also allow you to display the status of, and cancel, files waiting to be printed from the queue. Multiuser systems, especially, take advantage of these techniques because such systems often have several people sending output to the same printer—which is another advantage of print spoolers. Even print buffers do not always contain enough RAM memory to hold large amounts of output. But, because print spoolers use hard disk files for storage, large amounts of data can be spooled and printed without tying up the computer. Some print-spooling software even allows you to make copies directly from the queue—just like some print buffers—and, unlike a print buffer, most have the ability to display the jobs waiting to be printed and allow you to cancel one, or all, of the jobs, if necessary.

Paper Handling

There are a variety of methods for feeding paper into and through printers. For printers that accommodate single sheets—as with a letter—the paper is hand fed in the same way you would a typewriter; this is called a **FRICTION FEED**. Some allow the attachment of a power **SHEET FEEDER** which automatically feeds one sheet at a time. Other printers, mostly the laser type, have a built-in paper tray for single sheets. When continuous feeding of paper or forms is required, a **TRACTOR FEED** is attached—unless it is already built into the printer. A **PULL TRACTOR** pulls paper up through the printer, while a **PUSH TRACTOR** pushes the paper through from the rear or bottom of the printer. Tractor feeds work by grabbing the holes located along the edges of the paper or forms being used. This paper comes in continuous sheets and is referred to as **COMPUTER PRINTOUT PAPER**, **CONTINUOUS FORMS PAPER**, **TRACTOR-FEED PAPER**, or **FANFOLD** paper. The paper is available with perforations along the edges which allow you to tear off the tractor strips, separate the pages, and make the sheet look like a regular piece of paper. The terms **LASERCUT**, **MICROPERFORATED**, **MI-CROCUT**, **CLEAN-EDGE**, etc., mean the perforations are extremely fine and will separate easier, usually leaving few if any noticeable serrated edges. This is the type of paper you should use if using continuous forms paper for letters and correspondence. Virtually every kind of form or check used in business is available in continuous sheets, and many paper companies now offer continuous forms stationery—with or without your letterhead—for high-volume users.

One reason that typewriters will be around for awhile is because computer printers, while good at most things, are seldom able to handle nonstandard paper items with ease. Envelopes, 3 x 5 cards, Rolodex cards, and non-tractor-feed forms—such as those used for Fedex packages, Express Mail, and insurance claims—are not easy to align and print on. Some printers have optional envelope feeders available, but these may solve only some of the problems—and they don't always work well. For high-volume addressing jobs, continuous labels will go through most printers without a problem, and the labels can then be affixed to the envelopes. Window envelopes can also be used that allow the address on an invoice or other form to show through, thus avoiding the need to address each envelope. However, for smaller quantities a typewriter is often the fastest way to get the job done. Keep in mind that many printers are unable to handle carbon copies, NCR (carbonless) paper, multipart forms, or continuous labels. The **PAPER PATH** of the printer— the rollers the paper has to curve through as it feeds, etc.—often is such that labels peel off of their backing and stick inside the machine, and thick multipart forms may cause a **PAPER JAM**. Before purchasing a printer for this kind of use make sure it is rated for the job. Manufacturers often give ratings for the number of copies their printers are able to make through multipart forms. However, arranging an actual demonstration with the forms, envelopes, or labels you plan to use is the best way to learn a printer's true capabilities.

Bidirectional And Logic-Seeking Printers

Two common techniques used to increase printing speed are **BIDIRECTIONAL PRINTING** and **LOGIC-SEEKING PRINTING**. Ordinary **UNIDIREC-TIONAL** printers work by printing one line—from left to right—performing a line feed and carriage return (returning the print head to the left margin), and then printing another line—in other words, they print in only one direction. **BIDIREC-TIONAL** printers avoid the wasted carriage return by printing one line in one direction and another line when the print head travels back in the other direction. **LOGIC-SEEKING** printers seek out the shortest path for the print head to follow as it prints the characters on each line. Either of these methods can increase operating speed substantially over printers that do not use them, and most good printers use both. Keep in mind, however, that some printers create characters differently, and the methods just described are applicable only to printers with a traveling print head, such as dot-matrix and ink-jet units.

PRINTER PROBLEMS

Since all printers share some things in common—using serial or parallel connection, print buffers, etc.—printer users often have some shared problems. Following is a brief discussion of simple printer problems that can cause a great deal of frustration but are easy to solve. Make sure to check all of the symptoms described below until you have either solved the problem or made sure that none of these solutions apply. Your printer and computer manual should also contain information about troubleshooting.

Start by checking these simple items: 1) Is the printer turned on? 2) Is the ribbon installed properly (or, if a laser printer, the toner cartridge, etc.)? If not, the printer might print erratically or not at all. 3) Are the **DIP SWITCHES** properly set? (See "Dip switches," on page 245.)

The printer cable, though one of the least expensive components, can be one of the first causes of trouble. Assuming that you have the correct cable (judging by the fact that it has worked correctly in the past) make sure the connections at both the printer and computer ends are secure. No computer cable, especially printer cables, should be bent severely, twisted, crushed in closed doors, etc., and a close examination may reveal that such damage has occurred. Most modern printer cables are covered with rounded plastic insulation (Similar to the cable shown on page 175), and are the most reliable design. Some cables, however, especially older ones, are **RIBBON CABLES**, so named because they resemble a large, flat, plastic ribbon. Ribbon cables work fine inside of computers where they are not exposed, but they are a poor choice for most external uses and are very susceptible to wear and damage. Especially in systems where several users share a single printer and frequently connect and disconnect the cable, the cable can easily go bad and cause erratic results—or cause nothing to print at all. If examining or moving the cable does not solve the problem, try a different cable, or take the cable to a computer store and, if they don't mind, see if it will work with one of their printers.

All printers have somewhere on their control panel an **ON-LINE** indicator. When this indicator is on, the printer is electronically connected to the computer and is able to receive data. This also means that most, if not all, functions on the control panel are "locked out" and inaccessible to the user. If you are trying to access the control panel directly, such as in ejecting a page (called a **FORM FEED**), or moving the paper up a line at a time (called **LINE FEED**), the printer will not respond because while it is on-line it accepts instructions only from the computer. A printer should be on-line anytime the computer is sending instructions or data to it. Pressing the on-line button in the middle of a print job will interrupt the job and take the printer **OFF-LINE**, meaning that it is electronically disconnected from the computer. Likewise, when a printer is off-line it cannot receive instructions from the computer, and, if you are unaware it is off-line, it may not appear to be working.

With the exception of laser printers, and laser-type printers, most printers have a lever which allows the printer to be used in the tractor-feed mode for continuous forms, and in the friction-feed mode for single sheets. Trying to feed the wrong kind of paper with the wrong lever setting often results in an error, and the printer not printing. Naturally, if the printer is out of paper, or the paper has torn, broken, or jammed, the printer will also stop. By the way, even though most printers are supposed to stop if the paper jams, it is a good idea not to run large print jobs when no one will be around to keep an occasional eye out. If the paper should jam, and the printer fails to stop, the printer could be damaged.

If a printer is behaving strangely, you can also try canceling the print job, turning the printer off, and then turning it back on and trying to run the job again.

CHOOSING A PRINTER

The type of printer that is best for you will depend upon the type of printing you intend to do—and how often. If you will print only business letters which must conform exactly to a certain typeface or style, or if those you do business with require correspondence to be submitted in a specific typeface—such as Courier 10, the worldwide typewriter standard—then a laser printer would probably work best for you. A daisy-wheel printer would work here, also, but with laser printers becoming more popular—and less expensive—daisy-wheel printers no longer represent the best choice when buying a new printer. (Many manufacturers aren't even making them anymore.) If you will be printing only listings—like computer programs or accounting reports—need high speed, or will be printing continuously for many hours each day or around the clock, then a heavy-duty dot-matrix printer is probably the way to go. If you are in the publishing, printing, or graphics business, or if you have the need to prepare a large number of original drawings, charts, designs, presentations, etc., then, again, you should look into laser printers. If your needs fall into the normal category of most users—a mix of letters, some reports, an occasional chart or graph, etc.—a good letter-quality dot-matrix printer is almost sure to be your best bet. Before choosing any printer, however, make sure you find out what kind of printer the software you're planning on using requires, and that the printer meets these requirements.

This page intentionally left blank.

Chapter 7

THE WORKING ENVIRONMENT

When reviewing and planning the work environment for a computer system, never hesitate to involve the people who will be using it. Their input is not only valuable and can help you avoid making mistakes, but will give them a sense of involvement and satisfaction in having been a part of the process.

There are a number of things you can do to help make a computerized area or workstation productive, as well as pleasant for the people working there. Just as a typewriter requires a surface a little lower than a desk or table for comfortable typing, so do computer keyboards. Work surfaces that are adjustable in height are even nicer, since different people can use the height that works best for them. A comfortable chair is needed as well; here, also, adjustable height is desirable, if not a must. If the workstation is located in a carpeted area a floor pad may be needed to allow the chair to roll smoothly. Where carpets are involved it is also very likely you will have to take precautions against static electricity, particularly in dry, dusty areas (See page 136 for more information on how to deal with this problem).

Are there enough electrical outlets with the proper load rating available? Are they properly grounded? (The outlets in many older buildings are not.) Has it been determined what kind of electrical surge-protection will work best at this location?

Dust And Dirt

Small, modern computer systems rarely require a room that is specially air conditioned. However, because computers and dirt just don't mix, every effort should be made to keep areas where computers are operating dust- and dirt-free. The cleaner its environment the longer your computer equipment will last. Dirt, moisture, dust, and cigarette smoke can all cause damage. Dust covers are available for almost every kind of computer and are a wise investment. There are also covers available for computers, printers, and even keyboards, that can be left in place during operation (See "Resource list," on page 273). These covers are a must in dirty environments, or where something could easily be spilled on equipment (especially keyboards). You'll also want to make sure air filters on fan-cooled equipment are kept clean or replaced periodically. Every so often, perhaps once or twice a year, a "checkup"—preventive maintenance—by a service technician may be in order.

If for some reason the computer must be located in an area that is dusty, such as a shop floor or parts area, at least try to keep the area and the computer as clean as possible. If you are in a bad environment try to locate the computer and other sensitive components in a cleaner area, perhaps an adjoining office, storage room, or closet, leaving only a keyboard and monitor or other necessary components in the dirtier environment (extension cables are available for this purpose).

Tobacco smoke is included on the list of things that are bad for computers. Smoking restrictions are an emotional issue among employees, but keep in mind that if you do decide to operate a computer in a smoke-filled area it is very possible you may experience data loss, or repairs necessitated by tobacco smoke. Hair spray, furniture polish, and similar spray-can-type products can also wreak havoc on storage media, disk drives, and precision components.

How often, and how hard, you use your system will have a large bearing on the amount of service it will require. Because computers have few mechanical parts it is not uncommon for a system that's been well taken care of to operate for years without a major breakdown. Like anything else, the better you take of your equipment the longer it will provide you with reliable service.

Screen Glare

Glare on your TV screen at home can be annoying enough. Having to work at a hard-to-see screen all day long, however, will at the very least leave you with sore eyes, and will probably also prevent you from getting as much work done. Screen glare should be considered both before and after a monitor has been installed. If glare is a problem, change the lighting by adjusting whichever lights can be moved or aimed, or by installing shades on outside windows. You can also move the monitor to an area with more suitable lighting, or obtain one of the inexpensive, easy-to-install, and effective antiglare devices that attach to a monitor's screen.

If none of these solutions seem practical, there remains the more expensive and long-term alternative of relighting the affected areas. While more costly, new lighting—and the improved look it can bring to an office—often pays for itself in higher productivity, improved employee morale, and a better impression on visitors. Studies have shown that the lighting and colors used in an office can make big differences in the attitudes of people who work there. If you decide to change the lighting, make sure you use a lighting contractor who has worked with and understands the special needs of a computerized office.

Accidental Spills

Care should always be taken, both during normal operation as well as when cleaning, not to allow liquids to be spilled on or into the equipment. If this should happen, unplug the unit while being careful to avoid being shocked. If a large spill has occurred—a fish tank or water cooler tipped over, etc.—and the floor is wet, it would be wise to turn off the circuit breaker serving the equipment. Dry off the areas you can easily reach using toweling and *immediately* call a technician or take the equipment to one. Never use a hairdryer or similar device to try to "dry out" the equipment. It may work, but if not used properly a hairdryer can damage some heat-sensitive components. (See page 71 for instructions on how to handle a floppy disk that has had something spilled on it.)

ELECTRICAL CONSIDERATIONS

Under *ideal* conditions, electricity is "**CLEAN**," supplied to an outlet at a steady voltage level. Unfortunately, the electricity from the power company has usually suffered various forms of interference before it reaches your computer. You've no doubt observed the fluctuations in power that often occur over electrical power lines: lights mysteriously become brighter for a short time, or someone turns on a large appliance like a washer or dryer and the lights dim for a moment or go out entirely. (This problem can be worse in and around manufacturing plants, especially in older buildings). Such an electrical environment is, shall we say, less than "computer friendly."

Spikes And Glitches

Widespread electrical fluctuations are created by lightning, problems with the power company's transformers and substations, or other conditions affecting the distribution network. Extremely brief increases in voltage in an electrical line that last only a fraction of a second are referred to as **SPIKES** or **GLITCHES** (which may show up as a crooked line on your TV screen, or as a pop heard through the speakers of your stereo), while an increase in voltage that lasts longer is referred to as a **SURGE**. A decrease in voltage may be in the form of a brief **VOLTAGE DROP**, or may last longer and turn into a **BROWNOUT** or a total **POWER FAILURE**.

Significant fluctuations from any source can have a disastrous effect on computers. Severe drops, or a power failure, will cause the loss of *all* data in the RAM memory of your computer. If this problem occurs at just the right instant, even the data stored on disk can be wiped out. Strong power surges can burn out electronic components within your system or shorten their life span. In fact, most manufacturers specify that you void their warranties by operating their equipment without proper electrical protection. Insurance companies and service contract providers also give discounts to clients whose equipment is electrically protected. Just a point worth mentioning here: while computers are especially sensitive, these fluctuations don't do other electronic equipment any good either. Stereos, TVs, electronic typewriters, etc., can also be affected, and their warranties may carry a similar disclaimer.

Surge Protection

Protection against sudden power increases is accomplished at the outlet using a plug-in device called a **SURGE PROTECTOR**, sometimes referred to as a **SURGE SUPPRESSOR, LINE CONDITIONER, LINE FILTER,** or **LINE STABILIZER**. While many inexpensive versions are available, these vital devices are not a place to skimp. Look for one that offers protection against surges, spikes, noise, and hash, and one that has equipment isolation and protection against electromagnetic and radio frequency interference. The more of these features you can find, the better your system will be protected.

Good protectors also come with good warranties. Look for at least a year or two; some are guaranteed for five years or more. One possibility that some warranties take into consideration—not as rare as you might think—is that of a lightning strike. Even though lightning seldom enters a piece of equipment directly, a nearby strike during a storm can cause tremendous power surges through electrical lines. Few protectors guarantee to stop a direct lightning strike from damaging your equipment. However, many systems have been saved, or the damage reduced, because they were connected to good surge protectors. The warranties on some of the better units offer to replace the protector if it is damaged by lightning. If it is possible to shut the system down during electrical storms or periods of prolonged power-line disruptions it is a worthwhile precaution, even if your system has good protection.

Power Failure Protection

An **UNINTERRUPTIBLE POWER SUPPLY (UPS)**, also known as a **BATTERY BACKUP** or **EMERGENCY POWER SUPPLY**, continues to provide electricity to a computer system in the event of a power failure, giving you time to properly shut the system down to avoid file damage and/or data loss. (Remember, your current work is in RAM, and RAM is erased by even the briefest loss of power.) For this reason, few UPSs are designed to provide more than 10 to 30 minutes of power. Even so, you must make sure the voltage, amperage, or wattage rating of the UPS is equal to or greater than the maximum drawn by your computer system. To do this, total the watts or amperes required by each piece of equipment you intend to attach to the UPS. Unless there is good reason to do so, do not plan to hook up external—and non-critical—equipment such as printers to your UPS. Do, however, include the monitor and any equipment your system would not be able to function without. Once you've added up all of the electrical requirements, figure in at least a 10 to 20 percent safety margin.

A major consideration in selecting a good UPS is how fast it can provide power when there is an electrical failure. The speed at which this occurs is known as the **SWITCHING SPEED**. If it is not fast enough, data corruption, data loss, and even equipment damage may result. While by no means a substitute for accurate specifications, one way to determine whether a unit's switching speed is too slow is to simply pull the UPS's power cord while the unit is connected to a computer.

Many computer dealers have demonstrations like this already arranged in their showrooms. If there is *any* noticeable disruption in the screen display or other components, you can rule out that UPS. Keep in mind also that a UPS may or may not offer surge protection. If you should choose a unit that does not, you will still have to plug in a surge protector between the UPS and your computer.

Static Electricity

Besides the spikes, surges, and voltage drops which are carried over electrical lines, computers are exposed to the environmental hazards of static electricity. This is the kind of electricity that sometimes gives you a shock if you touch a metal object after walking across a carpet. Like electrical line interference, static electricity can wreak havoc with computer systems.

If you frequently get a spark when touching metal objects, you have a static problem. If it happens all the time, and/or the sparks are large, visible, and perhaps even painful, then you have a moderate to severe static electricity problem. Because static electricity does not come through your electrical outlet but is carried by objects—usually people—that come into contact with your computer, it is harder to control than power line interference. For this reason, preventing or minimizing static electricity is your best form of protection against it. But first, you must identify any static electricity problem areas that exist around your computer. Brick or steel walled buildings with cement or tiled floors seem to have the fewest static-electricity-related problems, while floors with carpet—especially shag carpet—and wooden frame structures usually create the most problems.

The first defense against any form of static electricity—and against electric shock—is to make sure your computer system is properly grounded. All newly constructed buildings are required to have 3-prong grounded outlets. If yours is an older building you should have the building engineer or your own electrician tell you whether the circuits are grounded; they often will not be. In an older building you will find 2-prong outlets, which are definitely not grounded even if the wiring in the building is; the 3-prong adapter you will need to use modern electrical equipment can be obtained with a grounding tab, which in turn is secured to the screw in the outlet cover. (This has no effect, of course, if the circuits themselves are not grounded, and the same is true of supposedly grounded 3-prong outlets.)

For occasional static problems, making sure you touch something metal before touching computer equipment should prove effective. Any static charge being carried by you or your clothing will then have been safely discharged. If your desk is wood or plastic, or it is inconvenient to find a metal object to touch, there are a number of products on the market which can help. Some are in the form of metallic touch-strips or pads—designed to be placed on or near your keyboard—that you touch before using the computer. Touch-strips safely discharge the static through a wire that is connected to a grounded outlet or other object.

If you have a high degree of static electricity at your location it may be because your computer is located in a carpeted area. Walking on carpets can generate enormous amounts of static electricity. If carpet can't be removed or the computer relocated you can purchase antistatic mats to place over the carpeting in the area it occupies. Pump-bottle sprays are also available to reduce static in carpets and other high-static areas. Before handling floppy disks or tapes in an area where static electricity is present, it's a good idea to first touch a grounded metal object. This will discharge any static electricity picked up by you that could cause data loss.

Any, or all, of the forms of electrical interference mentioned above can usually be expected to be worse in commercial and industrial locations than in a home or apartment.

Radio And TV Interference

In addition to external electrical hazards, you should also be aware that computer equipment itself gives off various forms of electrical and radio interference. While modern computers are designed to reduce such problems to a minimum, it is possible for computers and their connected devices to interfere with each other on occasion. This interference can also affect nearby radio and TV sets. However, this seldom causes a major problem—especially in office and commercial settings—and is usually easily corrected by relocating the computer or radio or TV it is affecting. If this doesn't help, you may be able to have a service technician install shielding inside the computer that will reduce or eliminate the interference.

You are required by law to correct the problem if someone should complain that your system is causing interference. All computerized devices are required by the **FEDERAL COMMUNICATIONS COMMISSION (FCC)** to be classified as either a **CLASS A** or **CLASS B** device. Class B devices generate the least radio interference and are thus well suited to residential use. Class A devices are primarily designed for use in office and commercial settings where the increased interference they give off is less likely to cause a problem. The rating of any computer-related device can be found on the label that lists its model and/or serial number.

Chapter 8

THE CRITICAL NEED FOR BACKUPS AND THE DANGERS OF DATA LOSS

A computer can be an incredible time-saving tool. You can use it to produce more work faster than you would have ever dreamed of doing by hand. However, this very same advantage—incredible speed—can work against you at a time when you need it least. True, computers are fast, but they can destroy data equally as fast as they can help you maintain or create it. Hitting the wrong key, for instance, can cause a computer to wipe out—in only fractions of a second—hours, weeks, even months of work. Occasionally this happens as the result of some glitch or bug in the system, but more often the computer is only carrying out the instructions it was given. It happens all the time: someone accidentally opens the disk drive door before the light goes out, or pushes the erase button instead of the button he or she intended to. Whatever the cause, sooner or later it will probably happen to you. That's why you should *never, ever, overlook the importance of making BACKUPS!*

Backing up your files is merely the simple process of making a copy of the information stored in your computer system so that if something happens to it you can recover the lost information. If you do not make backups you will *without any doubt* join the ranks of those who did the same and regretted it when it was too late, for in today's computerized society there are now *three* things certain in life—death, taxes, and totally unexpected data loss! So if you commit *anything* you've learned from this book to memory, and practice it every day, please let it be the very gentle reminder that follows.

Never

To

Back-

Fail Make Ups!!!

At one time people complained about making backups, and avoided doing it, because they said it took too much of their time. However, there are now many products on the market which drastically reduce the time it takes to make a backup—so time is no longer an excuse (See "Resource list," on page 273). Unfortunately, *many* people using computers have never been made aware of how important it is to make backups. It's this simple: If you don't have backups, and something should happen to the information stored in your computer, you have just lost that information for good. Certain kinds of information, such as that used for research or statistical purposes, once lost, *may be irreplaceable*. (The same is true for creative work of any kind.) Even if the information could be recovered, the time it would take to reassemble it and enter it into the computer all over again could easily be too expensive or impractical. The effect could range from a disruption in your normal activities to being unable to continue to work at all. Some businesses have gone under and school courses have been failed because of a major data loss. Hopefully, the thought of less-than-pleasant possibilities like these will encourage you to back up your system regularly.

There are many philosophies on making backups. Some people always back up everything on their systems while others only back up information which has been changed or added. Some people perform backups at the end of the day, others at night, and yet others early in the morning before work. With so many options available, how do you know what to back up and when? Simple: Make backups of *anything* and *everything* that if lost would be irreplaceable, would have to be reassembled and reentered, or would take more time to replace than you could reasonably afford. For most data this means backing up at least once a day. If a great deal of information is being entered or changed, backing up several times a day may be required.

Remember that you should also make copies of the floppy disks your software came on, in case the original disks should become unusable. This will not only allow you to avoid the delay—and expense—of obtaining new disks from the manufacturer, but also gives you protection in the event the manufacturer goes out of business. (A not-so-small number of people have loyally made regular backups *of their system and data*, suffered a loss, and then been unable to recover the information because they had failed to make backups of their backup software and the company that made it had gone out of business!)

Most backups are reused—written over again and again when new backups are made; however, it is highly recommended that you also make *permanent* backups on a regular basis. This is most commonly done once a month but can be as often as once a week or more frequently, depending upon your needs. Permanent backups are typically retained for at least a year before being used again; some companies retain them indefinitely. Permanent backups are kept not so much to guard against data loss but so that you can go back and reconstruct previous information should you need it; this happens more often than you might think. For instance, you might want to review a financial analysis that was done earlier in the year, but was then erased from the system. Or perhaps you'd want to go back to last year to see how your profit or inventory profiles compare with the current ones. If you should ever want to review information that was in your system at one time, but was then removed when it was no longer needed, permanent backups will prove to be invaluable.

In a small system, with only floppy disks and no hard drive, your choices for methods of backing up are usually limited to making copies of each floppy disk. Hard-disk systems can be backed up in a number of ways. One method is to transfer (back up) the information to floppies. Depending on the type of disk drive you have and how much information is stored in your system, backing up to floppies can be a relatively fast and effective method. However, for larger systems with greater storage needs you will want to look into more efficient back up methods. By far the most convenient and cost-effective method for backing up most systems is to use a **TAPE DRIVE**. These drives are about the same size as a floppy-disk drive; most can be mounted inside the computer like a floppy drive, or purchased as an external unit. An external drive offers the added advantage of portability. If you have several computers at your location, you can carry an external drive from computer to computer, backing up the hard disk of each one. A computer **TAPE CARTRIDGE** resembles a very heavy-duty version of a regular cassette tape. (Computer tape drives should not be confused with systems that actually do use regular audio cassette or video tapes. While some of these systems do work they are usually not as versatile, reliable, or cost-effective as tape cartridges and drives designed specifically for computer use.)

Tape cartridges come in two commonly used sizes. The most popular is the **MINI DATA CARTRIDGE**, such as the DC 2000 by 3M, which is slightly smaller than an audio cartridge. Depending on the brand and type, a data cartridge will hold anywhere from 10Meg to well over 100Meg. A backup that would take an hour or more, and require several boxes of floppy disks, can be reduced to one or two data cartridges and should take only 5 to 30 minutes.

Whatever backup method you use, make sure you keep an accurate record of what was backed up, and when. One of the most popular methods is to label your disks or tapes with numbers, starting at 1. (Using the days of the week is another popular method, but you will find it is not as convenient or practical as using a number-based system.) Since you will constantly be reusing the same disks or tapes for storing new backups, using numbers allows you to easily change your backup and storage records without having to actually relabel the disks or tapes themselves. Your backup log should be kept on paper, not on the computer; if it were on the computer and you suffered a data loss you would have no way of knowing which backups to use. A simple notebook, or 3 x 5 cards, work fine as a backup log. The cards are nice because they can be placed in the disk or tape storage box right along with the backups. Small Post-it notes, or removable labels, work especially well because you can affix them directly to the tape or disk. This assures the backup record can't be lost, and for that reason Post-it notes and removable labels are great for backups that will be carried around in your pocket or briefcase. Naturally, removable labels aren't the best choice for backup media that will not be kept inside a case or cover, since Post-it notes come off easily. Following are examples of what typical backup entries might look like:

8/3/91 - Total system, Tapes# 4 & 5.
8/6/91 - Word processing directory, Floppy# 1.

You can never have too many backups. To start, determine the number of working days each month that you think the system will be used enough to require a backup. The most reliable method—and the most expensive—is to have at least enough disks or tapes on hand to make backups each day for a full month. Keep in mind that more than one disk or tape might be need for each backup. If buying this many disks or tapes is cost-prohibitive for you initially, then start out with enough to make backups every day for a week. When reusing old backup disks or tapes, start with the one that has the oldest date; this way, if you should need one of the more recent backups, it will most likely not have been written over yet. Remember also to purchase extra disks or tapes to use for permanent backups.

At least two backups should be kept in a location away from the computer site, such as a safety deposit box, another office building, or your home. Such backups are referred to as **OFF-SITE BACKUPS** and provide protection in case the backups at the site of the computer should be lost through fire, theft, flooding, etc. The easiest way to set up this safeguard is by rotating backups between the computer's location and the alternate sites. For instance, once each day, week, or month, a current backup can be exchanged with one at the alternate site. Many people perform backups daily and make off-site backups on a less frequent basis, but obviously this method does not afford complete, and perhaps not even adequate, protection for most systems, since if the on-site backups were destroyed you would lose all data input since you last delivered a backup to your off-site storage location.

The only way to avoid such a loss is to make two backups at the same time—a regular backup, and one which will be kept off-site. True, this is a more expensive and time-consuming method, but it is the *only* way to make sure you will be able to recover *all* of your data in the event of a loss. (By the way, if you label, and number, your off-site and regular backups separately—both starting with the number 1—it will be much easier to update your backup log. Off-site backups could start with the prefix OS, for instance, e.g, OS# 1, OS# 2, etc.)

Backup While Working

Many people do not know they can make quick backups of individual files as they work—nor do they appreciate the need for it. Making backups only after the shift or work day is over is not enough; it is equally important to make regular backups even while work goes on. The reason lies in the way a computer handles the current work displayed on screen. Because access to needed files on floppy disks and hard disks is relatively slow, most software pulls the information you are working with from the disk drive into RAM memory. (Remember, RAM is a *temporary* high-speed working area). The changes you make to a letter while in a word processor, for instance, are not actually stored permanently on the disk until you exit the program or deliberately SAVE the file. While your work is still in RAM memory it is in constant danger of obliteration—total loss—from numerous threats: 1) Your striking the wrong key and erasing or "messing up" the data. 2) Electrical problems—power failure, etc. 3) Software or hardware defects and internal errors. 4) Unknown causes; even the best of systems are known to suffer from an occasional random "glitch" that corrupts or destroys data.

145

Using the **SAVE** feature built into most word processing, database, and spreadsheet programs easily allows you to avoid lost work. The **SAVE** command causes the data you are currently working with in RAM to be copied onto your floppy or hard disk, and then returns you to the place where you left off—usually in just a few seconds. This is not to be confused, however, with the normal **SAVE**, or **SAVE-ON-EXIT** command which is utilized by virtually all software. Unlike the work-in-progress-save (often referred to as **SAVE-AND-RESUME**), a normal save may not only fail to return you to where you left off but may also require you to exit the software program before your file is safely copied to disk.

How often should you use save-and-resume? Often! While using a word processor it is not uncommon for some people to use save-and-resume even before they finish typing a single paragraph! This is because the few seconds it takes are less important than would be losing their train of thought, and perhaps many minutes of work, should the information be erased or lost. As a rule, you should use save-and-resume as often as you can without slowing down or interrupting your work. This way, should you suffer damage to, or the loss of, the data you are working on in RAM, *and you will sooner or later*, you can simply reload the file and continue along your merry way with the smug knowledge of how well you handled such a potentially disruptive situation.

If despite all of the above you should find yourself staring at a blank screen on which data has been scrambled, damaged, or erased, all may not be lost. Most software has yet another safety feature in addition to save-and-resume. Rather than simply overwrite the previous version of a file with the new, most software instead creates a "backup" of the old file before saving the current copy. Most programs give these backup copies of files a file extension that includes the letters B and K. WordPerfect, for instance, uses the extension .BK!, while some programs use .BAK, .BK, or a similar extension which makes it easy to tell which is the current file and which is a backup copy of the previous version. For example: if you decided to save a word processing document named LETTER1.DOC (using WordPerfect for this example) the word processor would first create—or replace if it already exists—a backup file named LETTER1.BK!, then save the document currently on screen as the new LETTER1.DOC. If you suddenly realize that the previous version was what you wanted, you can easily retrieve your former document by using the .BK! extension (See also "Erase," on page 77, and "Head crash," on page 73).

146

Chapter 9

OPERATING CONSIDERATIONS

COMPATIBILITY

When talking about computers, compatibility refers to how well one computer, software program, or component, can communicate or work with another. While it would be nice if all computer systems were compatible, such is still not the case. There are, however, certain generally accepted standards you can take advantage of.

When it comes to small-business systems and personal computers, by far the most popular are the IBM PCs and compatibles. This group of computers and related products is both vast and highly interchangeable. The capabilities of today's micro and personal computers are powerful enough to handle many applications—ranging from keeping your personal files more organized to handling the needs of a fairly large business. Assuming your needs fall within the capabilities of a personal computer, or PC, let's discuss the extent and types of compatibility you can expect.

Virtually the entire PC market as it exists today sprang from the concept of the original PC marketed by IBM. As the IBM PC quickly caught on and started to become somewhat of a standard, naturally, other companies followed. Before long, it seemed as if new companies making computers which they claimed to be IBM PC compatible were springing up almost overnight. Most tried to compete with IBM by offering a lower price. Almost as rapidly as they appeared on the scene, many of these companies went out of business amidst the fierce competition.

While the IBM PC was becoming the accepted standard in the field of small computers, the term **COMPATIBLE** began to take on a new additional and separate meaning—different from the traditional dictionary definition. So now when you're talking about small computers and someone brings up the question "Is it compatible?" they are probably referring to whether or not a program or device is IBM compatible—or, more specifically, IBM PC compatible. Another term that has cropped up is **CLONE**. Advertising that says a computer is a clone of the original is claiming that it is truly 100 percent compatible.

Compatibility is probably easiest looked at as a percentage. Two or more products which are fully compatible—meaning there is no limitation to how well they will work with each other—may be referred to as **100 PERCENT COMPATIBLE**. Two or more products that do not work together at all have zero compatibility. And then there is the broad range between these two extremes. For all practical purposes, however, any machine which is not 100 percent compatible can be considered not compatible. Finding out which computers are *truly* compatible is not always easy. Despite all the claims, there are only two ways to be sure. The first is to buy only equipment made by the original manufacturer whose equipment you wish to be compatible with. The second is to actually run all the hardware or software in question to see if it does everything it's supposed to do. The word *everything* is used here to reemphasize the fact that a system may only be partially compatible; just because it works with some, or even most, of your software or equipment does not mean it will work with it all.

Even if a component does work, not all of its features may be available if the computer isn't 100 percent compatible with that component. For instance, a monitor may work in its low resolution mode but fail to display properly when switched to a higher resolution. A computer might work fine with hard-disk drives 20Meg in size or smaller, but not allow the full use of the larger drives which are now available. The only way to know which components will work with each other is to be thoroughly familiar with the operation of each, and to test to make sure all features function properly. If you are not this familiar with the products you need tested, secure the help of someone who is. If you intend to do a lot of comparison shopping, taking along a program you are familiar with may help you isolate systems that are not PC compatible. As a rule, the more sophisticated a program, the better a testing device it will be.

148

Business programs such as Lotus 1-2-3, analytical programs such as Sargon Chess, or programs with sophisticated graphics routines, such as Flight Simulator, are good for compatibility testing. Most stores will carry and be able to demonstrate these or similar programs. You may also wish to pick up a copy of Flight Simulator. It is economical, and has a DEMO mode so you won't have to learn how to use it right away to run it on a computer. Sargon Chess, or other such programs, could also serve the same purpose and help you rule out poor machines quickly. Not only will it give you a low pressure introduction to actually using computers, but you'll get many hours of enjoyment out of the programs afterward.

Computers that are compatible with software like that just mentioned can probably also run most of the other popular software written for PCs. Keep in mind, however, that none of these informal tests guarantees complete compatibility. Once you have decided which hardware and software you want to buy, make sure it runs properly on your computer before making a final decision. While there are exceptions, most stores that sell computers and software will not allow you to return something once you have purchased and used it. Outside the realm of the IBM PC, compatibility can refer to any component required by a computer system—right down to the cables used to connect them together. Many established computer manufactures make available a list which shows exactly which products their computers are compatible with. While these lists can almost never be complete, due to the large variety of products, they do concentrate on products that are popular and may help you in making a selection.

USER-INSTALLABLE PARTS

It is not uncommon to see the phrase "user-installable" in a computer instruction manual, or on the package of a plug-in circuit board or other product. *In most cases*, the advertisement or manual is telling you that you may install this device yourself. This is OK as long as you know how to install the device properly. If not, you could damage the new device and/or your computer system. If you read the fine print—in some of the same instructions that tell you the product is user-install-able—you will often find a notice stating the warranty is void if you make improper installations or repairs.

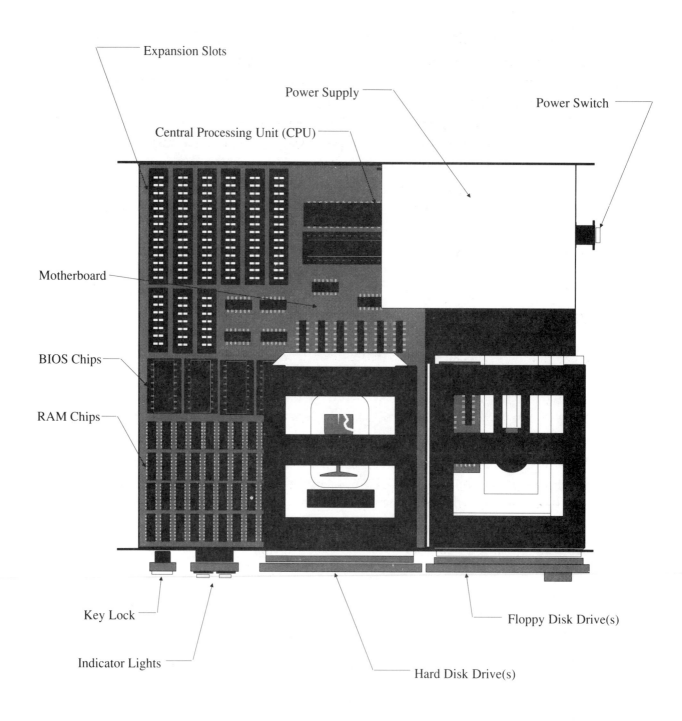

Expansion Slots

Power Supply

Power Switch

Central Processing Unit (CPU)

Motherboard

BIOS Chips

RAM Chips

Key Lock

Floppy Disk Drive(s)

Indicator Lights

Hard Disk Drive(s)

A Computer from the inside out

If you are not experienced in the handling of computer components the following guideline may be of help: If you are installing a new device—a modem, graphics board, etc.—and the installation requires you to disassemble either the computer or the device itself, you are probably better off having it installed by a qualified service technician. The small charge you'll have to pay could be far better than taking a chance on damaging something or voiding your warranty. Static electricity is a major cause of damage when handling electronic components. If you are carrying even a small static charge just touching the wrong area of a circuit board, or some of the exposed areas inside your computer system, can easily cause damage and/or electrical shock. (Believe it or not, some electrical equipment can cause shock or electrocution even when it is turned off or unplugged!)

EXPANSION CAPABILITY

Modern computers can be given increased capabilities (and versatility) by attaching additional components to them. While these components can be designed for either external or internal use, expansion capability is determined primarily by what will go inside the computer. Inside, on the bottom or side of a computer's cabinet you will find a large flat circuit board called the **MOTHERBOARD**, or the **MAIN BOARD**. This is the basic circuit board the critical components of the computer, including the microprocessor (**CPU**), are placed upon. On the motherboard you will find a number of **SLOTS**. These slots allow additional circuit boards (or just **BOARDS** or **CARDS**) to be installed in your computer. You will find a corresponding opening in the back or side of the computer which allows access to any cables or connectors used by the newly installed board.

Expansion boards can hold many internal components and devices. One of the most common expansions is adding more RAM memory; other possible expansions are RS-232C serial communications interfaces, parallel printer interfaces, monitor cards, high-resolution and color monitor cards, disk-drive cards, backup storage system cards, internal modems, and many, many others. Often, a board designed solely to operate a specific device is referred to as a **DRIVER**—as in the case of high-resolution and color monitor cards.

Although it is possible to purchase a single board which combines several functions, or attach an expansion cabinet which contains additional slots, for most systems when you have used all of the available, or empty, expansion slots your computer is said to be "full"—meaning no additional devices can be installed. In most cases, this also means you will no longer be able to add external devices. Exceptions might be small internal components for which a special slot or connector has already been provided on the motherboard. For instance, even if you have used all of your expansion slots, you may still be able to add an additional disk drive if a connector has been provided for it on the motherboard. These are referred to as **DEDICATED SLOTS**, or **DEDICATED CONNECTORS**.

MATH COPROCESSOR CHIPS

Another component for which a dedicated slot is provided in many MS-DOS machines is a math coprocessor chip, which takes a great deal of the processing load off the computer's CPU when handling numbers and also gives programs increased math capabilities and precision. Math coprocessors greatly enhance the capabilities of accounting, business, and other packages which rely heavily on computation (often referred to in computer lingo as "number crunching") and, in fact, there are quite a number of programs on the market that will not work without one. The availability of a math coprocessor, as well as the number of expansion slots, varies from computer to computer. Before buying a computer make sure it has enough slots to accommodate any extra memory or other devices you are likely to be adding.

TECHNICAL ASSISTANCE

Most makers of software and hardware maintain a phone-based service designed to assist customers. While many companies have general customer service departments, technical assistance lines exist primarily to answer specific questions—the answers to which customers might not readily obtain from the instruction manuals or other documentation that came with their systems. However, when technical assistance, or "help lines," first became popular, people had a tendency to call for the slightest reason—to find out how to adjust their printer, load new software, or perhaps why their program appeared to be calculating taxes incorrectly. These are all perfectly reasonable questions; however, answers to the very basic questions can almost always be found in the documentation that comes with the product.

The barrage of unnecessary calls received by many companies began to tie up their phone lines and prevent callers with legitimate technical questions—the people the lines were intended for—from getting through. Manufacturers responded by making changes to reduce the abuse of help lines. For example, toll-free 800 numbers, which in the beginning were common, were converted to toll numbers by many manufacturers. Even so, the number of calls received by some companies is growing at such a rate that no matter how much they enlarge their staff and facilities there are still too many calls to handle.

This background information is to give you some idea of why many technical assistance lines are set up the way they are today. It is not uncommon to get a busy signal when calling, or to be told all technicians are busy and someone will have to call you back. When this happens, such companies are not trying to ignore the importance of your call, they are simply trying to handle the huge flow of calls as fairly as possible on a first-answered, first-served basis. Following are some of the ways help services are now offered.

The first (and becoming less common) is the regular or toll-free number which you may call after becoming a customer. Some companies offer their customers so many weeks or months of free access to these lines, after which they are required to pay service charges. Next are lines available only on a pay basis. Some charge a flat rate per call while others charge by the minute—sometimes with a 15 or 30 minute minimum. These amounts are paid in advance, on account, or by credit card at the time of each call; very few companies will agree to send you a bill for time already used. Be prepared: while there are exceptions, rates for phone time are relatively high. You can expect, in some cases, to pay as much as $25.00 per call, or more; flat rates exceeding $200 per hour are not unknown. In 1990, pay-as-you-go 900 numbers began seeing use for the first time in technical support applications. 900 numbers bill the cost of technical support directly to your telephone bill. (Just a word of caution: not all advertisements or literature clearly state that you will be charged when you call a 900 number, or the fact may be in fine print—but charged you will be.)

Discounted technical service plans for high-volume users are also available. One plan, which is a money-saver for those who think they will be making frequent calls, is the prepayment plan; you pay in advance for the amount of time you think you will need in the near future—the more you pay in advance, the lower the rate. A number of companies also offer a yearly subscription service. Often, yearly subscriptions include newsletters and other benefits designed to provide helpful information for new and experienced users. Yearly service contracts are usually the most economical method of obtaining technical service, and can end up costing a small fraction of what you would have paid using one of the other plans.

A good attorney or doctor may be happy to have your business, but they will also encourage you to do whatever you can to avoid problems rather than correct them later, and the same is true of technical assistance lines. Before you call a technical assistance line you should first review the problem to see if there might be an easy solution. We have all probably experienced the frustration of spending minutes or even hours tinkering with a TV, stereo, VCR, or some other device, only to find out the problem was something embarrassingly simple like a cord not being plugged in, or a button that was in the wrong position. Always make sure you've checked to see that all cables, connectors, and switches are connected properly.

Have you completely checked *all* of the instructional materials to see if they explain the problem you are having? Sometimes the answer will be there, but it may be in a different section of the material than where you're checking; look for cross references in the text and check the index. Did you push all of the right buttons or keys the way the instructions indicate it should be done? Are there help screens or diagnostic tests built into the product you are using that could prove helpful? You may well be able to find the answer and save yourself the time and expense of a phone call.

If you cannot find a solution, or if the nature of your question is such that the answer cannot be found in the documentation, that is when you should seek experienced technical assistance. Before you call a technical assistance line you will need to organize and have ready the essential information. First, make note of what your questions are so that you will not leave anything out when you call. In most cases you will at least need the serial or registration number of your product so that your warranty or service status can be verified. If you have a technical assistance contract, you will need that number as well. Lastly, keep in mind that lines are usually less busy in early morning and late afternoon. Be prepared to make it convenient for someone to call you back if the technicians are busy, and make sure you mention the time zone you are in and when you can be reached. Technical assistance lines can be indispensable when you need them. By keeping in mind guidelines like those above, we can all help to make sure they remain available.

One last, important point should be made about the business of technical support. While it is certainly true that many people simply fail to read their instructions, all too often software publishers and hardware manufacturers do not provide good instructional materials. A customer reading a manual that is missing vital information, contains incorrect information, or lacks a good index or table of contents, has no choice but to seek additional assistance in getting answers to his or her questions.

While it is good to thoroughly check documentation in an attempt to solve a problem yourself, and avoid calling technical support unnecessarily, this can hardly apply to software or hardware companies whose documentation does not even answer basic questions. Not only are such companies greatly inconveniencing—and often frustrating—their customers, but, in many cases, forcing customers to pay for technical support as the only means of getting answers to questions that should have been covered in the documentation in the first place! Try to avoid software and hardware that is complex to operate but does not come with clearly understandable instruction manuals and documentation.

NEVER TURN ON A COLD COMPUTER

We are all familiar with different forms of moisture: rain, dew, humidity, etc. But there is one kind of moisture that—because it's hard to see—sometimes wreaks havoc on unsuspecting computer owners. At some point in time, you've probably had the experience of fog or frost (condensation) forming on the inside of your car's windows, or beads of water forming on the outside of a glass which contains a cold beverage. This can happen any time the glass (or other object) is colder than the surrounding air. Many people, however, are not aware that this same type of condensation can occur on the metal and plastic parts inside electronic equipment— including computers—that become chilled and are then moved into warmer surroundings.

Try to keep anything electronic as dry as possible, and always exercise caution when moving equipment from one temperature extreme to another. If it's cold out, and a computer or other piece of equipment is exposed to low temperatures only briefly while being transported to or from your warm car or some other heated area, you'll need to let it warm up only for a matter of minutes before turning it on. If, however, your computer has been in a car or other cold environment all night, it may take hours for it to warm to room temperature.

Aside from the fact that a system that has not had time to reach room temperature may not operate properly, the moisture can be hazardous—to both the equipment and you. The same goes for systems transported, or stored, in humid environments, such as damp basements. A cold or damp piece of equipment can take as much as a full day to dry out once it has been placed in a warm, dry area. Even if you have work to do, better to wait and be able to work tomorrow than spend the day taking your system to a repair facility, or receiving an electrical shock.

Chapter 10

BUYING AND USING A COMPUTER

DECIDING TO COMPUTERIZE

Deciding to computerize a business, or even to begin using a computer in your personal or professional life, is a daunting decision for someone who has never gone through the process before, but there are a number of approaches that have proved to be worthwhile. Let's look at a few of them.

First, if other people are involved, talk with them. You may find any number of people in your organization who have been anxiously waiting for a chance to computerize. If you do find this to be the case, they may already have a lot of the information and input you will need to computerize. If not, you can always bring in outside help, whether someone you know or a computer consultant who could help you determine a good route to take.

Choosing and buying a computer should actually be the last step, not the first, in a process of several steps on the way to computerization. First, try to write down on paper *all* of your reasons for wanting a computer system. Write down every possible application your system might be used for. Be sure to include not just ideas about the things you want to do now, but also things you might want to do within the next year or two. Try to think ahead. Take all the time you need to make sure your computer wish list is complete. If you already know from studies that you have a definite need for a computer, but have been putting off making a purchase, you may already have accumulated most of the information you'll need for your list.

Go through the list line by line, rating each idea in one of three ways: 1) Should be done now. 2) Will probably need to be done in the relatively near future. 3) Desirable, but of no great importance now or in the future. Be sure to get input from others who will be using the system, and from anyone you know who is already using a computer for similar purposes. From this information, create a single list of the most important reasons you can see for getting a computer right now.

Then, for each item on the list, try to get a rough idea of what each application will require in the way of **INPUT** and **OUTPUT**—input being information to be entered into the computer, output being any on-screen results, or printed reports, you expect the computer to produce. This includes information (based upon your current methods or a careful estimate) about what will be involved to produce the input and output, such as: 1) *Exactly* what will the input consist of? How many pages are currently required? How many words or keystrokes will typically be entered on each page? How many of the entries are always the same and could be filled in for you automatically by the computer? Is there information that would be helpful if the computer could look it up and provide it—such as filling in the city and state simply by having the operator enter the zip code? 2) *Exactly* what will the output consist of? What kinds of results do you expect to appear on the computer screen? Will a great deal of math be required to obtain the results? Will graphs, artwork, or pictures be required? If so, will they need to be in color, and do you need the ability to print them out on paper also? What quantity of printed output are you expecting there to be? Will printed output primarily be in the form of letters and other correspondence, financial and business reports, invoices, etc.? What level of print quality will be required?

For example, if one of the projects on the list is to computerize your accounting, you would want to outline the way your manual accounting system is currently set up. Are you using just a simple bookkeeping system, or a full system which includes general ledger, accounts receivable, accounts payable, payroll, etc.? How many accounts do you currently have listed on your chart of accounts, and how many accounts do you anticipate needing to add in the future? Is accounts payable a big part of your operation, or accounts receivable, or both? How many customer accounts do you currently have on accounts receivable, and how many do you anticipate adding? How many vendors will you need to enter into the accounts payable system? What kinds of codes, terms, shipping methods, advertisements, notices, or other information will need to be printed on your invoices and/or purchase orders? Do you need the ability to simply print bill-to and ship-to addresses, or do you need multiple location capabilities? What size invoices, and/or purchase orders, will be needed to include the information you would like to print on them? Do you want mailing and shipping labels to be built into the invoices, and/or purchase orders, or do you want labels printed on a separate roll? How many transactions are typically processed per hour, per day, and per month? What reports are you currently having prepared based upon this information, and how detailed does each need to be? You may find out a lot about your business that you weren't aware of in the process of determining your requirements.

DON'T COMPUTERIZE A SYSTEM THAT ISN'T WORKING

It's not uncommon for employees, managers, and business owners to discover ways of improving their operations and cutting costs as a result of this gathering of information before computerizing. As you proceed, you may even become aware of operations that just aren't working well the way they are currently being done. If this is the case—as it is more often than people might think—start getting things under control now. Don't wait until you actually computerize to make the needed changes.

Many people expect that getting a computer system will somehow make existing problems that have grown up under manual systems automatically disappear. In fact, the opposite may be true. Trying to computerize when you know the manual systems you already have in place aren't as good as they should be may be asking for trouble.

It is true that a computer can improve many operations where increased speed, efficiency, and accuracy will be of benefit. But, if you try to computerize a manual system that doesn't work now, there is no reason to expect that the same system will work better if computerized. For instance, although a computer can help a sales department do its job better, and thereby increase sales, it cannot improve sales that are low because of a poor sales force or mismanagement, such as a weak marketing program, failing to follow through on leads, etc. The computer is simply no substitute for good marketing and salespeople. First, you should solve the

159

"people problems" related to low sales, and then computerize. On the other hand, if sales are low because information on prospects and orders is being lost in a manual filing system, a computer could make a dramatic difference immediately.

GETTING COLD FEET

During the information-gathering process required to properly computerize, perhaps you will begin to get cold feet. Maybe you talk to a few employees who don't like the idea of getting a computer. Or you talk to a business friend who says computers didn't work for his or her company. Perhaps you get involved with another project. Or, as time goes on, the busiest time of the year has rolled around and is taking more of your time than usual. If you could really benefit from a computer system, and you let common excuses like these stop you, the decision not to computerize can only hurt you later.

The damage might come when you need a computer to keep up with a spurt of rapid growth—but you aren't computerized. Or when you lose customers who want to coordinate their computer systems with their suppliers' systems, or lose other customers to competitors who have computerized and can give better, faster service. You could also lose business, or not grow as fast as you could, because you didn't have the timely, accurate, and abundant information a computer could have given you to help make critical business decisions. (According to Better Business Bureau statistics, one of the biggest single reasons for business failure is a lack of information on how a business has performed in the past, where it is now, and where it is going.) A computer can organize and present you with this vital information quickly and accurately. As a matter of fact, unless a computer system can't do the things you've assembled on your list—which is unlikely—about the only valid reason for not getting a computer would be if you *were* going out of business.

FINANCING

If you decide to finance or lease computer hardware or software, try to use a bank or leasing company that is familiar with the type of computer you are looking at. Even today, not all lenders are familiar with the computer marketplace, and, if they aren't, this may be reflected in their terms, rates, and how flexible they are willing to be in working with you. The biggest things to watch out for are financing rates, the trade-in and/or buy-back policy (if you're leasing), and (whether leasing or borrowing) how much the lender will allow you for software. Some lenders that aren't familiar with computers may not allow you to include any software in the loan or lease, while others, more experienced, may allow your software costs to equal or exceed that of the computer. This is an important point since many software packages cost almost as much as the computer itself—or more.

INSURANCE

While small computers and PCs are no longer new to the insurance industry, because of the complexity of potential hardware- and software-related losses many standard policies still lack satisfactory coverage. You should check to make sure you are protected, now and in the future, because many standard loss policies offer no coverage for computers at all, and, if they do, coverage may be severely limited. If you think one of your existing business or personal insurance policies already covers your equipment, check with the issuer. Make sure that you have from the company *in writing* any explanation of coverage that applies to computer systems. Even if you find you have some protection through an existing policy, if the coverage is not complete you may wish to look into a special computer policy.

Good insurance coverage takes into consideration the complexity of computerized components and the unique circumstances under which a loss could occur. For instance, if your system should be damaged or stolen, would your insurer refuse to replace your software because it was not considered to be a part of the equipment, not a "tangible" item? What if the cost of your software far exceeds the value of the actual computer, as it often will these days? Will you be reimbursed for the expense of rebuilding the information that was stored in the computer but not backed up? (Actually, you'd be lucky to get this coverage even with a special policy, so remember to make backups!) What if you brought a laptop home from the office and someone spilled a soft drink on it? These are just a few of the many unusual situations that are unique to computers.

Good insurance policies for computers are available for less than you might think. The average PC-based system can be insured for less than $100 per year. Even a larger system, set up more for running a small business, can probably be covered for less than $200 If your system is a large business system, or if you have a substantial investment in software, polices can be tailored to suit your needs and provide coverage at a reasonable cost. There are a number of good nationwide insurers that specialize in computers. A quick glance through the index of any good computer magazine will provide you with names and numbers of computer insurers (See also "Resource list," on page 273).

THE CHANGEOVER TO A COMPUTERIZED SYSTEM

There are differing opinions as to the smoothest way to switch from a manual to a computerized system. Some people prefer to jump in with both feet and do everything at once, while others ease into it gradually—computerizing system by system, and one department within the organization at a time. While both methods can be successful, the gradual method usually proves to be the least disruptive and least subject to serious errors over the long run. When a new system is first installed, and employees are getting used to doing things a new way, it is likely things will be confusing enough without adding more changes than those that are not essential at the time. (In addition, unfamiliar people may be in and out of the office, files are likely to be scattered about more than normal as information is fed into the computer, and furniture is likely to be moved around to make wav for cables and power cords.)

If you start by learning only one procedure at a time, training can be handled more effectively since the people using the system will have less to absorb at each sitting. If errors arise, as they are likely to in the very beginning, they will be easier to isolate. For example, in a system that involves integrated accounting, inventory, and job control, if an error shows up you may have to look through all of the modules of the software, as well as talk to each person who made entries, before you isolate where the error originated. If you had started out by getting used to only one part of the system, say the accounts receivable module, for instance, if an error arose it would be much easier to isolate and correct because you would only have one area of the program to deal with. True, the entire system will eventually have to be learned. But by taking a systematic approach people will not feel overwhelmed, it will be easier to track down and prevent mistakes, and you should be able to get your system up and running faster.

162

The Six-Month Rule

Regardless of how you start using computers, there is one piece of advice almost everyone has come to agree upon: the six-month rule. This simply means that you should operate the old manual system side-by-side with the new computerized system for about six months. The exact length of time can vary, but the purpose is the same: to maintain the integrity of your records and to have a "safety net" to fall back on without interrupting your business if the new system develops problems. This is a time-proven method and offers more advantages than disadvantages. True, the duplicate operation will require more work and be more expensive than simply abandoning your old system. But consider the expense, loss of information, lost time, and loss of business that could result from *not* having the old system to fall back on. Even after your system is up and running smoothly it may still be a good idea to maintain copies of certain important records—such as check registers, customer lists, etc.—in a manual filing system. With this backup you can still carry out the critical functions of your business in the event of equipment malfunctions and won't have to operate totally blind until repairs are made. Copies of invoices, receipts, and other forms used by many businesses are filed in addition to records kept on computer, and can also serve as back-up records.

How do you determine how far to go in maintaining duplicate information? Simply review your system to see if you could continue to operate with a major piece of equipment—such as a computer—down for any length of time. While it is true that a current set of backups will preserve your data and allow you to restore it, backups do little good if you do not have a functional computer to restore them to. It is especially important to keep this in mind when attempting to drastically reduce or eliminate paperwork (such as in a so called "paperless" office). In order to *totally* rely on a computerized system you must have—or have access to—enough backup hardware to keep running in the event of equipment failure. Until, or unless, your system is large enough to include equipment that could be used as a backup in an emergency, keeping some form of written records is highly advisable.

Following Up After You Install A Computer

From golf to baseball, it's been said that, no matter how good your swing, without the proper follow-through your efforts may be wasted. Likewise, whatever type of computer system you eventually end up installing, make sure that you, or someone appointed by you, will be available to follow up on problems to keep things running smoothly. In the very beginning, as and after the system is installed, you may have your hands full just keeping things organized, but both then and, especially, later, you also need to be attentive to the needs of the people using the system so that they do not become discouraged. If someone is having difficulty, find out why. Provide extra training for him or her if necessary. If hardware or software problems should arise, always remember to document them in writing and have them taken care of promptly. And never fail to acknowledge good work or enthusiastic participation. In all likelihood, if you do your homework well and provide good follow-up, the transition from a manual system to computerization will be a smooth and trouble-free process.

COMPUTERS REPLACING PEOPLE

Many people wonder if, when installing a computer system, they should plan on reducing the number of people working in the affected areas. As a general rule, the answer is no. In fact, because of necessary training and orientation and the need to operate old and new systems in parallel for a time, it is not uncommon for the normal day-to-day work to get backlogged during the initial transition to a new system. Once the system is running smoothly, and everyone is using it effectively, it is more likely that the time saved by the efficiencies of computerization will allow the same people to complete more work than it is that jobs could be eliminated. Unless you foresee drastic changes that would make such a promise impossible to keep, help maintain employees' morale during this period of stress and uncertainty by letting them know that normal attrition from retirements and resignations—and not layoffs or firings—will be used to reduce the number of employees in overstaffed areas. Announcing an intention to fire people after computerizing is one of the worst things an employer can do—the end result of which is not good for you or the employees involved.

SERVICE AND MAINTENANCE CONTRACTS

SERVICE CONTRACTS are simply a kind of insurance. When the warranty runs out on a computer, you the owner are responsible for repairs and maintenance. A service contract allows you to pay a monthly, quarterly, or yearly fee and thereby amortize maintenance costs and protect against catastrophic breakdowns or computer damage. With the best contracts, you would not have to pay any costs for regular repairs or maintenance beyond the annual fee. Basically, in buying a service contract the computer owner is protecting against breakdowns that will require repairs costing more than he or she pays for the service contract, and the service company is gambling that such breakdowns won't occur.

Should you get a service contract to cover your system? The answer to that question depends on the type of system you have, and the use you intend to put it to. If your system consists only of an inexpensive personal computer worth less than $5,000, for example, then a service contract is probably unnecessary. If, on the other hand, you have a large investment in equipment that substantially increases the value and complexity of the system it would be wise to consider a service contract, because the more equipment you have in your system that is mechanical—printers, disk drives, etc.—the more likely it is to break down. If your system will be operating in an unusually dusty, dirty, or smoke-filled environment, or will be moved from location to location frequently, a service contract is a good idea. If your operation puts heavy or continuous use on the system, or if a system failure would seriously cripple your business, then a contract is probably a must.

A large variety of service contracts are available. They may be offered by the manufacturer of your hardware, the dealer you purchased it from, or a third-party company providing computer service. Contracts are available which cover repairs or breakdowns only, regular preventive maintenance only, or both. They can also be arranged so that a service person comes to your place of business (called **ON-SITE SERVICE**). A contract is cheaper if the system is taken to a repair facility, but lugging equipment around may not be the best use of your, or someone else's, time. In addition, in the process of having various cables unplugged, and being packed and moved, it could be subjected to further damage which would increase the costs of repairs. This is why on-site service contracts are popular for so many systems, and are almost a must for a business operation of any size.

In addition to using guidelines like those above, you should also weigh the cost of a service contract with the potential costs of repair if you went without a contract. Find out from an independent repair facility (not a computer salesperson) how often the equipment you are buying, or already own, needs repair: What is the cost of the average repair? What is the most expensive single breakdown that you are likely to suffer? You want to avoid asking a salesperson or a dealer's service department these questions because they may give you a less than honest answer in an effort to complete the deal. Talking to an independent service facility is the best way to get an unbiased opinion. You may also be able to dig up magazine reviews on the product that discuss its reliability.

Next, get out a pad and paper and see how the figures add up. For example: If you were considering a $550 yearly contract for a $3,000 system, the cost of the contract is nearly 20 percent of the cost of the entire system, *and* you have to pay that amount each year. It is unlikely that repairs or breakdowns on such a system in a single year would amount to the $550 cost of the service contract. The money would probably be put to better use elsewhere in your business—or even in an interest-bearing account set aside for repairs and maintenance. If little or no service was required you would end up being $550 richer per year.

On the other hand, let's say you had a larger investment in your system, $18,000. Let's also assume you are in a business where you can't operate without a computer. The service contract for this system would cost $1,500 per year—only about 8 percent of its entire cost. And the regular preventive maintenance the contract provides would help you run smoothly and avoid frequent breakdowns. Through your earlier detective work, you have learned that the cost of the average repair on this system runs $600, and for every day you would have to operate without the computer you estimate you will lose $700 in business. You've also been told that—for your use in your type of business—at least one breakdown a year would not be uncommon. Under these circumstances a service contract with a preventive maintenance feature could not only help you avoid major breakdowns and **DOWN-TIME**, but might save your company money when service is needed. The figures above are only rough examples to help you make a decision based upon the type of system you have and the contract rates a service provider quotes you. Every computer system and business has different requirements, and service contracts differ widely in what they provide. If you do decide you need some kind of contract, make sure you *fully* understand the terms of contracts you are offered, and that the one you select will suit your company's needs and budget.

TRYING A SYSTEM ON FOR SIZE: COMPUTER RENTALS

Renting a system could be a possible option for someone like you, who does not yet have a system, or for computerized businesses that temporarily need more capacity. You could rent a system for a while to see if it is what you wanted, and how well it does the job. This way, if you decide to go with something different, you'll have made only a small expenditure. Another possibility is to buy a relatively small and inexpensive system to start with. A PC with dual floppy-disk drives and a hard-disk drive, plus a printer, can accomplish a surprising amount of work, and can be moved from department to department, or shared by a number of people. Keep in mind that renting for "trial run" purposes should be limited to one computer, and one or, at the most, two software packages. The object is not to literally computerize your business but merely to get a taste of what computers can do. You should be able to accomplish this with a one-week rental—one month at most. Such a short trial period will not allow anyone to master computers or a complex software package. However, during this time you can experiment with the various features a system can offer, in contrast to the mostly hands-off, and sometimes hurried, demonstration you might receive as part of a sales presentation. In fact, many of the publishers of popular software packages offer free—or for the cost of the disk(s), shipping and handling, etc.—a demo version of their program which you can actually run on your computer. Once you are satisfied that a computer can do the job, it's time to make a final selection of software and hardware, and commit to the purchase of a system which can become a permanent part of your business operation. (See "Resource list," on page 273.)

BUYING A COMPUTER FOR YOUR CHILDREN

Today computers affect almost every aspect of our lives, directly or indirectly. In the future—and not too far off at that—a knowledge of computers will not only be helpful, but a must. This will be true whether someone is directly involved in the computer field or not. Those "someones" of tomorrow are the children of today. We are now a computerized society. No longer are people such as scientists and engineers the only ones who need a knowledge of computers. Office workers, auto mechanics, doctors, appliance-repair people—all are now affected by computers. Computer illiteracy can mean fewer promotions and raises, fewer opportunities—and can even make getting a hoped-for job an unlikely prospect.

Typewriters are rapidly being replaced by computer-based word processing. There are already people who can say they've never used a typewriter. Even modern electronic telephone "switchboards" are being replaced by totally computerized telecommunications consoles, complete with a monitor and keyboard. Schools, realizing that computers have today made possible a leap forward in communication just as typewriters did in the last century, have already taken the lead by introducing computers to children of all ages—from those just able to read all the way through high school and college. Studies have shown that, with proper guidance, children exposed to computers enjoy what they are doing and learn more in the process. Many students say that homework just seems more fun when they do it on, or with the help of, a computer.

In high school and college a student who knows how to use a computer can have a tremendous advantage over others. Studies have shown that papers turned in by students who do them on word processors get higher grades than those who turn in written or hand-typed papers. A student who uses a computer at home *and* at school has a big edge over a student who uses one only at school—or not at all. Parents may be skeptical about the wisdom of buying something children may not use but, in fact, most kids jump at the chance of having their own computer.

Now that you've thought about some of the advantages of having a computer at home, what kind should you get? If your sole purpose for buying a computer is to help your children in school you may want to look at what's being used in their classrooms—and to reassure yourself that the school intends to use the same type of computers for a while. If some of the lessons can, or are expected to, be done at home if your child has a computer, you will need a computer that is compatible with those used at school.

Even then, if a number of different types of computers are being used at school, it is unlikely yours will be compatible with all of them. Your children could also end up being moving to other grades or classes, or to a school where different computers are used.

Keeping factors like these in mind, you may be better off getting a system with the features you like best than trying to be compatible with the system(s) used at school.

The Apple II, Commodore 64 and 128, Texas Instruments TI 99, and the TRS-80 by Radio Shack were among the first computers to see widespread use in schools and homes. During the 1970s home computers became extremely popular because of their low cost and ease of use. By the mid-1980s, however, the rapidly decreasing prices of the more powerful IBM PC and compatible computers—as well as the popularity of computer games like Nintendo—all but eliminated the simple equipment formerly sold to the home computer market. By 1991 a moderately to well-equipped IBM PC-compatible computer could be purchased for as little as $1,000—sometimes less. For these reasons, most people are now purchasing PCs for use at home. And, while home computers can still be found in classrooms across the country, almost all new computers being purchased by school systems are IBM PCs or compatibles.

Parents getting a computer for their children should also consider whether they will be using the system themselves. Parents have a habit of getting hooked on computers as much as the children they supposedly bought it for. However, even if you don't become a fan, you'll probably have an interesting experience when you help your children to use their new computer, and you'll learn more about computers, and your children, in the process.

As you begin to see just what a computer can do, it's very likely you will start using the system more yourself. Maybe you just want to learn more out of curiosity, or perhaps you want to computerize your family's finances. Computers are great for keeping track of names and addresses, recipes, or perhaps helping you keep in touch with members of a club you belong to. Programs are available for everything from trip and vacation planning to programs that help you watch your or your family's diet. And, of course, not all computer games are designed for children. If you do get hooked, just remember to let your kids use the system every once in a while!

This page intentionally left blank.

Chapter 11

PROMISES, PROMISES: DEADLINES AND DELIVERY DATES

At times it has seemed that promises were more often made than kept when it came to product delivery dates in the computer industry. 1988 was possibly one of the worst years for consumers, who were promised one new version of software or hardware after another only to be disappointed by an announcement that the product's release would be delayed, or that it was unavailable.

In earlier years such problems were usually associated with small companies that had poor management and limited resources. In recent years, however, missed delivery dates and deadlines have plagued even the largest and most established makers of software and hardware. Probably in a race to beat the competition to the market with new products, many companies lowered their standards and became less concerned with meeting their promises for on-time delivery.

IBM introduced the AT (Advanced Technology) computer in 1984. Most people are unaware that many of the original promises made about the AT's advantages and capabilities—running more than one program at a time, multiuser and networking capability, etc.—remained untrue for years. In fact, most of these capabilities were instead provided by third-party hardware manufacturers and software publishers that saw the gap in the market and stepped in to fill it. Only with the much later introduction of IBM's OS/2 operating system were some of the original features promised for the AT actually made available by the company which built it. The only real advantage an AT offered when it was first introduced was its faster processing speed. And, now that software and hardware have finally arrived that make use of the AT's capabilities, it is quickly being replaced by the more advanced 386 and 486 computers.

Fortunately, some manufacturers seem to be moving back in the right direction and are improving their records of on-time delivery after a product announcement. There are also a number of companies that have consistently kept their promised delivery schedules for new products—and only announced products that were actually going to be produced.

Although there is little you can do to reduce the frustration of waiting for a product that is behind schedule, you can at least take steps to avoid it costing you money. First, never buy a new type of computer system from a company that promises: "New software and hardware will be available soon." If it is not one of the computers already accepted as a standard—like an IBM PC or compatible, Apple Macintosh, etc.—then what are you going to do with it after you buy it? Without a large variety of software and hardware to make a computer handle your applications your new system may end up being virtually useless. However, because PCs are now so widespread, few manufacturers try to introduce a new computer system anymore that is not IBM PC compatible.

Never pay in advance, or place a deposit on, hardware or software if its manufacturer or publisher is not already shipping the product. Many people have done this only to find that the manufacturer is still working out bugs in the product, or is having supply problems that prevent it from shipping on schedule. Also try not to commit your business to a major product that is not yet available. It's better to go with a proven product that is available than end up waiting for a one that is promised but never gets to market. Likewise, keep in mind that, as with new models of cars, more defects usually turn up in a brand-new software or hardware product than in one that's been around for awhile. You might patiently wait for a new product only to learn that it contains numerous bugs that still have to be worked out.

The same applies to upgrading an existing product to a newer version. While this is usually a straightforward procedure, on occasion the newer version of a product will contain bugs that did not exist in the previous version. Before upgrading you may wish to see if any magazine reviews have been published on the new version of the product. Asking people who are using it, as well as checking with a computer dealer and possibly even the manufacturer of the product, may also prove helpful.

Chapter 12

COMMUNICATIONS

Computer communications, in their various forms, are extremely important, not only for computers to work with other devices, such as monitors, printers, disk drives, and so on, but in the beehive of communications activities taking place within the inner workings of the computer itself. We will concern ourselves here not with these more routine and essential internal functions but instead with external, computer-to-computer, communications over connecting cables or telephone lines.

THE RS-232 INTERFACE

An interface is anything which is placed between two devices to make reliable data exchange possible. Most of today's computers come equipped with the first component that's needed for external communications, an **RS-232** (or **RS-232C**) **SERIAL INTERFACE**, installed internally on a plug-in circuit board. Although external RS-232 interfaces are available, they are mostly used only with devices too small to contain an internal interface, such as some portable computers.

The RS-232 interface is an international communications standard. It helps make communications between many different devices easier to accomplish. As the name implies, this is a **SERIAL** form of electronic communication. This means that each small piece of information, or **BIT**, must line up single file before being transmitted to or received from another device. (See "Bit-by-bit communications," on page 174.) In this way, a wide variety of otherwise unrelated, and sometimes incompatible, devices can be connected to each other; the possible uses for RS-232 are almost endless. (The connectors used for RS-232 communications are standard, but a newer, smaller, 9-pin connector has experienced some popularity and the connectors on some devices may not be set up properly. Check ahead of time to make sure the connectors and cables you intend to use for communications will work. If not, adapters are available. A service technician can usually make any necessary modifications.)

In addition to the more common use of RS-232 for communication from computer to computer, it is also used as a way of connecting computers with the "outside world." Using RS-232, and appropriate software and hardware, a computer can "talk" to and control devices ranging from home alarm systems to manufacturing machinery and equipment (also referred to as **CAM, COMPUTER-AIDED MANUFACTURING**). Lighting, heat, air conditioning, fire detection, and other operations can also be controlled automatically in a similar fashion. Companies that automate their lighting, heating, and air conditioning experience tremendous savings as a result of increased efficiency.

BIT-BY-BIT COMMUNICATIONS

Data must be converted into individual **BITS** of information before serial communication can take place. The device or computer on the other end will reassemble the data in the correct order, if needed. Each device must be **CONFIGURED** (set up) to correctly interpret and handle these signals. Because serial communication must take place a bit at a time it is slower than most forms of parallel communication.

The two devices communicating with each other must "talk" at the same speed. The speed of serial communication is determined by how many bits are sent or received per second (**BPS**). Communications rates are also stated in thousands or millions of bits per second, and 1 thousand or 1 million bits may sometimes be expressed as a **KILOBIT (KB)** and **MEGABIT (MB)** respectively. However, this speed is more commonly referred to as the **BAUD RATE**. Rates ordinarily used for personal computers range from 300 to 19,200 baud, although speeds many times these are not unheard of. Whatever the baud rate, you will find that it is always a multiple of 2, since all computers use the binary, or 2-based, numbering system. The very slow 300 baud was used on early small and portable computers but the more common speeds today are 1,200, 2,400, 4,800, 9,600, and 19,200.

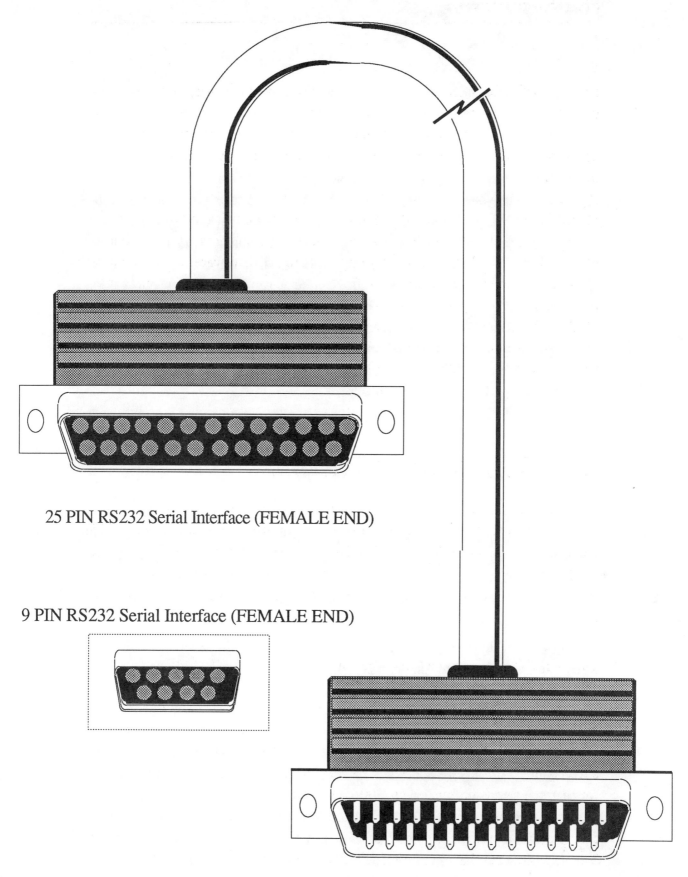

25 PIN RS232 Serial Interface (FEMALE END)

9 PIN RS232 Serial Interface (FEMALE END)

25 PIN RS232 Serial Interface (MALE END)

Since it is hard to picture baud rate itself, an easier way to get an idea of how fast a certain baud-rate setting will be is to picture text appearing on the screen of a monitor. Remember, even though information may seem to appear on the screen all at once, the screen is actually being "drawn." Each character appears separately from left to right, line by line, until an entire screen of data has been displayed. Normally, when you use a computer or terminal you are seeing information being sent to the screen at 19,200 baud or faster. At this speed, the screen fills too fast for the eye to see. At 2,400 baud, the screen no longer fills faster than the eye can see, but it is still fast enough so that you will probably not be able to see each separate character appear. At 1,200 baud, character generation is slow enough for you to see each individual character being displayed; even so, the screen still fills rapidly. At 300 baud, however, you can easily watch each character being displayed and each line slowly filling the screen. (These slower speeds are the ones you've seen used to dramatize computer displays in movies and TV.)

Another way to get a feeling for the differences in baud rates is by how long it would take to send or receive a page of text. It's easy to picture a letter you've written, and how long you think it should take to communicate it. If you were to send a one-page letter, typically 2,000 characters or so, to someone at 300 baud it would take up to a minute, or more, before the entire letter was finished being transmitted and received. On the other hand, one company advertised that its modem, operating at 19,200 baud, could transmit three of Shakespeare's plays—*Hamlet*, *Macbeth*, and *King Lear*—in their entirety in just under three and one-half minutes! Before rushing out to buy the latest in high-speed transmission technology, however, remember that the modems at both ends must have the same capabilities. Sometimes exactly the same brand and type of modem must be used on both ends to achieve ultrahigh speeds. And commercial services often charge higher rates when you use a higher transmission speed, thereby eating up much of the savings gained by cutting the time spent on long distance phone lines.

It is difficult to determine exact rates of transmission because the makers of communications hardware and software use different coding methods to send information. For this reason, two devices made by different manufacturers, certified to operate at the same baud rate, will usually vary in speed. One modem, for instance, might be rated at 1,200 baud, but, if used with special high-speed communications software, may achieve an actual throughput of up to 2,400 baud. The more efficient and sophisticated the software and hardware, the faster the communication.

MODEMS AND THEIR USES

Regardless of the method used, when communication takes place over a telephone line—i.e., any time a direct cable connection is not used—it is done using a device called a **MODEM**. The modem is in turn connected to an RS-232 interface inside the computer.

A modem (**MODULATOR/DEMODULATOR**) is connected to each of two electronic devices (usually computers or terminals) to enable them to send and receive data over telephone lines in situations where cable is too expensive or distances are too great for direct connection by cable; the maximum allowable cable run is about 1,000 feet, depending upon the system. (Remember that a modem is needed for both the computer that is transmitting as well as the one receiving.) Modems are often used on telephone lines even within the same building where cables would work, because long runs of expensive computer cable may cost more than using modems over existing phone wires or even installing new phone lines. Modems are also easily moved and relocated, but cable is not. In effect, the telephone company has already installed a worldwide computer communications network.

A modem can be connected to the telephone line by using the **DIRECT CONNECT** method or by using an **ACOUSTIC COUPLER**. An acoustic coupler is used when you do not have access to a modular plug-in telephone jack into which you can plug the modem. Some offices, most motel rooms, and all pay phones, have their telephones "hard wired," i.e., not easily unplugged—making a coupler a handy device to have. It consists of a device with flexible rubber cups that are slipped over both the earpiece and mouthpiece of any telephone. The device is called "acoustic" because it produces an audible signal which is transmitted through the telephone mouthpiece. The earpiece side of an acoustic coupler receives data being transmitted.

You may hear two different types of sounds through the small speaker built into most modems—the pure **CARRIER TONE** (also called **CARRIER FRE-QUENCY** or **CARRIER WAVE**), and the raspy, noisy sound it makes when it is being modulated, i.e., when the line is carrying data. When a modem receives an incoming phone call, or signal, from another modem, it must first detect the carrier tone before communications will start; otherwise, if it is an automatic modem, it will simply "hang up." When actual communication has been established it is known as **CONNECT**, or being **CONNECTED**. **CONNECT-TIME** ends when all communication has stopped and you, or a software program, instruct the modem to "hang up" and end the call.

As is the case with many computer components, modems are available on boards which plug into your computer for internal use and as external devices which require their own power. Most of the better portable computers on the market, the laptop variety, offer the option of a built-in modem to make them more convenient to carry and use. Whether or not you get an internal modem will depend upon both how many open slots for plug-in circuit boards are left inside your computer and your uses for a modem.

Like many other devices which attach to computers, modems are available in both **DUMB** and **SMART** versions, although most modern modems are smart—meaning they contain their own microprocessors and memory. Some of the more popular features found in modems are: A built-in clock; **AUTO-DIAL**, which saves your having to dial the telephone yourself every time you place a communications call; telephone number memory, which allows you to store the numbers you call most frequently; **AUTO-REDIAL**, to redial a busy or unanswered number; and **AUTO-ANSWER**, which allows the modem to automatically answer the phone and place itself **ON-LINE** if another computer is calling. As a rule, the more sophisticated modems tend to be external models—partially because they have certain features which are directly accessible to the user on their front, rear, or bottom panels. Internal modems are controlled entirely through software.

Modem Compatibility

Just as the world of computers has popular models which are used and copied more than others, so it is with modems. The IBM of modems, so-to-speak, is the **HAYES MODEM**. In the same way IBM was first to become popular with the small computer, Hayes produced the first modems which offered computer users the features and reliability they wanted. In the same way the IBM PC was copied, other companies followed by introducing **HAYES-COMPATIBLE** modems. There are many good modems on the market manufactured by a number of companies. The important thing, however, is to make sure the combination of hardware and software you select will be compatible.

Example of an External Modem

(Hooks directly to a modular phone outlet)

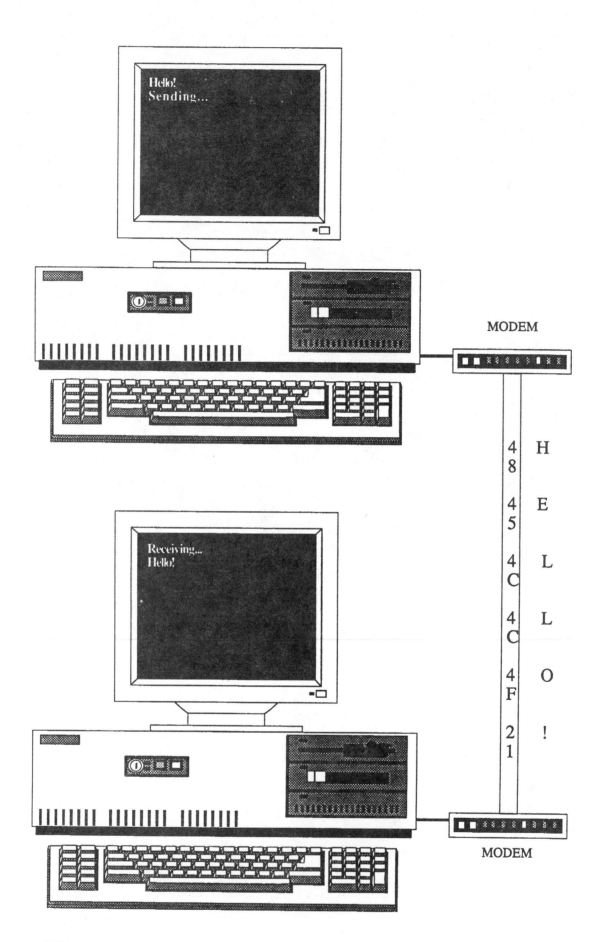

PHONE-LINE CONSIDERATIONS

Formerly, phone-line communication at speeds over 300 baud required a **LEASED LINE**—a phone line especially "tuned" or selected to be free from the static and background noise which interferes with reliable data transmission. Because leased lines are expensive, and because they are seldom available for use with portable computers, more and more modems incorporate **ERROR-CORRECTING** techniques which compensate for interference and make possible high-speed transmission over standard phone lines. Error correction, while an involved subject, basically works by checking all data that is sent and received. If an error is detected, the information which became garbled, or was sent incorrectly, is retransmitted.

With good software and equipment, virtually 100 percent error-free communication is possible. The higher the speed of the modem, and the more sophisticated it is, the more you can expect to pay.

Modems can be operated over the same lines used by telephones, or a phone line can be designated (**DEDICATED**) for computer and modem use only. If you use a modem only occasionally there is nothing wrong with plugging it into the phone line, or placing it on-line, only when needed. If, however, you use a modem often, or your system needs to have 24-hour access to a phone line, it is best to use a separate phone number and line just for this purpose. Otherwise, someone picking up the phone, or features such as call waiting, paging, etc., may interrupt communications and cause data loss. For the same reasons, it is best to use an unlisted phone number for your modem, unless, of course, the line is listed as being specifically for computer access, and not regular voice calls.

COMMUNICATIONS APPLICATIONS

One of the most common uses for modems is to connect small computers and terminals to larger computers, including mainframes, over phone lines. Why would you want to do this? First, your computer system might not have the storage or processing capacity of a mainframe but there may be times when you need the extra power a bigger system has to offer; when this is the case, you arrange for phone-line access to a larger **HOST** computer. Using this method, you gain the benefits of a larger system without paying all of the associated cost. In addition, because much—if not most—of the workload is on the smaller computer, the resources of

181

the larger system are not as easily overwhelmed. This is why many companies equip their offices with PCs, or other small computers, and allow them to tie into a central mainframe when needed.

Communications Software

To communicate using a modem there must be appropriate communications software running on the computer. The software must be compatible with not only the computer being used but the modem itself. Good communications software has the ability to receive and send files, as well as to operate unattended. Unattended operation comes in handy on occasions where you don't want to take the time to go through all of the information on a certain topic that is being offered by an on-line service. The same could be true of sending and receiving files. If your system is able to operate unattended, you can take advantage of the times when your system, or someone else's, is not as busy. You can probably also save money by using the lower evening phone rates.

ON-LINE INFORMATION SERVICES

Another good reason for tying into other computers over the phone is to gain access to **ON-LINE INFORMATION SERVICES**, "on-line" simply meaning you are on-the-line with, connected with, a computer which has an information database. There is a tremendous amount of information stored in many different systems around the world. Some of these services are general, appealing to the home and personal user as well as the business user. Others are designed primarily for use by those in a particular profession, such as law, medicine, finance, science, etc. On-line options can range from playing games to researching computerized encyclopedias to making extra mass storage available for those computer users who need it.

Once you know the commands and protocols, on-line information can usually be found, and researched, many times faster and more thoroughly than by searching manually in conventional resources, and computerized resources are often far more exhaustive. Almost all on-line services require a subscription, and a password, before you are allowed access. From then on, you usually pay in blocks of so many minutes per hour—such as $10.00 every 6 minutes, or $6.00 per half hour, etc. Sometimes, you actually pay by the individual minute, just like you would for a long distance phone call. Printed directories are available to help you find the kind of on-line information service you are looking for. Many on-line services provide on-screen help for using their services, and the larger services often make software and instruction manuals available through computer dealers. It is not uncommon to receive an introductory package to an on-line service when you purchase certain hardware or software packages—especially communications hardware and software. On-line services are also advertised in computer magazines as well as in trade journals intended for specific industries (See also "Resource list," on page 273).

Message Centers And Bulletin Boards

Two popular services for modem users are the **MESSAGE CENTER** and **BULLETIN BOARD**. While technically they are two different types of services, most people associate both terms with the same functions. Message centers, as the name implies, are used primarily for the storage, retrieval, or distribution of electronic messages; intercompany memos and mail are prime examples. Computerized bulletin boards, however, usually offer many additional features and services, many more than their cork-board counterparts. Message centers and bulletin boards are also unique in that, unlike most on-line services, many are free of charge. They are usually maintained by computer users, special interest groups, or businesses. Even when no cost is involved you will usually still need a password to access these systems. Systems operated by individuals or groups often make public domain software available to anyone calling in. Businesses use these services to give employees a more efficient way of leaving and picking up their messages from anywhere in the country, or the world. They are the method of choice for news reporters and writers to get a story back to their magazine or newspaper. A growing number of computer-oriented businesses are making customer information and services available via computer bulletin boards. These range from product and technical information, to an on-line connection direct to a service representative. Company policies vary as to whether or not a charge or subscription is required for these services.

Electronic Mail

ELECTRONIC MAIL can be in the form of messages exchanged through computer bulletin boards, or a much more sophisticated system designed to accommodate a paperless office. Most companies use a system with capabilities in between these two extremes. Mail, letters, memos, and other information can easily and rapidly be distributed to one employee or many. Electronic mail is not always totally electronic—or paperless—since it is sometimes routed to a computer printer, printed out, and then distributed to the appropriate individuals. In an informal system, mail is sent, received, and read as the need arises, while in other systems schedules are set up for the sending and receiving of certain types of mail—a company newsletter, or daily information bulletins, for example. The uses for electronic mail are almost as limitless as those for regular interoffice, intercompany mail. The type of computer system will determine how sophisticated an electronic mail network can be. Obviously, electronic mail systems must be implemented on multiuser networks or on-line facilities.

The U.S. Postal Service at one time made it possible for computer users to send correspondence electronically from their computers to post office computers nearest the addressees, thus saving the time needed for collection and sorting at the sender's end and for long-distance transportation of the mail. The receiving post office then took care of stuffing and addressing the envelopes and sending them on their way. Unfortunately, according to the Postal Service, this service was discontinued for lack of interest. This was, and, perhaps could become again, another form of electronic mail.

Downloading And Automated Communications

DOWNLOADING refers to the process of transferring information, usually an entire file rather than just a portion of one, from another computer system to yours. **UPLOADING**, as you might expect, is just the reverse—transferring information from your system to another. Downloading is certainly preferable to wading through a large file on-line while you are paying phone and service charges by the minute. Once you have downloaded the information you can review it at your convenience, obtain a printout of part or all of it, and revise it just as you would a file of your own creation.

An important application of downloading is the mass transfer of huge amounts of business and financial operational data each day. Many businesses automate their communications operations to allow users to have the full computing power of the system to themselves during peak busy periods, usually during the day. For non-peak periods, however, the system can be programmed to automatically send and receive any required information (sales records for the day, electronic mail, banking information, etc.). Many do this to take advantage of lower phone and service rates even if their computers aren't tied up during the daytime.

Because downloading from sources outside your organization is one of the few ways in which a virus can enter computer systems, some caution should be exercised, mainly by making sure you know the reputation of the people operating the computer on the other end. For instance, some bulletin boards allow anyone who calls in to upload files, including software, to that system. If such a file contains a virus, intentionally or otherwise, anyone who downloads the file to his computer will also receive the virus as well. Most reputable public bulletin board operators check uploaded files, and insist on knowing who sent them, before allowing callers to download. Commercial on-line information services and company-owned and technical service bulletin boards are usually much safer—but keep in mind that there are no guarantees. Any time you access another computer, there is always the risk that something you don't want could be introduced into your own system.

PHONE-LINE SECURITY

Computers not connected to a phone line are relatively easy to secure—by limiting access to them. However, any time you have a computer system which allows automated phone-line communications—by which your computer is accessible to almost anyone in the world with a modem—you should also make sure you take appropriate security precautions.

Computer security is an involved and technical subject that occupies books all by itself. Obviously, we cannot cover here every possible detail. These, however, are a few of the key principles: 1) Each employee should be issued, and made accountable for, a personal password, without which access to your computer is impossible. This allows you to assign different restrictions to individual employees, change individual restrictions, and to remove a password from the system if an employee leaves—all without affecting others. 2) Passwords should be required not only to enter the operating system but also to use individual programs. 3) Make sure that access for regular users is restricted to only those areas and programs they need to use. With this additional restriction, even if an unauthorized person were to discover a password he would still not be able to roam through, or damage, the entire system. 4) Monitor computer usage carefully, keeping in mind that a person who is a threat is not always someone from the outside but may be an employee who is attempting to access restricted areas of the system. 5) Don't count on an unlisted phone number to provide much additional security. Anyone intent on espionage or trashing your files might learn your number in several ways, including using a software program designed just for that purpose.

One of the best ways to protect an automated communications system from improper or illegal access is to use the **DIAL BACK** procedure. Using this method no one is allowed to call and access your system directly. Instead, the phone numbers of all computers authorized to access your system are stored by your security or communications program. When someone phones your system and logs on, the program stores the log-in and password of the caller, and then hangs up on him. Next, the program checks its records to see if the caller and the number given are listed among the authorized users. If so, the program returns the call and the caller is allowed to proceed. If not, an unauthorized caller has been stopped cold. More and more communications software is starting to offer this almost foolproof protection. It is also available from a number of manufacturers in the form of a "black box" you place between your modem and computer. If your needs are more sophisticated, you can also have a security system custom designed and programmed for you.

Chapter 13

MULTIUSER COMPUTER SYSTEMS

The term **MULTIUSER** applies to any computer system that allows two or more people to work independently of one another at the same time, with each person having the ability to be doing something different. One person might be using a word processing program, for instance, while another is using inventory control software. Traditionally, the term *multiuser* has been associated with large computers—mostly mainframes. However, advances in technology have brought multiuser capabilities, in one form or another, to all but the smallest of modern computers. However, whether a multiuser system is to be large or small, a good deal of thought needs to go into its planning before a purchase is made.

As is the case with computers themselves, multiuser computing is an area where the sometimes fuzzy definitions of computer classification and power can become almost meaningless. At one time, only mainframes had multiuser capabilities. With today's advanced PCs, however, and with the appropriate hardware and software, even desktop computers can be given multiuser capabilities. Unlike mainframes, which have always been relatively standardized, with smaller computers there is seldom such a thing as a "standard" multiuser system. The very competition which has made multiuser technology a reality for the small computer has also created a wide variety of different systems, hardware, software, methods, and technologies. Because multiuser technology first came about on mainframes, let's begin by exploring the way larger systems work.

At one time, *all* computers were large, expensive, and had to be staffed and operated by trained technicians or scientists. For these reasons, computers were mostly used by large companies, the government, and the universities who could afford them.

Because computers were such a valuable resource people had to make sure they made the best use of them. This often meant that only projects high on the pyramid of importance were allowed to use valuable computer time. And, unlike today, few people were allowed hands-on access to the actual computer. Most turned their data over to a programming and operations staff, who in turn programmed the computer, ran the programs, and returned the results to the appropriate person. The frustrations, inefficiency, and inconvenience of those arrangements was partially, if not largely, responsible for the development of multiuser technology. Few people had the desire to delay their work while waiting for a slot of computer time to open up.

Because even early computers were so fast, it was eventually realized that, since they already appeared to do more than one thing at a time (See "The computer is quicker than the eye," on page 42), there was no reason why the same illusion could not be applied so that it appears as if more than one person could have a computer all to himself or herself.

Most of the work a person does on a computer does not use all of its capacity. There are even small amounts of idle time when a person pauses between thoughts, or words, when entering information, or when a slow typist is working. True, these *slices* of inactive time are hardly even noticeable. But a computer is so fast that it can do other things even during these brief periods of idle time. (See also "MULTITASKING," on page 227.)

Methods were developed which allow a single computer to divide idle time between two or more users. Multiple users each appear to have the full use of the computer individually. But, in reality, the computer is rapidly switching back and forth between tasks. First it works on processing a portion of one user's work, then it leaves that job for a moment and gives a certain amount of time to another user's instructions. Each time the computer switches, it remembers where it left off so it can resume either job when it needs to. Because this all happens so fast, users seldom notice, and are seldom interrupted by, what is going on inside the computer (although at times of peak usage processing is a little slower).

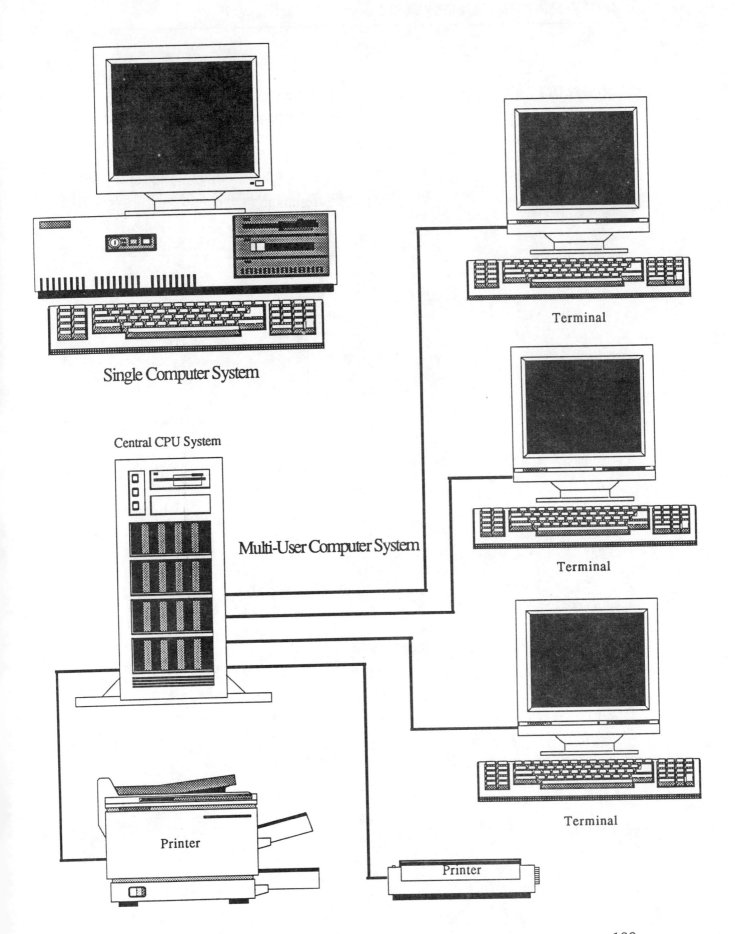

Single Computer System

Central CPU System

Multi-User Computer System

Terminal

Terminal

Terminal

Printer

Printer

189

TIMESHARING

After the bugs were worked out of the system and a few more features were added, the computer was able to perform this high-speed juggling act between more and more users. The process was then known as **TIMESHARING**, and it opened the door for more people than ever to gain direct access to a computer. Companies no longer had to buy as many computers, more work got done, and money was saved in the process. These are the same reasons that make such systems attractive today—although now they are more commonly referred to as **MULTIUSER** systems.

In a multiuser system all equipment is connected with, and all work eventually goes through, only one CPU. The number of users the system can handle at one time will vary depending upon the power of the CPU. This type of system—as do other methods of serving multiple users—has its advantages and disadvantages.

The biggest advantage is relatively low cost. Regardless of how many users you add—until you reach the capacity of the system—you only have to buy one computer, one set of memory boards, one mass storage system, etc. One computer also takes up less space, and there is only one repair bill if something goes wrong. Besides the fact that you are buying only one computer, less supporting hardware is usually required for this type of system, so there are increased savings in that respect, also.

A major disadvantage of a multiuser single-CPU system is that, as already mentioned, the system's single CPU slows down as it divides its time between more and more users and tasks. This is also a factor which limits the number of users this type of system can handle. Each user added puts a greater workload on the CPU, and it can only handle so many users before it becomes too slow for efficient operation. Speed is a major consideration with a single-CPU system, and if you overload the system so that workers sit idle waiting for the computer to process their input, and if your system does not offer the capability of being tied in with another computer for more power, you could indeed have a problem.

DOWN TIME

Another factor to consider when planning a computer system is **DOWN TIME**. *Down time* refers to periods when you are not able to use your computer. It does not necessarily mean that something has malfunctioned. The system might be unavailable (down) because backups are being made, or because its hardware or software is being modified or upgraded. Actually, especially on larger systems, most down time is *scheduled*—usually late at night or early in the morning when few, if any, users are likely to be affected. Because all work goes through one computer in a single-CPU system, however, when maintenance or repairs are required your entire operation is disrupted until technical service is completed. (Note: *Down time* is a term not limited to multiuser systems. Any system, regardless of size, can be referred to as being *down* whenever it cannot be used to perform its normal functions.)

UNIX AND XENIX

While most small computers use operating systems that were originally designed for their size class, there is also an operating system called **UNIX**—originally developed for mainframes—which is now available for smaller systems such as PCs. A variation of this operating system, **XENIX**, has since been created specifically for small computers and PCs. UNIX and XENIX share one thing in common: In terms of the instructions and programs needed to run them, UNIX and XENIX are both *huge*, compared with the operating systems usually associated with small computers.

For example, most versions of MS-DOS, which is the most popular operating system for small computers, require less than 1Meg of disk space, but a complete version of the UNIX or XENIX operating system can easily require 10 megabytes of disk space, or more. This is because many more capabilities are built into these operating systems. UNIX and XENIX are also systems- and programmer-oriented, meaning that to use them to their fullest extent requires a good deal of knowledge about the computer system itself, as well as the operating system.

MS-DOS usually comes with one relatively small operations manual adequate for most small computer users. In contrast, a complete set of documentation for the UNIX or XENIX operating systems may span a number of detailed manuals which are sometimes larger than encyclopedias. Because in-house programmers were common in the UNIX mainframe environment, it was designed and primarily intended for use by programmers and systems specialists and administrators. These people take care of any programming or configuration of the system that might be needed by the end users. Because it was realized that many users, especially small computer owners, will not need full versions of UNIX or XENIX, they are available in sections, or modules, and only those modules necessary for your application have to be purchased and installed. If you require in-house programming, or if you will be modifying your software, you will probably need a complete installation of XENIX or UNIX.

UNIX was developed in answer to growing demands for standards in the computer industry. System owners were frustrated because they could not easily transfer programs and data from one type of computer to another, and coordinating activities between two or more computers, even within the same company, was difficult. A program that would run on one system might not run on another without extensive modification. Often, when companies outgrew a computer and went to a larger system, their software was not compatible with the new system. This has even happened with systems made by the same manufacturer!

So, with UNIX or XENIX you will find a great deal of compatibility and flexibility. You will have access to the mainframe world, and be able to run most of the languages developed for serious applications. You should keep in mind that while UNIX and XENIX software is relatively standardized, the same has not yet happened with mainframe and minicomputer hardware. Also, while UNIX and XENIX themselves may be highly compatible, programs written on, or for, a specific computer system may not run on another brand of computer, even if they are using the same operating system. Be careful about expecting a program to run on your system "as is" even though its publisher claims it works on machines running UNIX or XENIX.

If your UNIX or XENIX software doesn't run it may not mean that you are entirely out of luck. Even though some hardware and specific computers may not be compatible, the operating systems, and the language the software was written in, most likely are compatible. If this is the case, there are two possibilities you can look in to. One is seeing if the software you want to use can be modified or adapted to run on your system. The other is that, if you can obtain the original source code of the program, it is very likely that you can simply recompile the program on your system, after which it should run properly. Either of these techniques will require a programmer. However, using this same process, you can often utilize software on small computers that was originally designed to run on mainframes.

TERMINALS

Multiuser systems increase efficiency and economy by allowing a number of people to use the resources of a single computer. Rather than equip users with complete individual computers; they instead need only a keyboard and monitor to access the main computer. A **TERMINAL**, sometimes crudely referred to as a **TUBE**, consists of a keyboard, a monitor, and a means of connecting the two to a computer. Some terminals get their power through the same cable that connects them with the computer. Most, however, contain their own power supply and other supporting components and circuitry. This arrangement allows terminals to easily be placed at a distance from the computer—sometimes, with a modem, at a considerable distance—and to be used with a variety of computer brands and types.

Terminals, like computers, are available in many different brands and varieties, but they fall into just two categories: **DUMB**, or **SMART**. As with other computerized devices, the term *dumb* refers to a terminal that relies entirely on a computer for processing ability. A *smart* terminal contains its own CPU and memory, and allows the user to control some features from the terminal itself—such as cursor size or type, screen colors, etc.—that would normally be adjusted at the computer. Some of the more advanced terminals, such as those usually associated with mainframes, contain enough memory and processing power to allow users to perform some operations **OFF-LINE**, i.e., independently of the main computer. This reduces the workload on the computer's CPU and increases overall system speed and efficiency.

Another thing terminals have in common is the way they communicate. All terminals use the international ASCII standard to transmit and receive information to and from a computer (See "ASCII," on page 27). Other than models which receive their power from the computer, most terminals are connected using another communications cabling standard called **RS-232**, or **RS-232C** (See "RS-232," on page 173). The connectors and cables may have to be **CONFIGURED** by a service technician before they will work properly. Before a terminal is used for the first time it will also need to be configured to match the brand, type, and setup of the computer it is connected to, as well as your personal tastes.

Smart terminals offer more customizable features, and convenience, than do dumb terminals, and many can be configured (set up) to better accommodate the user. This configuration process can range from changing the type of cursor displayed on the screen to varying the character size, or style, used. Some terminals have a feature which makes the keys "click" when pressed to give you a better feel of the keyboard—to make it more like a typewriter. Many terminals also have a **SCREEN SAVER** feature that makes the screen go blank after a specified time. Blanking the screen prevents screen images which are displayed for long periods of time from being "burned on" (leaving their impression on the screen permanently) and distorting subsequent images.

WORKSTATIONS

At times, trying to describe the equipment being used in a multiuser computer system can be very confusing, to say the least. You might be talking about a terminal when the person you're talking to thinks you are referring to an entire computer system, and vice versa. Or, when talking about a network, someone might be describing a terminal equipped only for being connected to a computer system, when you may be thinking about a computer capable of performing all functions independently. Partly to help avoid confusion, the term **WORKSTATION** is often used instead of computer, terminal, etc. A workstation can be described as any physical location, as well as *everything*—many features or just a few—that goes along with it, which allows a person to access a multiuser system. The term workstation has been applied to the main computer and monitor in a multiuser system, as well as to the computer, monitor, and keyboard of a single-user system. It is more common, however, to hear it mentioned in reference to a terminal or keyboard being used in a multiuser system.

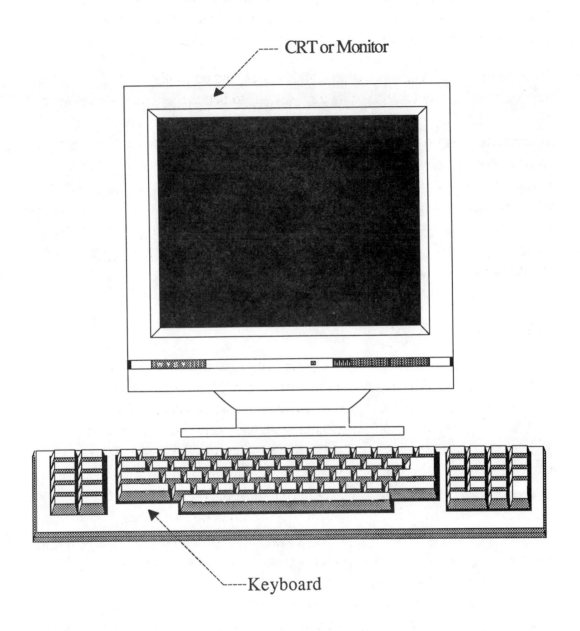

CRT or Monitor

----Keyboard

Example of a Terminal

195

NETWORKING: COMPUTER NETWORKS

This is a term that most people didn't began to hear until the 1980s—and one which can still be confusing. Just because a computer system is networked does not automatically mean it is also a multiuser system. But since we're already on the subject of multiuser systems, let's cover that area of networking first. Unlike the original multiuser concept, which requires one computer to do all the work, in **NETWORKING** two or more computers are linked together to achieve the same result. While, as with the traditional multiuser system, this method has its advantages and disadvantages, networks tend to have more on the positive side. One advantage is that, since users actually have their own computers, a networked system is not as subject to slowdowns as a system where everyone must share a single computer. Because each user that is added does not necessarily slow the system down, there are fewer limitations as to how many users a network can handle. In fact, networking systems have been put into operation which linked together hundreds, or even thousands, of users—a feat not possible with a single computer, no matter how powerful!

Networks which operate largely within the confines of a single office or building are often referred to as a LAN (**LOCAL AREA NETWORK**), while systems spread across different buildings and linked by phone line and modem—possibly in different cities and states—are called **WIDE AREA NETWORKS**.

Since users in a networked system are using their own computer or CPU, they can usually operate independently of the network if they choose to. For instance, someone might have a special program on his own floppy or hard disk just for department or personal use. One disadvantage is that, even when relatively inexpensive PCs are used, the cost of a networked system often exceeds that of a single-CPU system. This is because, instead of just buying an inexpensive terminal when you want to add a user, you must buy a complete computer. With steadily dropping prices, however, the issue of cost is becoming less important when comparing a network to a single-CPU system. Most networks only require each user's computer to have a floppy-disk drive installed—individual hard disks are usually optional—so there are usually savings as opposed to a fully equipped computer. Each computer does, however, have to have its own RAM memory—and possibly a few other components like a video card, RS-232 interface, etc.

File-Sharing Techniques

While a network can be assembled with each user having a complete computer to himself—with hard drive, etc.—this is usually not done. Instead, one computer acts as a manager of the entire network. That computer may be referred to as a **NETWORK SERVER, SYSTEM SERVER, FILE SERVER, FILE MANAGER**, or any number of other terms. Because different manufacturers use different terms, some having slightly different meanings, we will use the more generic term **NETWORK SERVER** in this discussion. The network server is a computer in the network that is equipped with whatever hardware and software is to be used by other computers (workstations) on the network. The remaining computers need to be equipped only with the hardware needed to operate as terminals, workstations, or stand-alone units, and can cost considerably less than a computer equipped as a server.

The networking software or operating system itself is stored on the hard drive of the network server. Because this hard drive probably has to store the programs and information needed by every user on the system, it is usually larger than the drive that would normally be found on the same type of computer in a single user configuration. The network server does not actually run programs or do any processing for the other users; their own computers do that. The server instead coordinates the use and transfer of files and programs. When someone wants to run a particular program from his computer, he enters instructions just as he would if he were using an isolated computer. The network server then processes his request and sends the needed program or module to the memory in his computer, where it is run. All of the files that user uses, or creates, will be stored by the network server on its hard drive. On some systems, rather than send entire programs over the network, the programs each user needs are stored on the hard drive of his or her own computer—and only the data files being worked on are sent to and from the network server. This arrangement greatly reduces **NETWORK TRAFFIC** (the amount of information that has to be sent over the network) and increases overall speed and efficiency.

Because the network server carries the greatest load, as far as disk drive usage is concerned, its hard-disk drive should not only be larger than normal but as fast as possible. A drive with the standard access time of the original PC XT (65 milliseconds) would prove too slow for most multiuser and networking applications, because a number of people will be sharing the same hard drive—often at

197

the same time. In a computer that is used as a network server, its disk drive should have an access time no greater than 28ms. You'll find such drives—or faster ones—already installed on most high-performance computers. If not, you can specify a faster drive when you order the computer.

Nodes

There is usually a limit to the number of additional computers, and users, that a single network server can handle. Some networking systems solve this problem by allowing each computer to, in effect, act as a system manager. Instead of all information being stored on the hard disk of one network server, these systems allow information to be stored on the hard drives of more than one computer in the network. If the programs or information one user needs are not on his own computer, he can access the hard disk of someone else's computer to get it. Some systems are combinations of both of these methods—with one or more main or primary network servers, and one or more auxiliary or secondary servers. It is more common—and more organized—however, to add another computer to serve as a network server for additional users than to place applications randomly on the hard disks of computers throughout a network.

In a system built around servers, each server is referred to as a **NODE**. If a single network server in the system you are using can only handle 8 users, and you want to add 8 more for a total of 16 users, you would first buy another computer set up, like the first, to serve as a network server. The first network server would be linked with the second, which in turn would serve as the network server for the 8 additional users. If a user on the second node (the additional computer and disk drive serving the second 8 users) needed to access information on the first node (the first computer and disk drive serving the first 8 users) the network software (operating system) would handle the necessary juggling without its being noticeable to the users. This is referred to as **TRANSPARENT OPERATION**, meaning the system automatically handles everything in a such way that the users do not have to be concerned about which computer or hard drive their programs or data are on. Using multiple nodes, you can build large networks with little, if any, practical limitations on size and number of users other than those imposed by the brand and type of network you are using.

This same technique can be used to link shared-CPU systems together—including mainframes. Sometimes, depending on the type of network you are building, it is possible to link different types and sizes of computers together, and perhaps even

198

Central CPU

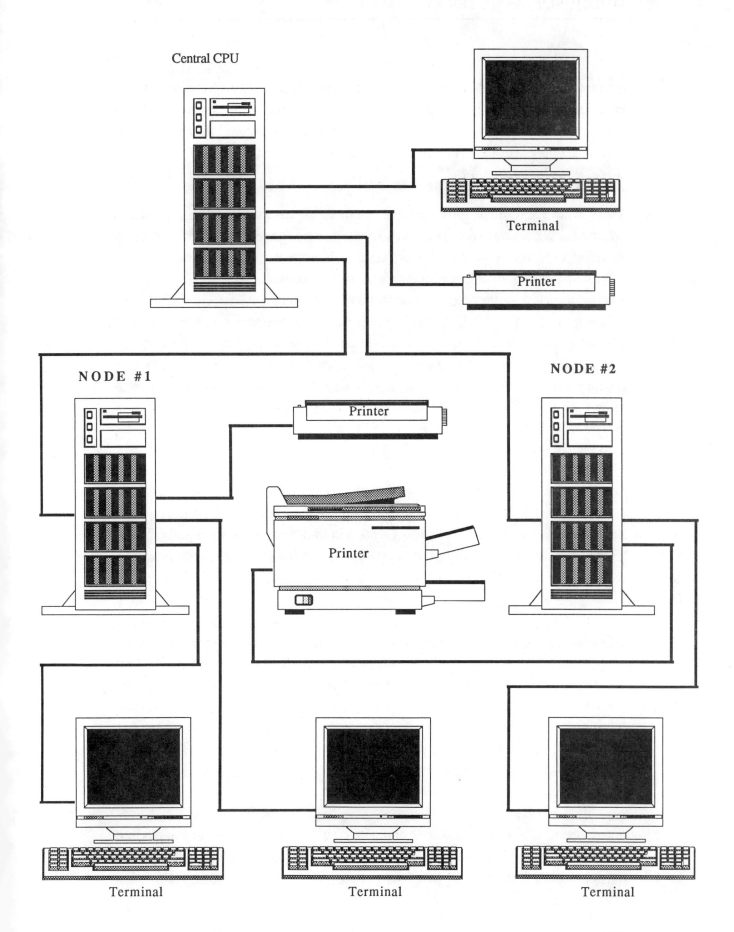

Terminal

Printer

NODE #1

Printer

NODE #2

Printer

Terminal

Terminal

Terminal

199

different brands. It is not uncommon to find networks where PCs are connected to mainframes, but call on the mainframe's power only when more capacity is needed or when it is necessary to access information stored on the mainframe. It's like having the power of the mainframe at a fraction of the cost.

File-Sharing Systems

Now that we have covered the area of multiuser networks, let's take a look at a different way the same concept is used. It will be easy for you to picture how **FILE SHARING** works because it operates using most of the same ideas as the networking systems just described. As was mentioned earlier, networking does not always refer to a system that has true multiuser capabilities. The term *networking* can be more accurately described as any system where more than one computer is connected to another. The type of network we are referring to now is one in which more than one computer can access and share the same files—but not at the same time, as it can in a multiuser system. This is why this type of network is most often referred to as "file sharing." Remember to keep in mind, however, that a file-sharing system can still be, and often is, considered a network.

File-sharing systems offer the same advantages to purchasers that networking does, except the ability for more than one person to use the same file at the same time. For instance, two users might be able to use the same accounting program at the same time. But if they both tried to access the payroll files the **FILE SERVER**, which operates in much the same way as the network server described earlier, would allow only one to do so at a time.

File-sharing systems vary in their degree of sophistication, as well as in the capabilities they provide to users. Because most file-sharing systems do not allow true multiuser capability, their main attraction is that they offer most of the other benefits of networking. Only one computer has to be fully equipped with a hard drive, printer, etc., and office users can share the same programs and information—even though they cannot do so at the same time. There can also be savings in software costs. Even though most software on the market is for single users, there is usually nothing to prevent a file server from allowing more than one user to load the same program into their own computers' memory. This should not pose a problem as long as each person is using different files, or files that are on a hard disk in their own computers. Care should be taken before such a system is put into operation to make sure that no conflicts can arise from two people trying to share the same files. Copy protection schemes will prevent some software from being used in this manner—although this is becoming less the case. Also, some single-user software is designed so that it cannot be loaded onto more than one computer at the same time. Some software publishers also require you to pay an additional charge for a **SITE LICENSE** to use their programs on a multiuser system.

File, Record, And Field Locking

Besides dividing computer time between users, a fully capable, or true, multiuser system must also handle the important job of allowing only one user to change the information stored in a file at the same time. This is accomplished using three common methods, **FILE LOCKING**, **RECORD LOCKING**, and **FIELD LOCKING**.

In order to understand the several forms of **LOCKING** you will need to be familiar with the way computers store information on mass storage devices. First, to help you understand the computerized method, let's take a look at how a manual filing system in an office might handle payroll records. For this example, we will assume that all of the payroll records for employees are in one file drawer. Each drawer is organized by employee name. The information for each employee is kept in individual file folders. A computer would refer to the entire file drawer as one **FILE**. Just as with a manual system, every file in a computer must have its own unique name; in this case we will call the file **PAYROLL**. What we would refer to as file folders a computer refers to as **RECORDS**, just as in a manual system where each file folder contains the record of one employee. While there can be only one payroll record for each employee, a file can contain separate records, on many different employees—just as a file drawer can contain as many file folders as there is room for. Now, let's pull out one of the file folders to take a closer look at *some* of the information it contains.

```
EMPLOYEE NAME........: Jane Doe
EMPLOYEE ID NUMBER: EMPID-1OO-A
HOURLY RATE...........: $14.70
HOME ADDRESS..........: 911 UPCOMING EXECUTIVE LANE
```

If we look at this file folder as if it were in a disk file named PAYROLL, it would be considered one record. The name of the record, the **RECORD HEADER**, would be the same as the name of the employee. Individual pieces of information within each employee record are stored in what are called **FIELDS**. The name, number, rate, and address are each a separate field. So, a computer stores information in FILES. Every file has its own name, PAYROLL in this example, and each file is further divided into separate RECORDS. In this example, each record is used to hold the information on a different employee. Finally, each record is further divided into FIELDS to hold the separate types of information that pertain to just that one record and employee. You will notice that what was used as the record header, in this example, is also repeated in a field. This is because *all* information contained in a record must be stored in a field of some type.

Now that you have a better understanding of how computers store files, let's see how multiuser systems use those files. **LOCKING** refers to a process whereby a program electronically "locks" a certain file, record, field, or all three, and prevents changes by other users of the information that is locked, although most programs will still allow someone else to view the information. If the user actually wants to change it, he or she must wait until the first user has finished, and the information is **UNLOCKED**. Although record locking is the most common arrangement, locking can also take place at the file or field level.

A multiuser computer usually does not automatically perform any locking functions itself. Instead, the operating system running on the computer, and/or the software you are using, must have multiuser capabilities. If you are having software designed and written for you, the programmer will have to design into the system the level of multiuser capability you need. This is why you should always make sure that software you expect to run in a multiuser mode will actually perform as you expect it to. This is especially true with PCs, since they were—and to a large extent still are—primarily designed as single-user computers. Although multiuser technology is becoming available for more and more small computers, and multiuser PC software is likewise increasing, most software available for small computers is still designed for a single user.

Because multiuser software requires more programming to create, and is more expensive for its publisher to support, you can usually expect to pay more than you would for the same program in a single-user version. In the most basic systems, locking takes place only at the file level. File locking is the easiest and most economical locking level to program into a system. For a small system, or one where it is unlikely that more than one person will need to use the same files at the same time, this method may prove adequate. When one user accesses a file, causing it to be locked, no other user can access *any* part of that file—none of its records

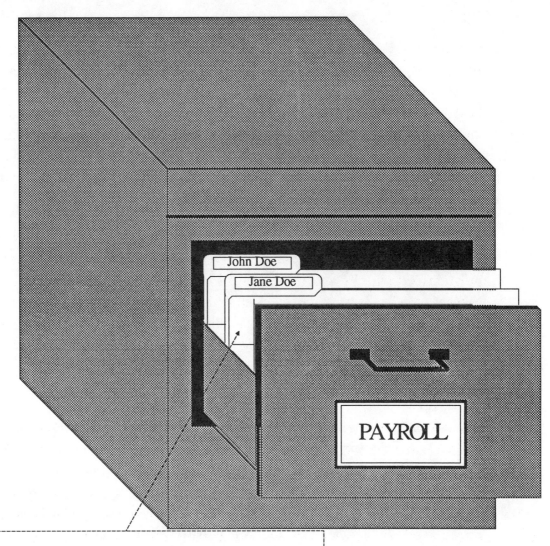

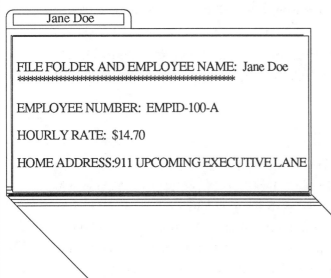

FILE FOLDER AND EMPLOYEE NAME: Jane Doe
****

EMPLOYEE NUMBER: EMPID-100-A

HOURLY RATE: $14.70

HOME ADDRESS:911 UPCOMING EXECUTIVE LANE

nor its fields—until the first user has finished and the file is unlocked. Using the payroll example given earlier, this means that if one user was working in the payroll section of the program everyone else would have to wait before they would be allowed access to *any* of the employee records.

The next, and most practical, method is to lock only the record being used. This way, as many people can access as many different employee records as they need to, at the same time. One user might access the Jane Doe record used in our example. A second user might, at the same time, be working in the record of John Doe. Another user could access yet a third record, and so on. Users on a system utilizing record locking would experience few delays, because, in most cases, only one user would need to work with the record of any given employee, at one time.

The last method, field locking, is usually not found on small computer systems. For those applications which can benefit from field locking, however, it represents the ultimate in multiuser convenience. Field locking allows more than one person to access and work not only in the same file but in the same record, as well. For instance, in the payroll example, two people could both be in Jane Doe's employee record. For this example let's assume she had been given a raise, and had moved to a nicer neighborhood. The bookkeeper in the accounting department could be changing the **HOURLY RATE** field while at the same time someone in the personnel department also corrected the **HOME ADDRESS** field. Neither user would be affected by the other, unless they both tried to change the same field at the same time. It is unlikely a real-life application would use as few fields as in the example above. Working payroll systems often use hundreds and, sometimes, even a thousand or more fields to maintain all of the necessary employee information. In such a system, it is very unlikely two people would ever need to update information in the same field at the same time. Therefore, conflicts rarely occur in systems which utilize field locking.

You may still be wondering why locking is necessary in multiuser systems. To illustrate why, let's use the same payroll example again, only this time without locking of any kind. Jane Doe's employee record must be updated with the newly changed information. The bookkeeper accesses Jane Doe's record and changes her hourly rate from $14.70 to $16.20. The bookkeeper double checks to make sure the figures have been entered correctly. The program appears to accept and display the new information. So the bookkeeper leaves Jane Doe's payroll record to do other work in the general ledger. What the bookkeeper never realized was that, at the same time, another user in the personnel department was also using Jane Doe's employee record to enter her new address.

Now it's two weeks later, Jane is excited about the thought of getting the first paycheck since her raise. But when she opens the envelope she is surprised to find that her check is for the same amount as before. She also notices that, while everything else is correct, her hourly rate is still at $14.70, not $16.20 as it should be. How could this have happened? It happened because more than one user accessed the same employee record at the same time, and no file or record locks had been written into the payroll program. If the bookkeeper had changed the hourly rate, and then, later, the personnel department changed the address information, everything would have been fine. But in this case both were using the record at the same time. Even though the system appeared to accept the bookkeeper's entries, someone from personnel was still using the record when the bookkeeper finished.

When there are no locks on a record or file, and more than one person is using it at the same time, the file is *usually* updated with the entries made by the last person to use it, which means that entries made just before the last change might be lost. In this example, the hourly rate, as well as any other entries the bookkeeper made, were lost because the bookkeeper was not the last person to use the file. Although this is an example of what would *usually* happen in such a situation, whenever a clash of users occurs the results can range from all of the information in a record being erased, to the entire program being **LOCKED UP**, or a program **CRASH**. Both of these terms refer to what happens when a program malfunctions and can no longer be used properly until the problem is corrected (and it is sometimes not even clear what the problem is!). The bottom line is: having multiple users of software that has not been designed or modified for multiuser purposes is simply an accident waiting to happen.

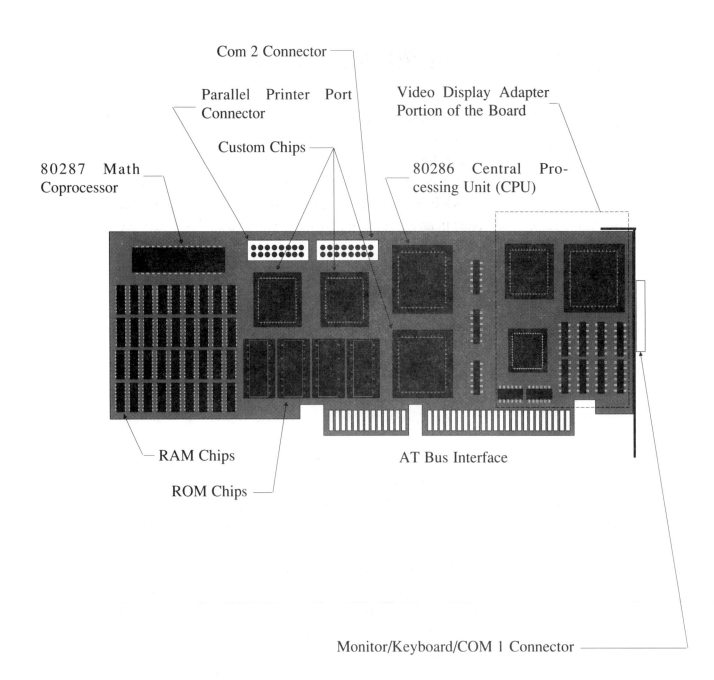

Com 2 Connector

Parallel Printer Port
Connector

Video Display Adapter
Portion of the Board

Custom Chips

80287 Math
Coprocessor

80286 Central Processing Unit (CPU)

RAM Chips

AT Bus Interface

ROM Chips

Monitor/Keyboard/COM 1 Connector

Computer on a Board

COMPUTER-ON-A-BOARD SYSTEMS

The processing power of most modern small computers has been reduced to the single microchip referred to as the microprocessor, or CPU. The hardware that surrounds the CPU—such as the power supply, cooling fans, disk drives, etc.—merely provides supporting functions. Computer-on-a-board systems take advantage of this fact by placing all of the external, or "support," hardware in one cabinet, often referred to simply as a **BOX**. The box contains slots into which circuit boards may be installed that contain any other components that are needed. Most of these boards will contain CPUs. However, boards containing modems, hard drives, floppy disks, and other components, can be installed as well. One board containing a CPU would be required for each user of a multiuser system. Because virtually an entire computer—including minor support circuitry—can now be placed on one plug-in circuit board, the cost can be saved that would have gone into support hardware for separate computers for each user, as well as a cabinet to put them in. Instead, each computer-on-a-board has only to be connected to a terminal (a monitor and keyboard) before it is fully functional. Even though users see only a terminal, they have the full use of a complete computer all to themselves.

Board-oriented systems can be found in many varieties and configurations. Most are installed as part of a multiuser system, or in custom-designed systems for engineering or scientific use. Whatever the use, computer-on-a-board systems all have at least two big advantages: the same low cost as a shared-CPU system, and the independent speed and reliability of a networked system. Like a multiuser system where all work goes through one CPU, here the work all goes through one box. That box, however, contains multiple computers (CPUs) to handle the workload. True, the cost is higher because each user essentially has his own computer, but because the computers (CPUs) are mounted on relatively inexpensive boards which draw power and other support from one central box, the cost is still usually lower than it would be if each user were given a computer system complete with box, power supply, etc.

Because each user is connected to a CPU with its own memory he enjoys the same speed advantages he would in a network with his own computer. Also, a malfunction in an individual user's portion of the system probably won't cause downtime for anyone else because each computer is separate. On the other hand (unlike in a networking system where, even if the network server goes down, each user is usually left with a fully operational single-user computer) the same is not true of computer-on-a-board systems. Because the system box contains *all* of the support components required by each user's CPU, if a component in the box itself malfunctions the entire system will experience down time.

Just as with a networked system, there is a limit to how many users one box can accommodate. The capacity is determined by how many open slots are available for installing boards with CPUs on them. Also, the size of the power supply and the cooling capacity of the fan system can limit the number and type of devices that can be installed. When a box-type system is expanded by adding one or more additional boxes, many manufacturers use the same term, **NODE,** for the boxes as is used for central units of more traditional multiuser and networked systems.

OTHER SYSTEMS

There are many other methods than those just described of linking computers together and allowing more than one person to use them. They all operate on essentially the same principles, although manufacturers often use different software or hardware techniques. Whatever your needs are, remember: with small computers and PCs there are as yet few *true* standards (at least not like the ones that exist for water purity, motor oil, etc.). So, while some systems may be more popular than others, don't be talked into buying one just because someone says it's *"standard."* Make absolutely sure you know what your needs are before you even go shopping. When you do shop, make sure you are buying from a company that has been around for awhile—and looks like they'll be around tomorrow if you need them. Be sure the system will do *exactly* what you need it to do, and that your software will work on the system. If a programmer will be needed, check with him or her before you buy to make sure everything you want done is possible and within your budget. Lastly, make sure that you understand what is being explained to you. It is not uncommon for the prospective purchaser of a system to confuse a multiuser system for one that has only the ability to handle simple file sharing. Or, a buyer might mistake the capability for two users to run a program at the same time as being the multiuser capability he or she needs. Then, only after the system has been purchased and installed is it realized that just because two people can run a software program at the same time does not necessarily mean it is multiuser software.

Once you've decided on a system, it isn't a bad idea to summarize your needs and the expected capabilities of the system in writing, and have it signed by you and an *authorized* representative of the computer dealer you are working with, to make sure you understand each other before the purchase. If the system does not do what is outlined, the statement of agreement will make it easier for you to get the situation corrected. If you are uncomfortable with doing any of these things yourself, or you just want someone to help you with the details, get some unbiased help or hire a consultant. The money you'll pay will be well worth it if you can avoid buying a system that isn't suited to your needs.

This page intentionally left blank.

Chapter 14

COMPUTER SECURITY

Computer security is a large and complex field concerned, primarily, with the protection of large systems. We will touch on only on two areas that the small computer owner will most likely want to give some thought to. If you are the only person using the system, perhaps at home, there may be no need to observe even these simple precautions.

First, and easiest, is to control the physical access people have to your computer system. If you have information you want to protect it goes without saying that you should allow access to the system only by those people who need to use it, and only system users should be allowed to handle floppy disks or tape cartridges. Even if you are not concerned about theft or invasion of privacy you should discourage untrained persons from handling storage media or experimenting with equipment in order to prevent damage that would likely be innocent—but could nonetheless be serious. Most software for small computers stores information on disks using a method that is easy to access and read. Such files are almost always entirely unprotected. So someone taking one of your disks or tapes could easily read the information on another computer without difficulty. Software is available which "scrambles" the contents of files on your disks so that it can be retrieved and viewed only by you, through the use of a password. This process is known as **ENCRYPTION**, and is currently the most effective way to protect the data on any system, regardless of size.

Second, take advantage of the security feature built into many good programs which requires users to enter a password before they are allowed to use the program or to access certain portions of it. This not only provides a simple and effective means of internal security but, in some programs, also provides you with a history of each user's actions while using the program. This is known as an **AUDIT TRAIL**, which serves a function similar to the audit trails used in accounting but has a different meaning when referring to computer security. Audit trails keep track of such things as the number of times someone has logged in, the number of times someone has tried to access a restricted area and been denied access, and how much time a user spends in each area of a computer or program. Audit trails help you detect unauthorized activity, and can come in handy in situations where clarification is needed on who did what. In a computerized accounting system, having an audit trail can be a lifesaver when trying to balance the books or locate missing items. However, passwords and audit trails are effective only when used properly. If your system has multiple-password capability, meaning that you can assign each person a different password, and you instead use only one "master" password that allows everyone access to the entire system, you will lose the advantages such a system has to offer.

In a one- or two-person operation passwords may be all the security you need. However, where a greater number of users are involved more thought should be given to refining password use. You would not, for instance, want someone working in inventory to be able to access payroll and accounting records. You might also wish to limit a person's access even within a given area. This way, for example, a person whose only responsibility is to enter time card information would not also have access to more sensitive areas, such as employee salaries, bank balances, or check writing. By using reasonable care, the above precautions should prove adequate for most small systems. If your system is constantly accessible by phone line you will want to observe the precautions mention under "Phone line security," on page 185.

If your company is large, or you feel that greater protection may be necessary, check with your computer dealer for suggestions. You will also find firms that specialize in computer security listed in the phone book, computer magazines, and trade journals. Whatever methods you explore, extra care should be exercised whenever you are using your system to store confidential or proprietary information. This is especially true of information you are keeping on, or for, others, such as employee records, or client records if you are an accountant or attorney. You could easily be sued if such information were in your care and an unauthorized person gained access to it.

Speaking of which, let's take a look at an obscure area that vaguely concerns computer security—even if only for your own peace of mind. If you are thinking of using your computer to accumulate information on other people or businesses—without their knowledge and permission—it might be wise to first get an opinion from a legal professional. There are laws which make it illegal to acquire or compile certain kinds of information on a computer. This is an area that will affect few people, and, naturally, does not apply in the same way to those who have legitimate reasons for storing personal and confidential information—insurance agencies, attorneys, etc. However, because privacy laws can change dramatically, it is something to keep in mind.

VIRUSES, WORMS, AND OTHER NASTY THINGS

Just when you thought the flu season was over, you find out your computer can catch a virus! Or maybe a "worm" eats its way through your files, or a "Trojan Horse" sneaks into your system disguised as an ordinary program and devastates your hard drive. These terms, and others just as imaginative, are being used to describe types of stealthy damage encountered because of the growing problem of computer sabotage.

Once confined to governmental systems, giant corporations, and large universities, computer sabotage has now taken on a more subtle form that is affecting an increasing number of people. A small number of computer "experts" with nothing better to do, with malicious intent, or both, are designing clever ways of "infecting" computer systems with trouble-causing programs.

The effects these programs have on systems can range from mere inconvenience, with little or no actual harm done, to major disruptions of a system, to permanent data loss or other serious damage. Even as a prank such programs identify the saboteur as a person with little or no respect for others, and a disregard for the law. This is because "pranks" sometimes go wrong (as the saboteurs know very well that they can) and what some claim was intended as a joke ends up a very serious threat to important research groups, the nation's defenses, and firms providing hundreds of thousands of jobs and important services.

Most people not involved with mainframes or the computer industry were unaware of this problem until November of 1988. That month a graduate student made worldwide headlines after introducing a virus into a nationwide network of computers. (Technically, they say it was not a virus but a worm. However, the media referred to it by the more popular term, *virus*.) According to one Associated Press article, the virus affected over six thousand university and government systems. The author claimed he intended it to be just a high-tech prank—an experiment of sorts—but an error in the design of the program caused it to duplicate much more rapidly than he had planned. While apparently no data was destroyed, the virus caused damage by slowing down the processing speed of the computers and using up their memory. The costs of the resulting losses of computer time and the clean-up necessary to get systems back to normal ran well into the millions.

Unlike many prior incidents, the extent of the damage caught the immediate attention of federal authorities. An intensive investigation by the FBI located the young man—a college student who was later expelled from college—in a matter of days. In 1989 the former student was indicted on a felony charge by a federal grand jury in Syracuse, New York. He faced a possible prison sentence of up to five years, and a fine of $250,000, but was sentenced to only three years' probation, a $10,000 fine, and 400 hours of community service.

This was the most vigorous prosecution to date of such a crime, and, even with the light sentence, perhaps it will make most people think twice about designing such programs. But what can you do to protect your system against those who design them anyway? Currently, your best protection is to provide good physical security for your hardware, and password and software security for your data.

Systems that have been infected by "pranksters" up until now have usually been those which are available to at least a restricted but hard-to-identify public, through modems and telephone lines. Here also, if your system is accessible in this way you will want to take precautions such as those outlined in the section on "Phone-line security," on page 185.

Most computer systems are not accessible to outsiders by modem, however. The only way a system not accessible by callers can be infected is by an employee or a "visitor," either of whom might plant a virus directly, or through software voluntarily downloaded into the system via modem, purchase, or a software "gift" which has been modified to create various kinds of difficulties for the unsuspecting user. Public domain software and shareware (See "Public domain software," on

214

page 110) have been particularly vulnerable to such tampering. Obviously, the risks of virus invasions are best avoided by making sure you obtain your software from reliable sources.

Describing programs which sabotage computer systems is difficult because their structure and functioning vary greatly and are largely dependent on the people who create them. However, it may help you to know some of the signs that could indicate your system has been infected.

A sudden unexplained growth in the size of a file or a number of files is a major symptom. If the amount of memory remaining on your hard drive seems to be declining at a faster than normal rate, a virus may be duplicating itself there. Examine your hard drive to make sure all of the files it contains belong there. Be suspicious of overly large files, or multiple files that have similar or unusual names that don't appear to be a part of your software. Some viruses work not by duplicating themselves directly, but by attaching themselves to legitimate files or programs and then making them larger.

Unexplained decreases in file size and number also suggest a serious problem. These effects result from the operation of programs which work by destroying or corrupting files and software—causing data loss or erroneous results to appear in your programs. It can be difficult to determine if such a problem is actually a virus, or just a bug in your software or hardware.

And still other programs are designed to cause a computer system to crash and stop operating altogether. You should also keep in mind that some programs are, in effect, time bombs, set to "go off" in your system at a certain time or on a certain date.

Lastly, it should be mentioned that after the increased publicity about viruses, numerous antivirus programs appeared on the market. Sometimes referred to as "vaccines," these programs claim to offer your system protection from viruses and other damaging programs. However, as explained earlier, there is no such thing as a "standard" computer virus. Each new program seems, usually, to be designed by a different person, and each one can cause different kinds of damage. For these reasons, antivirus software cannot offer you total or fully reliable protection, but can only guard against known viruses and programs and check your system for general signs of infection. It is probably for these same reasons that many of the new antivirus programs that popped up in 1988 and 1989, after all the publicity, disappeared from the market almost as quickly.

This page intentionally left blank.

218

Chapter 15

THE BIG APPLE VERSUS BIG BLUE APPLE COMPUTER AND IBM

Perhaps it's only appropriate that there is as much contrast between the visual symbols of these major companies as there is between their product lines. The famous apple, with a bite taken out of it, projects an artful, imaginative image—matching the personalities of Steven Jobs, the equally famous originator of Apple Computer Company, and his associates, Steve Wozniak and Mike Markkula. The big, bold, IBM logo matches well the blue suit, strictly business, impression many people have held of International Business Machines over the years.

Apple Computer was truly an imaginative company. The Apple II, introduced in 1977, was ahead of its time and led the way for the personal computer industry that was to follow. It sported a modern streamlined look, an open architecture which offered easy expandability through plug-in circuit boards, color graphics, sound, and quiet operation (because it didn't need a cooling fan), most of which were industry firsts. Apple was the first computer to enjoy widespread use for education in schools and homes. More educational software was written at the time for the Apple than almost any other computer. Many business programs were available on the Apple as well, including VisiCalc, the first electronic spreadsheet. A large number of the original Apples are still in use today.

Apple introduced a number of other computers, leading up to its Macintosh series, which has also created a strong following. Like the Apple II that came before it, the Apple Macintosh (also referred to as a Mac) was ahead of its time, and was one of the first personal computers to make use of microfloppy disks, pull-down menus and icons, and the mouse input device. All of this was housed in an unusually small case which made the use of the term "small footprint" popular. Because it was a radical departure from the industry standards of the day, the Mac was not an overnight success. However, since it was superior at handling graphics and art applications it soon became a favorite with artists and illustrators. The Mac virtually invented "desktop publishing" and remains a good choice for this application.

Interestingly, the very features which made the Macintosh "radical" when it was introduced are now commonplace. Many computer systems now feature the same type of 3.5" (microfloppy) disk drives, a mouse input device, small footprint, and desktop publishing capabilities. IBM officially adopted the microfloppy disk format with the introduction of its PS/2 line of computers in 1987.

Even though a considerable amount of business software has been written for the Mac, desktop publishing remains its most popular application, while the larger variety of software and hardware available for IBM PCs and compatibles makes them the preferred choice for everyday business applications. In an effort to better penetrate the business market and compete with IBM compatibles, in 1987 Apple introduced a new line of Macs, the Mac SE and the Mac II. These machines offered more power, greater speed, and many of the features of IBM compatibles. In fact, through the use of a plug-in circuit board, the newer Macs can run most MS-DOS programs.

Until the introduction of the newer Macs, choosing between a Mac and an IBM PC or compatible was easy; if your applications were art or desktop publishing, you chose the Mac; for everyday business applications—accounting, databases, programming, etc., you chose an MS-DOS machine—a PC or a clone. Now, however, some people have a hard time determining which computer will best suit their needs.

If your needs are primarily business related, or if you must have certain software that is only available on PCs, then a PC or compatible is the obvious choice. Even though software is probably the most important factor, don't overlook hardware compatibility. There are a large number of plug-in circuit boards that are only available for PCs. If your application needs the features one, or several, of these boards offers, you may have little choice in your selection of a computer.

Obviously you will have to make the final decision as to which computer is best for you. However, there is a very easy way to cut through all the pros and cons and be assured you're getting the system that's right for you. As pointed out in the chapter on software, software will likely be the most important factor in your selection of hardware. Do your homework to find out what software will be best for your applications, and make sure you also find out if any special hardware will be needed. Then it's simply a matter of choosing whichever system can run the required software or hardware most efficiently, and provide the best value for your money.

While the above "formula" will help you come to a decision if you are comparing the Mac and the PC, you may also wish to weigh a number of other factors as they relate to the type of use you intend to put your system to. There are more IBM PCs and compatibles than any other kind of personal computer in the world (over 40 million by 1991). This, combined with an equally impressive selection of software, makes PCs the overwhelming choice for everyday business use. In addition, while at one time the best graphics and desktop publishing software was available only on the Mac, most of the same software is now available on PCs as well. Much, if not most, of what can be done on a Mac can now be done on a PC.

This does not mean, however, that a PC would automatically be the best choice. Expensive hardware such as graphics monitors and cards, a mouse, and possibly a mouse driver card—among others—may need to be added to a PC before it is suitable for desktop publishing. On a Mac, however, these features are standard. And even though a great deal of graphics software is now available for PCs, some of the best is still available only on the Mac. If you are intending to put your computer to only "light" business use, and are planning to do a lot of desktop publishing, you can hardly go wrong with a Mac. There are word processing, spreadsheet, and other general programs available for the Mac that may be suitable for your business or personal needs.

One area of graphics in which the Mac is not the leader is CAD (COMPUTER AIDED DESIGN). While CAD can fall into the same category as graphics design, more often it involves the areas of drafting, architecture, and engineering. A wealth of CAD software (and hardware) is available for PCs—and they are easily the best choice for these applications.

This page intentionally left blank.

Chapter 16

IBM'S PS/2 AND OS/2: A NEW STANDARD?

In 1987, just as it appeared IBM PCs and compatibles and MS-DOS had positioned themselves to remain the accepted standard worldwide, indefinitely, IBM announced its new **PERSONAL SYSTEM/2** (**PS/2**) line of computers and the **OS/2** operating system.

The introduction of the PS/2 series was somewhat similar to that of the IBM AT, in that many advanced capabilities were promised but little software or hardware was immediately available which made use of these features. The PS/2's most significant advance was in the design of its **MICRO CHANNEL ARCHITEC-TURE (MCA)**. The MCA bus greatly enhances the multiprocessing capability of the PS/2, as well as preventing conflicts between plug-in circuit boards and errors in their setup or configuration. Plug-in boards for the MCA bus automatically configure themselves into the system—unlike the boards for PCs, which often require the user to change dip switch or jumper settings. Other features include 3.5" 1.44 Meg microfloppy disk drives and VGA graphics. The promised OS/2 operating system became available during the following year or two. As of 1991, OS/2 still didn't provide multiuser capabilities—which was also one of the unfulfilled promises of the AT which came before it.

With the announcement of the PS/2 came dark predictions that it would be the end of PCs, compatibles, and MS-DOS—but none of this happened. Although PS/2s and OS/2 have seen slowly increasing sales, the world did not automatically embrace them as the new standard, as IBM thought they would. The reason is largely that, while many software houses provide both MS-DOS and OS/2 versions of programs, and while a PS/2 computer will run MS-DOS, OS/2 will not run the

MS-DOS versions of programs, nor is the MCA bus compatible with the PC bus. People are understandably reluctant to throw away the thousands of dollars worth of MS-DOS software and plug-in circuit boards they may own. By far, MS-DOS-based and Unix/Xenix-based computers still dominate the microcomputer market.

For reasons like these, it seems that many buyers of PS/2s have been first-time purchasers or those loyal to the IBM product line. Many people, and the computer industry as a whole, seem to be less than sure that PS/2 will replace the current PC/MS-DOS standard. In fact, although a number of manufacturers started out to clone the PS/2 when it was introduced, as they did with PCs, many dropped the effort because they didn't see enough potential, and because the design of the PS/2 was much more difficult to copy. This was yet another "feature" of the PS/2; IBM made much of its design proprietary so that it could not easily be copied the way earlier PCs were. In response, the computer industry invented its own version of the MCA bus architecture, called **EISA**. EISA (pronounced "eesa") stands for **EXTENDED INDUSTRY STANDARD ARCHITECTURE**, and offers many of the advantages of the MCA bus plus plug-in board compatibility with PCs.

If all of this sounds a bit confusing, it is! And it appears things will stay that way until the computer industry decides on a new standard for personal computers—whether that be PS/2, OS/2, together with the MCA bus or EISA or a new standard that hasn't been invented yet. It is to be hoped that, after all the years it took for PC compatibles and MS-DOS to become as entrenched as they are, improvements can be made that will maintain a high degree of compatibility between the old and the new. Change will come, though, because the current design of PC compatible computers has almost reached its hardware limit. In order to bring more advanced hardware capabilities to PCs, a new system will at least need to have the features the MCA and EISA architecture have to offer, plus multiuser capabilities.

Chapter 17

WINDOWS

The introduction of version 3.0 of Windows by Microsoft in 1990 was probably accompanied by more hype and hoopla, was the topic of more conversations, and was backed by more advertising dollars than any PC-based software product to come before it. Officially rolled out at a gala, Hollywood-style "grand opening," Windows 3.0 quickly rocketed to the top of software sales charts. But even in the wake of this early success there was also confusion. Let's try here to clear up the confusion by explaining exactly what Windows is, and what it is not.

Windows is a **GUI (GRAPHICAL USER INTERFACE)**, meaning that it provides a graphic or picture-based alternative to operating software and computers. Although Windows can be referred to as a graphical operating system, it is not an operating system in the true sense of the word because, like most software, it requires a separate operating system in order to function—in this case, MS-DOS.

Ease Of Use

One of the greatest attractions of GUIs for some users is that they offer greater ease of use than do character-based interfaces such as MS-DOS (although MS-DOS versions 4.0 and higher do contain an optional and relatively simple graphical interface called the **MS-DOS SHELL**). To take full advantage of a character-based operating system the user must first familiarize him or herself with its many commands and functions; the same applies to most character-based software programs. For instance, in MS-DOS users are usually greeted by the **DOS PROMPT** after first turning on the computer. The DOS prompt—which often looks something like this: "C:\->"—simply indicates that the computer is ready to accept input in the form of a typed command. No other information is given, so the user is required to already have memorized the information and commands needed to use the operating system, and to run software programs. Incidentally, in the above example the DOS prompt is telling the user that he or she is using the "root" directory of "drive C:" (See "Drive letter," on page 65.)

Every software program that is installed on a computer must have a unique name in order to be identified by the operating system (whether using a GUI or not), and this information must also be memorized by the user in order to start each program. In addition, once the user has started a certain program (a word processor, database, spreadsheet, etc.) he or she must also know the commands and control-key sequences required to operate it. For example, in a word processor made by one software publisher F1 might activate help screens, F3 copies text, and pressing control "S" causes your document to be saved. A word processor made by another publisher, however, might use F3 for help screens, alternate F4 + control "1" + "2" + "enter" to copy text, and F7 or F10 to save documents. A word processor made by yet another publisher might use still different function keys and control-key sequences to accomplish the same things. Add to this the commands that must be memorized to operate other programs a person is likely to have on their computer, and you can see why the learning curve for character-based operating systems and software can be substantial.

When using a GUI such as Windows, however, operating system commands and software programs are always displayed on-screen—although a number of windows might have to be opened before you find the command or program you are looking for. Because such information is always accessible on-screen, the user can be far less concerned about having to memorize the available options. In addition, GUIs tend to have consistent user interfaces. Unlike the user in the character-based examples above, a GUI user would have no problem locating and "learning" the on-screen commands needed to obtain help, copy text, or save a document—even if they had never used the software program in question. This is because software designed for use with a GUI uses the same interface that the GUI does. For example, most GUIs display available commands in a single line across the top of the screen, while files and programs appear as icons within the rest of the screen area below (known as the **DESKTOP**). In the upper-left-hand corner of the screen usually appears a selection named "**FILE**" which opens into a window with additional options for retrieving, naming, copying, and saving, files. A similar "menu bar" will appear when you run any software program designed for the GUI. Such an arrangement would have allowed the user of the two different word processors in

226

the previous example to accomplish the same tasks even if he or she was not already familiar with the programs. (Many users of GUIs can actually boast that they have never had to refer to their instruction manuals!)

Such extreme user friendliness does not come without a price, however, because even though GUI-based applications can be very easy to learn, the same features can get in the way and slow the productivity of an experienced user who is less concerned about learning problems than they are with being able to work quickly. This can be especially true since using a mouse to open one or more windows, and then making a selection, is almost always a slower process than it would be to type the same commands. (Most GUIs do allow limited use of typed commands, often called **KEYBOARD SHORTCUTS**, because of the speed advantages.) Many programs are ideally suited to use with a GUI. However, you should also consider your experience level and typing speed when deciding between GUI or character-based versions of similar software products. If you are a beginning typist and/or computer user, a GUI may be ideal. If you are an experienced user and speedy typist, however, you could purchase a GUI-based program only to find that it can't keep up with you and slows you down. (See also "User friendly products," on page 86.)

Multitasking

In addition to the graphical interface, Windows provides extended capabilities that MS-DOS alone does not offer, the major one being **MULTITASKING**. Multitasking is the ability to run more than one software program on the same computer at the same time. This differs from *multiuser* systems, which allow *more than one person* to use the same computer system at the same time (See "Multiuser computer systems," on page 187). With a multitasking system you can switch back and forth between the programs you have running. If, for instance, you were in the middle of typing a letter on a word processor and discovered that you needed some figures from your spreadsheet program and an address from your database program, you could leave the word processor, switch to the spreadsheet program to get the figures you need, then switch to the database program to look up the address, and then switch back to your letter. When you return to the letter, because the word processor has still been running all this time, you will be exactly where you were when you left off. To accomplish the same thing on a nonmultitasking system you would have to stop working on the letter, exit the word processor, obtain the needed information by using the spreadsheet and database programs, restart the word processing program, retrieve the file you were working on, and then find the spot where you left off.

Multitasking allows for additional increases in productivity when, as is often the case, you start a long process running while within one software program and then need to do something else on the computer. For instance, if your accounting program was posting the entries for the month—which can take many minutes on some systems—and you received a phone call which required you to look up information stored in a report on your word processor, you could simply leave the accounting program running and switch to the word processing program. On a nonmultitasking system you would have no choice but to wait until the accounting program finished posting, and then return the phone call later.

Virtual Memory

Another major feature of Windows is that programs are better able to use the computer's RAM memory. Windows does not restrict programs to the 640K memory limit which was long imposed upon most software that runs under MS-DOS alone. Instead, most programs are limited only by the maximum amount of RAM memory the computer will accommodate. Windows also has the ability to create **VIRTUAL MEMORY**. To a computer, and/or a software program, virtual memory looks just like RAM memory. However, virtual memory is actually created by taking advantage of unused hard disk space to simulate additional RAM. Because hard disks are slower than true RAM memory, programs using virtual memory may operate more slowly than they otherwise would.

WYSIWYG

While superior memory management techniques and multitasking are important features offered by Windows, the most visible feature is its graphic interface. Unlike text-based systems where only characters and simple lines appear on the screen—and a keyboard is the primary input device—Windows is entirely picture-based and relies heavily on the use of a mouse (See "Mice," on page 55). Text displayed within a Windows program looks much more like the text on a printed page than the boxy characters you usually see in a text-based program; pictures, drawings, and color are also easily accommodated. This method of display is referred to as **WYSIWYG** (<u>W</u>HAT <u>Y</u>OU <u>S</u>EE <u>I</u>S <u>W</u>HAT <u>Y</u>OU <u>G</u>ET), and is pronounced "whiz-ee-wig." WYSIWYG displays allow you to see what the attributes—such as <u>underlining</u>, **boldface**, *italic*, or even a different typeface—as well as the overall appearance, of a document will look like before you print it. A standard non-WYSIWYG display simulates the above attributes by highlighting text in different colors (on a color display), in different shades of gray on a monochrome monitor, or by marking the beginning of such text with special characters or codes (See "Control codes and characters," on page 28). For typesetters, artist, and others, WYSIWYG displays can save a great deal of time—and paper—and is also why they are so popular for desktop publishing.

Many non-Windows programs will run under Windows, but may not be able to take full advantage of the features offered by programs designed specifically for Windows. While most non-Windows programs can be made to work with Windows, programs designed for Windows will not run under MS-DOS alone, so you must have Windows installed on your computer to run a Windows program.

The most popular GUI before Windows 3.0 was probably that of the Apple Macintosh computer, and is also why the Mac has always been cited for its ease of use and better handling of graphics-related jobs. Because of the instant popularity of Windows for PCs, however, and the fact that a PC running Windows has a look and feel that is very similar to that of the Mac, the already questionable superiority of the Mac for graphics work and desktop publishing is growing more debatable. Before Windows 3.0 most people chose a PC for business and home use while a smaller number of people chose the Mac for graphics and desktop publishing. Now, for many people, it is not a matter of the Mac versus the PC but simply a matter of deciding whether they need a PC with or without Windows.

For all of the advantages Windows has to offer, it does have some drawbacks, a major one being that it requires considerably more computer power than most people are accustomed to using with their regular MS-DOS-based software. Most people who have used Windows agree that, for acceptable performance and speed, you need at least a 286- or 386-based PC that has at least 1 to 2Meg of RAM, plus a hard disk, because, among other things, more CPU time and RAM are required to generate picture-based displays. With a text-based display only the outline of each character on the screen must be stored and manipulated in memory. With a GUI, however, the tiny dots (pixels) which make up on-screen images (See "Pixels," on page 61) *always* fill the *entire* screen. Modern, high-resolution monitors can require the manipulation of over 1 million pixels to create the screen images that you see. Add to this the fact that each of the pixels on the screen is completely refreshed (updated) many times each second, and it is easy to see why some GUIs can literally slow screen response, processing times, and print speed, to a snail's pace on computers with limited memory and a slow clock speed. Even when running on fast computers, programs designed for GUIs almost always run more slowly than text-based versions of the same software.

In addition, almost all GUIs—including Windows—cannot be operated properly without a mouse. Many people feel that their productivity is reduced when they are forced to use a mouse and make menu selections to achieve results that could have been accomplished more quickly by typing on the keyboard. Word processors, databases, and spreadsheets are traditionally text-based programs that can usually be operated with greater speed by using the keyboard. Fortunately, Windows gives people a choice: they can choose to keep using MS-DOS by itself if they don't need a GUI; they can use Windows for running graphics-based drawing and desktop publishing programs; they can run regular MS-DOS software in the non-Windows text-based mode (just as it would run from DOS); or they can install Windows on their computer, use it as an MS-DOS machine, and only run Windows when they need to run Windows software.

In short, although it did not quite live up to the pre-introduction hype mentioned above, Windows is an excellent GUI for MS-DOS-based PCs, and is highly recommended for graphic and desktop publishing applications. It does not take the place of but enhances the MS-DOS operating system by adding improved memory management capabilities, multitasking, and greater ease of use, and is a formidable alternative to the Apple Macintosh for users who need a GUI-based computer.

Chapter 18

PORTABLE COMPUTERS AND LAPTOPS

The title of this chapter uses two names for portable computers as a reflection on the changes that have occurred in the industry since they were first introduced. Although many portable designs—ranging from what is acknowledged as the first "portable computer," the Osborne 1 introduced in 1981, to the Kaypro II, to the Apple Macintosh portable computer and compatibles—have been introduced over the years, MS-DOS-based machines have emerged as the accepted standard in the portable computer industry. We will, therefore, only briefly touch on a few of the important developments that lead the way to today's MS-DOS-dominated portable computer market.

The first portable computer to see widespread use was the Radio Shack Model 100, introduced in 1983. The Model 100 was truly portable, compact (about the size of a large, thick book), battery operated, had the ability to send and receive files to and from other computers, and had a very readable—although small—LCD screen. The Model 100 quickly caught on with news correspondents and writers worldwide because they could carry it to the site of a breaking news event, and even use it while riding an airplane or bus. They could take notes or write an entire article, edit their text and make changes, and then use the nearest available phone to transmit the story to their home office via modem. Even though news correspondents were largely responsible for the success of the Model 100, it became an important tool (and toy) for many others who wanted portable computing power. As much as the Model 100 had going for it in those early days, however, it merely paved the way for the more powerful machines that were to follow.

The subsequent generations of portable computers set about to develop the features needed to make such small devices truly usable and practical for a wider range of users. Even though some of these computers featured disk drives, and screens which could display the normal 80 x 25 characters of text, each one used its own nonstandard operating system and software and lacked compatibility with MS-DOS. The inability to run MS-DOS programs on the early portables meant that few were used for anything more than word processing, because little software had been written for the portables' nonstandard systems.

Unlike the Model 100, which was truly portable in every sense of the word, the first portable computer that was compatible with the IBM PC and MS-DOS—the Compaq computer, introduced in 1983—was about the size of a suitcase, weighed almost 30 pounds, and had to be plugged into an electrical outlet to power its built-in monitor, circuitry, and disk drives. However, because the Compaq was both portable *and* offered an alternative to the more expensive IBM PC, it took the computer world by storm, quickly catapulting Compaq computers and Compaq Corporation to star status with first year sales exceeding 110 million dollars—a first year sales record never before achieved by any American business. Compaq, almost singlehandedly, pioneered portable computers *and* IBM PC compatible technology, and remains today perhaps the most respected and closely followed manufacturer of PCs—portable or otherwise.

Other manufacturers quickly jumped on the portable computer bandwagon in an effort to duplicate Compaq's success. Both the original Compaq portables as well as the copies that were to follow retained the same basic design, which lead to coining of the terms **"TRANSPORTABLE"** and **"LUGGABLE,"** as more accurate descriptions of their "portable" but heavy-to-carry and AC-outlet-dependent natures. These dimensions were reduced by about half with the introduction of the more advanced **LUNCHBOX** portables—which still required AC power but were of about the same size, shape, and outward appearance as an oversized child's lunch box.

Next came **LAPTOP** computers, larger than the Model 100 but small enough to fit in your lap. They were battery operated (and/or rechargeable) units with LCD screens, and lighter (usually 10 to 20 lbs) and much smaller than any of the previous portables. These machines more closely approached the true portability of the Model 100 while offering IBM PC compatibility. But they still needed three major things for truly practical usability: a more practical disk drive arrangement, larger and more readable screens, and the option of a hard disk. Zenith Data Systems broke this final barrier in 1987 with the introduction of its Z-183 line of laptop computers. The Z-183 featured a refreshingly clear LCD screen that was almost as large as that of a standard 12" desktop monitor, a 10 megabyte hard-disk drive (then unheard of in a laptop computer), and a high-capacity 3.5" 720K floppy-disk drive.

Even after the introduction of such well-designed machines as the Z-183, and the even more advanced models that followed, laptops were still considered too limited for everyday business use. Most users rightly felt that laptop computer screens were still too small and too dim to be used in place of a regular desktop monitor for any length of time. The processing speed, disk drive capacity and speed, and memory capacity of most laptops also fell short of the needs of many users. Laptops were considered a high priced luxury by some users, and an auxiliary system to supplement and allow operation away from a desktop computer for others. Few people felt that laptop computers could compete with, or be used entirely in place of, desktop PCs. By 1990, however, portable computer technology had advanced far enough for laptops to offer the same computing power as could be found in most desktop PCs.

The **NOTEBOOK** computer, which as its name implies attempts to approximate the size and shape of a medium- to large-size book, started out with about the same limitations as the first laptops. However, even notebook computers now offer clear screens, ample hard disk size and performance, and plenty of memory capacity. Compaq set the pace here also with the introduction in 1990 of its LTE 386s/20 notebook computer. This machine weighed only 7.5 pounds, featured an Intel 386s microprocessor running at 20MHz, 2 megabytes of RAM as standard, a 3.5" 1.44Meg floppy disk drive, a VGA display, and up to a 60Meg hard drive that actually ran faster than the hard disk drives found in most full-size desktop computers. Like its larger, and formerly more sophisticated, laptop counterparts, the LTE 386s can be plugged into a "Desktop Expansion Base" to become a fully functional desktop computer.

Portable Color Displays

Most computer users felt that the full-size (80 x 25 character), high-resolution screens modern laptops were offering by 1990 were more than adequate for their needs, and that the lack of a color display was not a problem. However, there have always been those who felt that a *high-quality* color display was the last remaining obstacle which prevented a laptop computer from competing with—and/or being used in place of—a desktop computer. Although a number of computer manufacturers had produced laptops with color screens over the years, LCD color screen technology trailed far behind the often crystal-clear one-color screens that had become common on many laptops. Color LCD screens were dimly lit and could not display the variety of colors, or compete with the clarity, of desktop color monitors.

Even this last "barrier" was removed, however, in early 1991 with the introduction of two new laptops by Sharp Electronics, and Toshiba. These machines both featured **ACTIVE-MATRIX** (meaning transistors are actually bonded to their screens, making them very much electronically "active") VGA color LCD displays, as good as, if not better than, the displays of most desktop color monitors. As is the case with most new technologies, these laptops also came with a hefty premium in price, with pre-release prices ranging from $9,000 to $15,000—almost double the cost of similar laptops without color screens. Like early noncolor laptops, active-matrix color laptops will probably first see use by those who have deep wallets and feel that such a machine is a must—or would make the ultimate executive toy. As color laptops become more common, however, and as color LCD technology improves, prices will probably continue to drop until color is a standard feature on most portable computers. In fact, because new-generation color displays are so clear and take up far less space than a conventional screen, it is very likely that similar technology will find its way into desktop monitors and TVs. Perhaps one day—as many in the industry have said for years—we will really use flat screens mounted on the walls of our home or office, instead of the bulky monitors and TVs we have grown so accustomed to.

In any case, it is clear that portable computers are now machines which demand few compromises. Although—as with most electronic devices—you will still have to pay a premium in price for their compactness, laptop and notebook computers now offer the speed, disk-drive options, and clear displays, necessary to meet the needs of all but the most demanding computer users. In fact, by 1991 some retail stores were claiming that as many as 1 out of every 3 new computers they sold were laptops! So if you feel you need a portable computer, and you are willing to pay as much as 40 percent more than you would for a similarly equipped desktop model, it is very likely that you can find one that meets your needs. Just keep in mind the fact that expansion capability (See "Expansion capability," on page 151) is very limited with even the best laptops. Although many can be plugged into

234

optional expansion bays which allow the use of standard desktop circuit boards, this is usually an expensive add-on, and some models do not offer such an option. If you know that your computer will need to have expansion boards added—such as for a tape drive, network, etc.—check before buying to make sure the portable you have in mind is suitable.

OPERATING CONSIDERATIONS
Remember To Turn The Power Off!

While portable computers are electronic devices just as desktop computers are, there are some operational differences that many users tend to overlook—some of which may sound obvious. For instance: It is almost impossible to move a regular computer from room-to-room or building-to-building while it is running because the power cord prevents it. On the other hand, there is often nothing to prevent a new, careless, or forgetful, user from closing their battery-powered laptop computer and walking away with it while it is still running; perhaps destroying their hard-disk drive and the data it contains in the process! (See "Head crash," on page 73) Some portable computers will sound an alarm if you try to close them without first turning them off. However, it is a very good idea to make sure the power is off—by physically checking the on-off switch or the power-indicator light—before you close your portable. This is especially true since to prolong battery life most good portables have power-saving features that automatically shut off the screen, hard-disk drive, and other components, after so many minutes of keyboard inactivity—often referred to as the **"SLEEP MODE."** When automatic shutdown has occurred it is easy to falsely assume that the computer has already been turned off, if you are not careful.

Surge Protection

Portable computers need protection from the same electrical hazards faced by desktop models (See also "Surge protection," on page 134). However, perhaps because portable users do not wish to lug around any more equipment than they have to, surge protection is ignored by the majority of those using portable computers. Unless a portable is advertised as having adequate electrical protection built-in, you will need to make sure a good surge protector is plugged in between the outlet and the computer. If, as most portable users do, you need a surge protector that can easily be carried with the computer, compact models are now available which are designed just for laptops and notebooks.

Avoid Movement While Working

Computers, portable or otherwise, that contain only floppy-disk drives are not easily damaged by movement—and so can be used onboard an airplane, bus, car, etc. Hard-disk drives, however, are an entirely different matter. Despite the fact that advertisements, commercials, etc., would lead you to believe otherwise, few hard-disk drives can tolerate being subjected to movement while they are running. Unless the instruction manual of the portable computer you are using specifically states that the hard-disk drive it contains is designed to tolerate movement, *do not* subject the computer to movement once the power has been turned on. True, the computer *is* portable, but you may have to wait until *after* you reach your destination and have placed the unit on a *stable, vibration-free* work surface before its hard-disk drive can be operated. In fact, at least one model of laptop has been made that featured a switch which allowed the hard-disk drive to be turned off for use while in a moving vehicle—temporarily using only the floppy drive, instead. If the ability to use your portable while onboard a moving vehicle is a must, first make sure that doing so will not cause damage to the hard drive.

Battery Life

A few models of portable computers require AC power—most notably lunch-box designs, or those with color or gas-plasma displays (which consume far more power than regular LCD displays). Most modern portables, however, operate on rechargeable nicad batteries. Portable makers are getting better at providing instructions which tell you how to properly care for batteries. Following, however, is information that will help you achieve the longest operating time and longevity from your rechargeable nicad battery pack.

First, always try to run down the batteries completely before you recharge them. Nicad batteries have a "memory," and will adjust to the use-charge cycle that you subject them to. For instance, if the nicads in your laptop are rated to provide 4 hours of continuous use, and you repeatedly use the unit for only 1 hour before recharging, the batteries' operating time will continue to diminish until they can only operate the laptop for 1 hour (approximately). If you must recharge your portable before the batteries have run down, make sure that as soon as possible you "deep-cycle" the batteries—meaning that you allow them to run down completely and then recharge them fully.

Do not leave the batteries in your portable on charge any longer than the recommended time—doing so could result in reduced battery life and/or damage. Likewise, allow the batteries to recharge fully before operating the unit again on battery power. (Important: Make sure that you fully charge the batteries of a new portable before it is operated for the first time!) It is OK to operate a portable computer while it is recharging—unless it is the first time you are charging the unit, or the instructions say otherwise. If the above procedures are an inconvenience, or you need even greater battery life, many models feature removable battery packs—usually at an additional cost. By charging one pack while you operate the computer on the other you not only avoid running out of power at an inconvenient time, but can easily maintain peak battery life by completely running down each pack before it is recharged.

Handle With Care?

Despite the fact that portable computers are by nature designed to be tougher than desktop units, they are not indestructible. Treating a portable computer like a briefcase or piece of luggage can easily result in a trip to the repair shop that could have been avoided. Handle portables the same way you would any other delicate, electronic device. After all, you wouldn't throw your VCR into the back seat of your car, would you? Portable makers and salespeople have sometimes gone to great lengths to demonstrate the durability of their products, including throwing a computer across the room—while it was running! Nonetheless, the fewer bumps and bruises your portable has to endure the longer it will last, and the greater its resale value will be.

Protective cases are available for portable computers and are an excellent idea if you intend to travel. Handing an unprotected portable over to an attendant for it to be placed into a luggage compartment is a mistake that many people have regretted, not to mention the open invitation to theft and tampering. Even when you are only going from office to office, or from office to home, a case provides excellent protection from dust, dirt, and the weather.

This page intentionally left blank.

Chapter 19

DO YOU NEED A NEW COMPUTER?

OBSOLESCENCE

If you think about it, obsolescence, like beauty, is often in the eye of the beholder. Something that is obsolete to one person may be entirely adequate for someone else, because their needs and perceptions are different. A Model T may not be as fast or as flashy as some of the newer, more modern automobiles, but many people still own, collect, and drive older models and antique cars. If you are concerned about buying a computer system that will quickly be obsolete, don't worry—it will be. In today's rapidly changing world of technology almost anything you buy having to do with computers can be considered obsolete the moment you buy it. Some-where—in the United States, Japan, or elsewhere—someone has probably designed or is preparing to introduce to the market an even more technologically advanced system than the one you are buying. It may be smaller, faster, have more memory, or just look better, but when it is announced everyone will be calling it "The latest in technology." If it actually gets to market, and if it is not full of bugs, and if enough people buy it, and if it proves to be reliable, and if it stays around for awhile and the company doesn't abandon that product line—or go out of business—then, perhaps, just maybe, it might end up being accepted as the latest in technology.

It is because advertisers know how strong the appeal is for people to own "the very latest" that everywhere you look you see the label "New and Improved." But have you also noticed that these same labels stay on products for months, and even years after they were "improved"? While most manufacturers are always exploring ways to improve their products, obviously products which carry these labels cannot be "New and Improved" every time you buy one. The manufacturers realize, however, that people seem to get more satisfaction out of buying products that are perceived this way. The point here is: don't get too worked up over whether or not your system is making headlines as the latest in technology. If you're a computer buff, or you have lots of money you want to spend, or both, then maybe that's OK. Otherwise, the main criteria for judging your system should be how well it can do the job you need it to do and whether it can continue to do what you *need* it to do into the *foreseeable* future. The average useful life of a microcomputer system is generally considered to be around five years—or less. This does not mean the system will fall apart or stop running in that time, but that you will have outgrown its capacity, or a newer system will have come out that can do a better job. If, though, when you purchase a system, you carefully determine what your needs are now, and what they realistically will be in the *foreseeable* future, you will have a system that can provide you with years of productive use. Even if something better comes out in the meantime, your system should still be able to provide you with reliable service for the applications it was selected for. The word *foreseeable* is used here because no one can be 100 percent sure of what his or her future needs will be. And, of course, expected needs may change. For instance, even though a system you purchased two years ago is still working fine, you may find that, in order to use a powerful new software package, different and/or more powerful hardware is needed. Competition can also change your needs and prompt you to replace a system even though it is doing the job it was purchased for. If your competitors, by using more advanced computer equipment, are able to gain a substantial edge over you, it would surely be unwise not to update your own system.

When you are reviewing the ability of a system to cope with future growth and expansion in your business, remember to be realistic. Sure, you probably wouldn't complain if your business grew 1,000 percent in the next two years, but a more accurate profile of your future computer needs will most likely come out of checking your growth in the past. If the business is a new one and you have no past data to use, you can look at the growth similar businesses are experiencing and add on a little for optimism. After all, if your business does grow 1,000 percent, and you did manage to outgrow your existing computer system, it is likely that you would also be in a better financial position to spend more money for a larger system with greater capacity.

What If You Think Your System Is Obsolete?

If you think your system is obsolete, the first thing to do is try to determine why you think so. Is that just what someone has told you? Has a newer system been made available? The only thing that really makes a computer system obsolete, for *you*, is that it is not capable of performing the work you need it to. Before investing in a complete new system first see if there is something you can do which, for a reasonable cost, would allow you to use the system for your purposes— *reasonable* meaning either what you can afford to spend, or a cost significantly less than buying a newer system. Obviously, if a system is beyond repair, replacement is the *only* alternative.

The most frequent reasons given for considering a computer obsolete are incompatibility with other equipment or a lack of speed. Either the system never was compatible with the most popular standards for hardware and software, or, since its purchase, newer standards have become more popular. It's also possible that your model is no longer manufactured and parts and software are now hard to come by. If that's the case, make sure any repairs or extra equipment that has to be purchased to get your system running will not cost more than a new system. Also check to see if your system has a history of frequent breakdowns and repair; if so, it may be unwise to make anything but a small investment in getting it running. If you would simply have to purchase new hardware—such as a printer, modem, etc.—in order to make the system operational, and that hardware is compatible with the computers and standards being used today, then you could always use the newly acquired equipment with a newer system should you decide to purchase one.

As far as speed goes, if the system has really become just too slow under the load of more advanced software, or more users, you may have few options but to buy a new system. If, however, the reduction in speed has been caused by a defective, improperly configured, or outdated, component you may be able to get more use out of the system by reconfiguring, repairing, or replacing the component causing the slowdown. While a number of things can cause a computer to be slow, the most common is the hard-disk drive. As they are used, hard disks run slower due to a process called **FRAGMENTATION**. This is normal. However, if it gets bad enough it can slow a system down to almost a crawl. Fortunately, it is easily corrected using a disk-maintenance utility program. It is also possible that the hard disk is not set up properly and is not operating as fast as it should be. If you suspect this is the case you may wish to have a service technician check your hard disk (although you might first wish to try the defragmentation process that some disk-maintenance programs provide).

There is also the problem of software compatibility; the system you have may not be compatible with new software you need to run. Often, however, the publisher may still make a version of the software you need that will run on your system, but it is available only by special order. Check with a dealer who offers the new software. If they don't have or can't get a version suitable for your hardware, ask the publisher if such a version is available; often, it will be. If not, there is one other possibility.

Software designed to run on one type of computer can sometimes be modified, or what is known as **PORTED**, to another machine with which the program is not ordinarily compatible. The people to ask are the publishers of the software. They may offer this as a special service or may do it for you as a custom application. If not, custom programmers might help, as can companies which specialize in porting software; you can find their advertisements in computer publications under "Conversion."

WHY ISN'T YOUR COMPUTER BEING USED?

Around the country—in office corners and basements, in garages at home, and numerous other likely and unlikely places—there sit what are known by many people as the "Dust Collectors." These are computers whose use has either been abandoned altogether, or which are being used only occasionally. Sometimes these systems are in almost daily use, but for purposes far removed from—and far less important than—the applications they were originally purchased for. For example, a system might have been purchased to handle complex inventory needs but instead has been used only for casual word processing.

Assuming you wish to make greater use of your investment, it would be wise to try to determine why things ended up this way. There are usually only two reasons—either the people whose responsibility it was to utilize the computer fully, or the computer system itself. Believe it or not, one of the biggest reasons systems fall into disuse is simply a lack of interest. The people who originally thought a computer would be a good idea might not have kept in mind the obvious fact that someone would have to operate the system. It could have been that when the computer was first installed the intended operators had most of their time tied up in other projects. Or perhaps it was not fully understood what work was to be done on the computer. There also could have been a lack of training if the system required it. Whatever the reason, it usually falls into the category of lack of follow-through. If you think this might have been the problem, do some backtracking to find out what went wrong.

Find out, for example, if the system itself was installed properly. If training or instruction was needed, did everyone receive it who should have? Did the people expected to use the system express a lack of interest, or unwillingness to use it? If you determine reasons like these are why things never got off the ground, make a list of everything you think would have to be done in order to put things back on track. And, as you work on getting the system into regular use, remember that without proper follow-through the same thing may happen all over again.

The other possible reason a computer system is not being used is some unsolved problem with the system itself (probably one that wasn't corrected properly when the system was first installed). This could have been a hardware or software problem—or both. Care should first be taken, however, to determine whether an obstacle that appears to be a hardware or software problem is not actually due to a lack of operator training. Hardware and software combinations, despite the efforts of their manufacturers to make them easy to use, are still very complex underneath. It is easy for these kinds of user-caused problems to arise when the system is first being installed and is operated by inexperienced people.

When a computer system is installed, the hardware and software must be adapted to, or **CONFIGURED**, to each other and to the specific needs and requirements of the users. For some applications you can literally just take a computer out of its packaging and start to use it. In most cases, however, some—perhaps many—configuration or **SETUP** changes will have to made first. These changes usually involve both the hardware and software. Because of the enormous number of different software and hardware combinations, it would take several encyclopedia-sized sets of books to even try to describe the setup procedures for each. Even then, hardware and software specifications change constantly, making what was accurate information at one time invalid a short time later.

244

Many setup requirements are often customized just for your specific system or application. To give you an example, here are just a very few of the more common things that may have to be configured for your system: The computer itself must have the proper internal equipment, namely plug-in circuit boards (cards), installed correctly. These include the minimum amount of memory required, the correct video board for the monitor you are using, boards for any floppy or hard-disk drives, and any boards required for connecting external devices to your computer—such as printers, disk drives, modems, etc. Any device connected to your computer must itself be configured properly in order for the two to work properly. Cables or power cords used must be selected specifically for your system and application.

When all of the necessary components are installed there are sometimes **DIP SWITCHES** whose settings must be checked. These are not the same as the more familiar power on-off switches but tiny devices arranged in rows on the circuit boards themselves. They are usually too small to move with your finger, so the tip of a pencil or pen is most often used. There are also software switches. Software switches cannot be touched, but are instead changed by using special setup software.

Thus, you can easily see that there are many things that can make a computer system appear not to be operating correctly, when it really is just a setup or configuration problem. To avoid these kinds of problems, when you install new hardware or software be alert for any setups or fine tuning that need to be performed by the user, which will be described in the instruction manual. You should also be aware that some setups are primarily intended to be performed by a service technician. Lastly, even though a great deal of systems hardware and software comes in packages that say "User Installable," it may not be advisable to attempt it yourself. Often these same packages say that incorrect modifications made by the user will void the warranty. If you do not know exactly what you are doing, or if the instructions provided are not clear or understandable to you, call, or take your system to, the dealer or a service technician.

Once a system has been properly installed and is in operation, a problem similar to incorrect setup may appear that is easy to avoid if you know about it, namely, that some hardware and software will work with other hardware or software only if it is a *compatible* model or version. For instance, you may have purchased your computer system with MS-DOS version 2.1 some time ago. Now, years later, you purchase a new program. You're looking forward to using your new software, and have no problem installing it on your computer. Then, you notice that some things in the program just don't seem to be working right, or perhaps the program doesn't run at all. Before blaming it on the new software program, check to see that your version of DOS is compatible with the requirements of your new program. In this hypothetical example, the problem occurred because the software program required the newer 3.3 version (or higher) of MS-DOS that was made available since you first purchased your computer. Always make sure the hardware and software in your system are compatible versions; the specifications for equipment or programs will tell you which version of which operating system or which model of equipment is required (as well as other details of memory, power, etc., needed). Every piece of hardware or software is given a model or version number by its manufacturer or publisher. If a version number is not visible you can trace it through the manufacturer or publisher by using the serial number.

WHAT IF YOU'RE STUCK WITH A COMPUTER YOU DON'T WANT?

The reason doesn't matter, but you have a computer or other piece of equipment that you no longer want. What do you do? If you're of a generous and kind nature, or you could use a write-off, or both, you might consider giving or donating the system to someone who would have a use for it. In a large company, even though a system might have become inadequate for one department, perhaps it could still provide valuable service in another department or area. If this is not practical, trading it in on a new system, or selling it, are, theoretically, the next most likely alternatives.

Actually, however, because computer technology changes so fast, some dealers don't accept trade-ins of small systems. If they did, they would in turn be stuck trying to sell systems that were perhaps nearly obsolete or that would be competing with their inventory of newer systems. If you think new cars depreciate rapidly, wait until you see what happens after a computer has been "around the block" a few times. Remember that pocket-sized calculator that used to sell for over $100.00 when it first came out, and now, due to improved technology and mass production, can be bought for as little as three dollars? Well, computers aren't likely to drop that much in price, but they're not far behind either. Mainframes are a different story, but the resale value of a small computer can quickly depreciate to just a few percent of the original selling price.

Take heart, however, all may not be lost. Just as one person's loss may be another's gain, so it often is with computers. Someone, somewhere, may be looking for a system just like yours—possibly even for the same features you have found you have no use for. Perhaps they already have a lot of money invested in a compatible system, so, instead of buying something new, they are trying to find more equipment compatible with what they already have. The problem is letting people who could use a system like yours know you have one for sale.

You can advertise a computer system in a number of ways, but try the easiest and most economical first. This would include a talk with the computer dealer you purchased your system from, or, if he's not interested, a dealer who sells or once sold the same kind of system. Also check with those same dealers about local computer **BULLETIN BOARDS** you could use to advertise a system for sale. These are computerized message services and information centers which people can dial up and access with their computers. There is no cost for using most bulletin boards of this type. If you don't have the equipment to do this—a modem and communications software—you can probably find someone that would be willing to place your advertisement on a number of bulletin boards using their own equipment.

Next, there are the publications which contain a classified section. The best ones to use for a computer are your local newspaper, business publications, and, naturally, computer publications. Pick the one that best fits your budget, and that you think would appeal to the kind of person who would be looking for a system like yours. Don't, for example, place an ad for a home computer in a national publication that is primarily read by the executives of large companies. Likewise, it would do you little good to place an ad for a $120,000 computer in a publication that's read mostly by the users of smaller systems and PCs.

You will probably also find listed in your local phone book, or advertised in computer publications, businesses that specialize in buying used systems or selling them for a commission (which you pay, of course). This may be one of the fastest ways for you sell your system. (See "Resource list," on page 273.)

Above all, in selling used computer equipment, have patience. It may take time to find a buyer—or for them to find you.

This page intentionally left blank.

Chapter 20

CONSULTANTS

Computer consultants come in many varieties and specialties. Some specialize in small business systems. Others concentrate on specific areas such as manufacturing, accounting, publishing, etc. The main service a consultant provides is to supply clients with all the information needed to obtain and maintain suitable hardware and software. The consultant may simply assess your needs and provide you with a report and recommendations, or may actually be involved in supervising the design, purchase, and installation of the computer system.

The advantage to using independent consultants (who, being independent, are by definition not connected with someone who sells the actual hardware or software) is that they are under no pressure to recommend a particular piece of equipment or service provider. Instead, like an independent insurance agent, they are free to utilize any companies, products, or services they determine might best fit your needs. If the computer-related project you are facing is a large one, and you either do not know where to start or would find it too time-consuming to carry it out yourself, talking with a consultant to get some suggestions might not be a bad idea.

Your first appointment with a consultant may be free of charge if he or she is locally based (and if it is an exploratory discussion rather than one devoted to solving specific problems). If the software firm you are using has an in-house consulting service they may provide free consulting services as long as you are buying your system from them. You can choose to have a consultant do as much, or as little, as you would like. Keep in mind that because you are paying for their time, and the information they obtain, you may be obligated to pay regardless of whether or not you eventually decide to use their recommendations. You can expect to pay between $40 and $100 an hour for most consultants. In larger cities, or for a consultant knowledgeable about a specialized area, you can expect to pay more. Make sure that any information obtained by the consultant is provided to you on an ongoing basis and in a timely fashion. This way, you will still have use of the information even if you should decide not to use the same consultant all the way through the completion of the project.

Freelance programmers, although they may not think of themselves in such terms, are consultants able to help in many situations, and can be found through computer dealers, local schools with computer science departments, and computer bulletin boards. They may also sometimes be found through software houses or computer service firms (although such services usually prefer to sell their own time). Freelance programmers may be more flexible in assisting you with getting your system running than a service firm, and their rates are normally lower. On the other hand, the freelancer is probably not supervised by a more skilled person, as probably would be the case if he were affiliated with an established firm. The skill and experience of a freelancer also may not be on the same level as that of a true professional service provider. In hiring a freelancer be sure to take the precautions mentioned below for assessing any service provider.

As you start finalizing your plans, don't allow optimism and haste to cause you to overlook good business practices. In particular, make sure that everything that could later cause a problem is reduced to writing. No one can remember everything. You reduce agreements to writing not as a mere formality but so that everyone fully understands what is to be done, and so that important points are not forgotten as time goes by. See to it that changes in specifications and any other matters that affect the agreement are also confirmed in writing by the supplier or yourself.

It is very important to keep in mind that a custom program may take longer than you had planned. The main reason is that as the project progresses, or even when it is finished, you will almost certainly discover things you would like to change. Depending on how good an information-gathering job you do, and on how well your needs are communicated to the programmers and understood by them, some things may not have been conveyed properly at the start of the project. Or, there may be features you find you need, but they become evident only after you have worked with the finished system for awhile.

The main advantage offered by a custom program is that you can adapt it to your needs, or expand upon it as you see fit. In this sense it is often said that a custom program is never really finished because, often, it is constantly being changed, modified, and improved, especially in large companies. Be careful, though, not to get caught up in a premature circle of making constant program modifications, reviewing them, and then making additional changes. For one thing, you will have to pay for each change or modification made to the program. For another, you may end up spending time and money to make a lot of changes that you later find were unnecessary. The best approach is to get the program running as it was first designed (unless, of course, serious flaws are obvious), and then use it for awhile. As you use the program write down all the things you think you want changed or added, and then review the proposed changes in a few weeks or so. This way you can better evaluate which modifications would actually improve the program, and which modifications would add little value to, or detract from, it. In evaluating the program and possible changes, take your time and be thorough. The results will be well worth the effort, and far less expensive than doing things wrong and having to pay to make corrections later.

Unless you are very lucky, your custom program will have at least a few disappointing features. Perhaps certain parts of the program run slower than you thought they would, or you feel you would like to reduce the number of steps you must go through to perform a certain operation. Considering the complexity of situations where you have to resort to custom programming and the difficulty of communicating between yourself and the technicians, it would probably be impossible to avoid some disappointments. But you can avoid most problems by being thorough in the steps you take in the information-gathering and design process. If you do feel, however, that you are not getting what you paid for, get a second opinion from another professional in the computer field. He or she should be able to tell you if in fact the program appears to have been written properly and, if not, what steps to take. This is where a well-written contract is important. Your contract should have as many, *specific*, legally enforceable, provisions as possible that spell out what kind of program you want, what you expect it to do, how much it will (or could potentially) cost, and how long the entire process will take.

Whichever methods you choose to obtain custom services, make sure the people you choose can deliver what you need. The best way to do this is by looking at work they have already done for others which is similar to, or applicable to, what you are doing. As in architecture, in programming no amount of training can take the place of experience. If whomever you choose has done work that is similar to your application, and someone else is satisfied with it, the same programmer can probably do a satisfactory program for you. Although you may not be familiar with the technical points of programming, common sense and good judgment alone can be very helpful in selecting a service provider.

If, for instance, you know that a prospective software house has written a financial statistics program that has proven satisfactory, it's reasonable to assume the same people could provide you with an accounting package. If, however, you need a program written to control the manufacturing equipment on your shop floor and your prospective programmer has worked only on financial programs, it is very likely your application falls outside of his area of expertise. There are times when your selection of programming services will be limited because your application may be so unique or specialized that you can find no one who has done similar work. If it comes down to this, make sure the people you decide to deal with have worked with enough somewhat similar projects so that they have some feeling for what will be required for your application.

Once you have found someone who can provide you with the kind of program you're looking for, make sure he can also do it in a way you will be satisfied with. You might find that while two different firms can provide you with the same program, you like the methods of another firm better. Perhaps one firm has shown you other software they have created, and you liked the "look and feel" of their programs, or the ease of operation that they provide. Or, one firm might offer so many days of free training for the software they create. The bottom line is that you must determine what you will be satisfied with.

You would also want to know if the firm you choose can deliver the application within your time frame. Keep in mind that, no matter who does the work, once the program specifications are nailed down it is going to take a certain amount of time to create it. There is little you can do to cut time and still maintain quality, short of having the people involved work longer hours or adding people to the project (who will more than likely have to be pulled away from other jobs they are already working on), both of which will cost you more money. You can, however, get at least a general idea as to what the firm's workload is, and certainly they should tell you when they plan to begin work on your job. Once all the appropriate factors have been included in your written agreement it will be up to the service provider to make sure they meet their commitments.

Remember also that shopping for someone to do a custom program, and having one successfully created, are only the beginning. Once the project is finished, will the people you choose be able to provide training that will meet your requirements? Will they be the ones responsible for installing their software on your computer system, and seeing to it that everything runs smoothly? How available will they be afterward? You may need additional training at a later time, or, more than likely, you may need additional programming as you become more familiar with your new software. Obviously, you will be taking a chance on not being able to secure any post-installation services if you use a firm that does not impress you as being reasonably stable and run by professionals committed to their firm's continuation and growth.

Your involvement in the creation of custom software will make a big difference in how smoothly things proceed when the project starts, because your contractors probably will not be familiar with your individual business. Even if they have produced similar packages for others, your specific needs will almost surely be different because you run your business in a manner unique to yourself.

Someone, whether yourself or a person with authority to make decisions whom you designate, will have to be *readily available* to assist the people designing your system. Many people overlook this important point, only to be disappointed if the resulting system does not meet their expectations. A computer system and/or software can be designed only on the basis of information you provide about your needs and your business operation. Again, don't hesitate to involve other people who will be using the finished system; their input is very important.

This preprogramming stage is also a point where you may have the opportunity to save a considerable amount of time and money. The section on buying a computer suggests that before you start looking for software you reduce *all* of your requirements to writing. This advice will prove just as valuable when putting together a custom program and new computer system. In the initial stages the people designing your program will simply be gathering information about your business and what your needs are. Once gathered, this information will be used to actually write the necessary program code. The more you can organize this information— the better you can define exactly what you are doing now on paper, and how you would like for it to be done on a computer—the less work the programmers will have to do. In fact, you may be able to not only reduce the amount of time required, but in some cases reduce the cost of the finished program by as much as half. Before starting to write down your requirements, however, ask your programmers to give you a memo outlining exactly what information they will need, and how you can go about preparing it in a format that will save them time.

Chapter 21

COMPUTER PROGRAMMING

Everyone Used To Program

In contrast with today's readily available software, at one time everyone who wanted to use a computer also had to be a programmer. This was because, for one thing, there was no such luxury as being able to go to the local computer dealer and pick up the latest software program. For another, the first people to use computers were engineers and scientists with unique and special problems to solve, so it would have been unlikely that their computer-using colleagues would have already written programs that suited their needs. There were few professional programmers and, often, budgets were limited and there was no money to hire someone who did nothing but program—so everyone did his or her own.

Even when computers and programmers became more common, if you wanted something done on the computer, even something like a simple report, you had to go through the right channels—assuming that you ranked high enough to directly request such a use of the computer department's valuable resources. If your request was accepted, a programmer would have to write the necessary instructions (the program) for the computer. Then, your job would have to wait its turn until the computer was free and the program could be run to produce the results you needed. And if there was an error in the programming, or something went wrong with the computer, the process would have to start over again.

Today, almost everyone can have direct access to a computer—even at home or on his or her own desk. Having to go through someone else to get to the computer has all but been eliminated. In most cases, there are programs already available to do just about anything you might think of; they don't have to be written every time you want a computer to do something. Perhaps, though, you are curious about how such programs are made. You might even be interested in trying to make one yourself. If so, this chapter will give you enough of an introduction so that you will understand what programming is, and whether or not it might be for you.

SOURCE CODE

With the possible exception of instructions written in machine language (see below) the actual instructions a programmer writes to create a computer program are referred to as **SOURCE CODE**. This is simply the program in its *original* written or printed form, or as it appears on the screen. A printout of a program (the source code) is also often referred to as a **PROGRAM LISTING**, or just **LISTING**.

MACHINE LANGUAGE

In the early days, scientists and other professionals who worked with computers could just as well have been considered computer engineers and technicians. None of the modern methods or tools were available. This meant that, in addition to programming the computers, the users also had to have considerable knowledge about how computers worked. They were also required to write excruciatingly detailed programs based on that knowledge in what is now called **MACHINE LANGUAGE**, although relatively little of such programming is done today.

Machine language takes you as deep as you can go into the inner workings of a computer. It is the lowest level of programming because you are talking directly to the computer in its own language. Machine language was invented because it was easy for computers and electronic devices to use. It is not, however, the easiest language for people to work with. Machine language is based upon directly controlling the thousands of electronic on-off switches inside a computer or other programmable electronic device. Naturally, this requires a good working knowledge of the binary system (See "The binary system," on page 15).

To use machine language, in addition to knowing the binary system you also need to have a knowledge of the inner workings of the computer, including the way memory is handled. For the most part, RAM memory can be thought of as one long string of bytes—512,000 bytes, 640,000 bytes, 1,000,000 bytes, or however much your computer happens to contain. Each byte occupies 1 location in the computer's memory. In the house/mailbox example (See page 20) used earlier in the chapter about the binary system, the houses, each with its own mailbox, represent a location in the computer's memory. Now, however, instead of just eight houses, picture a row of houses that runs the length of the longest street in your town. Just as street addresses start at 0 and go up, so do the memory locations inside a computer. Some areas of memory are reserved for special use, while other areas are free to be used by software—such as a word processor, spreadsheet, etc. These locations are actually referred to as **MEMORY ADDRESSES**. Unlike actual street addresses, however, memory addresses always increase in increments of 1. Unused addresses are referred to as **AVAILABLE MEMORY**, or, sometimes, as **FREE MEMORY, REMAINING MEMORY**, or **UNUSED MEMORY**. Some areas take up only a short range of addresses—a block or two—while others may span an entire neighborhood or more. The lower-numbered memory addresses are usually restricted for use by the computer and its related components. Those memory locations contain such information as which keys have been pressed, what time it is, and other internal information the CPU uses constantly. Further down the block are the areas of memory left relatively free for almost any use. This is where machine-language programs are written, stored, and run. A diagram of the memory a computer contains, as well as what it is used for, is referred to as a **MEMORY MAP**.

In machine language you are almost entirely on your own; few things—even if simple—are done for you. For instance, if you wanted to print the word "HI" on the screen, you would first have to break the process down into its simplest components. This would mean finding out what binary codes would represent the letters *H* and *I*. Next, because every location on the screen has a corresponding location somewhere in memory, you would have to find out which memory locations—which parts of the neighborhood—the computer uses for its screen display. You must then determine where on the screen you want this word to appear, recognizing that screen memory starts at the upper left-hand corner of the screen and continues left to right, line by line, until the lower right-hand corner is reached.

For simplicity's sake, let's plan to print the word *HI* in the upper left-hand corner of the first screen. That way we can just start at screen memory location 0. (Computers always start counting at 0, not 1.) Since each line is 80 characters long, and there are 25 lines on the screen, our screen ends at screen memory location

1,999 (80 x 25 = 2,000, minus 1 because we started at 0). But, before we can print a word, we must first clear the screen. We don't want our word to print out on a screen that's already messy from something printed out by another program.

Since in machine language you have to do everything yourself, in order to clear the screen we must write a program which starts at 0, and places the number *32*, the decimal ASCII code for a blank space, in each memory location through 1,999. To do this we must convert the decimal number *32* into a binary number, 00100000, that the computer will understand, and write a program to store it in each screen-memory address in order to erase the screen. Finally, with a freshly erased screen, we can place the binary number which represents the code for the letter *H* in location 0. This will make it appear in the very upper left-hand corner of the screen. Next we place the binary number which represents the code for *I* in location 1; this will make it appear immediately after *H* on the screen. The screen is now welcoming you by saying "HI," and you have just completed your first machine-language program!

As you can see, programming in machine language is time-consuming, requires a good deal of knowledge about the inner workings of the computer, and, of course, lots of patience. Why then, does anyone still use machine language if he doesn't have to? Because systems software, the kind that actually tells the CPU and other components what to do, has to be programmed in machine language. This includes the special instructions stored in **ROM (READ ONLY MEMORY)** chips which enable the system to begin operating before instructions can be retrieved from a floppy or hard-disk drive, the operating system, and related software.

Machine language is also used for applications which require a great deal of speed. Machine language executes extremely fast because it is written directly in a language the computer can understand. Therefore, no translation has to take place between what the programmer writes and what the computer can run. This is why almost all fast-moving video games and graphics programs are programmed in machine language.

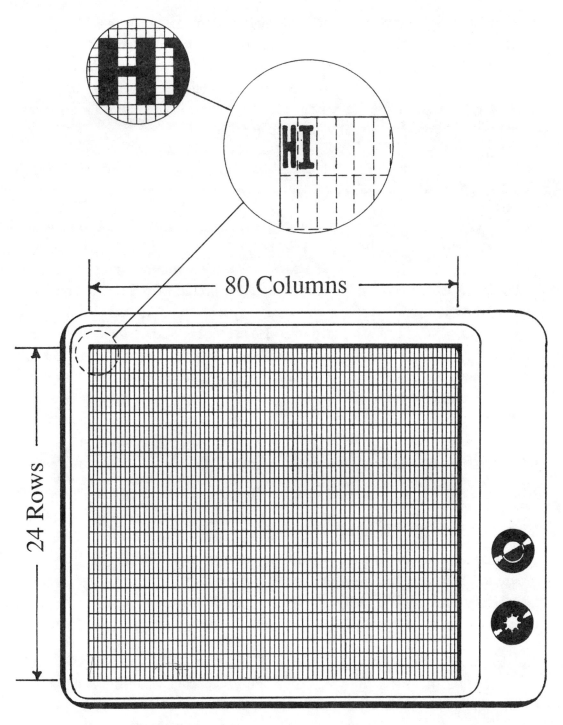

80 Columns

24 Rows

How a typical screen is arranged

Machine language was the pioneering language of computers. It is the language you must use if you wish to talk directly to a computer, and requires an intimate knowledge of how computers work. For these reasons, and because relatively few people program in machine language because it is considered difficult, there are some who learn it for no other reason than the challenge and satisfaction they get from having such a special skill with computers.

ASSEMBLY LANGUAGE

Because machine language is so awkward for humans to work with, as time went by a new alternative arose called **ASSEMBLY LANGUAGE**. All of the things that can be done with machine language can be done with assembly language. However, assembly language is much easier for people to work with because, instead of being limited to only the binary system—the numbers 1 and 0—a programmer using assembly language can also use the **HEXADECIMAL** numbering system. In addition, the programmer is no longer limited to just using numbers. Easier-to-understand symbols can be used to represent the more-difficult-to-remember machine-language instructions.

OTHER COMMON COMPUTER LANGUAGES

Even though it offers advantages, assembly language still requires all of the same knowledge needed to program in machine language; it is simply a way of making things easier for the programmer. That is why, as more time went by, the people who programmed computers continued to develop new, and easier, ways to program. The results of these efforts are seen in the large variety of programming languages we have today. Many languages were developed for specific purposes, others were designed from the start to be used for many different applications.

The language **FORTRAN (FORMULA TRANSLATOR)**, for example, was developed primarily for engineering and scientific applications, and other purposes which require the extensive use of numbers and calculations. **COBOL (COMMON BUSINESS ORIENTED LANGUAGE)**, on the other hand, was designed to be a language better suited for business users. COBOL was easier to program in, read, change, and operate for the kinds of information most businesses use. **Pascal** (developed by Niklaus Wirth, and named after French mathematician Blaise Pascal) and **BASIC (BEGINNER'S ALL-PURPOSE SYMBOLIC INSTRUCTION**

<u>C</u>ODE) primarily saw early use as learning tools but developed into more widely used general programming languages. Even after small computers started to become widely available, most languages being used were still those developed earlier for large mainframes. BASIC and Pascal were among the first programming languages that were practical for use on small computers.

HIGH-LEVEL LANGUAGES

The number of programming languages available has now grown into the hundreds. However, they do share some things in common. Most languages can be classified as **HIGH LEVEL**, which means they are far removed from machine language and are much easier to program in than machine language, or **LOW LEVEL**, meaning they are closer to machine language and are therefore not as easy to program in. Some languages—like the mainframe-oriented language relatively new to micro-computers, referred to simply as **C**—fall somewhere in the middle, in that they display characteristics of both high- and low-level languages. All of the languages mentioned in "Other Common Computer Languages" above are considered high-level languages—with the possible exception of **C** which was just mentioned. The C language also has the ability to extend into the low-level spectrum of machine language. "Low level" does not mean that a language has less capability than a language that is considered a high-level one. It simply means that the higher-level language will probably be easier for a programmer to work with, but provide less easy access to machine language-like functions. All languages, with the exception of machine language, must be translated from the conventional language used to make programming easier, into the machine language the computer can understand. Programming languages which remain in their original format until they are run are referred to as **INTERPRETIVE** languages and programs, while those that are first compiled before being run are referred to as **COMPILED** programs; the differences are explained in the sections that follow.

Interpretive Languages

Probably the best example of an interpretive programming language is BASIC. Such languages are called *interpretive* because programs written in them remain in their English-like format. Program instructions are translated (interpreted), while they run, into the machine-language instructions the computer understands, by a special software program called an **INTERPRETER**. Then the computer is able to execute the instructions, and, if called for, generate results. As you might imagine, this process is extremely time-consuming. Because computers are so fast, however, many people are not aware of, or are not inconvenienced by, the inefficiencies of interpretive languages, just as most of us are satisfied with the performance of the automobiles we drive, but to someone who has driven a race car anything less seems sluggish and unresponsive.

Despite their inefficiency, interpretive languages offer a major advantage: they execute instructions "as is." There is no wait between the time you finish writing a program in an interpretive language, and being able to see it run on the computer. Because there is no difference between the source code and the instructions the language executes, you can also test certain instructions by typing them directly into the computer. This allows you to make sure the instructions work before taking the time to integrate them into the program. Features like these make interpretive languages ideal for people just learning how to program.

Compiled Languages

Compiled languages include all of the programming languages we have discussed so far. (Some languages, such as BASIC, are available in both interpretive *and* compiled versions.) Compiled languages run much more efficiently than interpretive languages because they eliminate the time-consuming process of converting each instruction into machine language as it is read. Instead, they work by first converting, or **COMPILING**, the *entire* finished program completely into machine language, which the computer can then execute directly. The part of the language which performs this conversion is referred to as the **COMPILER**. Once compiled, the program is always ready to run, and does not have to be compiled again (**RECOMPILED**) unless changes are made to the original source code.

A compiled program will usually run many times faster than the same program written in an interpretive language. In most cases, however, compiled programs written in languages like C, BASIC, Pascal, etc., do not run as fast as programs written directly in machine or assembly language. This is because, in order for a compiler to do what it does, it has to operate according to a defined, yet general, set of rules to generate machine language code. Just in the compiling process alone some efficiency is lost. Also, any time you make something more general there are certain tasks for which it will be less suited. For instance, if you live and drive in the city and own a car, it will serve you fine. If, however, for some reason you need to drive on rough country back roads or need to haul something, your car will probably do the job, but less efficiently than a specialized vehicle such as a pickup truck would. This is why some programs are still written in assembly or machine language. A program written in a high-level language may not always be fast enough, or may lack the needed ability to directly control the computer as machine language does.

SOFTWARE PORTABILITY

An advantage of most compiled languages is **PORTABILITY**, the ability to run on many different computers. This characteristic comes from the fact that machine language is what is known as **HARDWARE DEPENDENT**, or **MACHINE DEPENDENT**. Because machine language resides in, and relies on precise relationships with, other components, a machine-language program that will work on one computer will not run on another of a different design. Put another way, machine language expects to find everything in the same place every time it is run. The computer's memory, and the memory map and addresses used, like those in the previous house examples, must always be the same for machine language to function properly. If they are not the situation is the same as it would be if you moved to a different neighborhood and expected to find the same identical houses that were on your old block, complete with the same addresses.

While a program that has been compiled and converted to machine language will run only on similar, and compatible, computers, the source code (See "Source code," on page 256) is a different matter. If the language has been around for a while and is a popular standard (like C, Pascal, BASIC, etc.) it probably is available for almost any computer system. The original source code can then be entered into the new computer and compiled by a version of the language that runs on that machine. Because the compiler is made for that particular computer the resulting machine-language program will be specifically tailored to work with that machine's internal hardware and components. This means you can literally take such a program, even one written on a home computer, and compile and run it on even the largest mainframe. The word "standard" is used here because while there are published and international standards for most major languages, many software publishers change or improve something about the way the language works to create an **ENHANCED** version. When this is the case, the instructions which are enhanced may not run properly, if at all, on another publisher's version of the same language.

A compiled program includes yet another advantage over one written in an interpretive language—theft protection. If programs are written to sell to others (which includes virtually all commercially available software) or if the programs contain proprietary information, compiling them is an excellent security and protection measure, because compiled programs have been returned to machine-language form from the high-level languages in which they were written and are thus harder for dishonest competitors to use as a basis for their own programs. The original source code of a program not only more closely resembles the English language but usually also contains comments and notes (**SOURCE CODE DOCU-MENTATION**) put there by the programmer to explain how each part of the program works. Machine language, on the other hand, contains few English-like words, and is understood by relatively few people even in the computer world. It is unlikely that most people would even know how to view the machine-language instructions of a program, and, even if they did, it is very difficult to program in machine language, as you have seen. Undocumented machine language is virtually impossible for even a very experienced programmer to convert back into source code. Thus, the original program, and any unique, copyrighted, or proprietary ideas it might contain, are available only to those who wrote it or have access to it.

One last word on compiled languages: There are a few interpretive languages also available in a compiler version. Likewise, a number of languages that were originally designed to be compiled have now been made available in interpretive versions. If compiled languages are so much better, why would anyone also make an interpretive version? Because interpretive versions, being interactive, allow program developers to quickly test, or debug, part, or all, of their program code. (To **DEBUG** is to remove errors from a program. See more below in "Bugs And Glitches.") Since beginning programmers find themselves constantly testing and debugging programs, using an interpretive version of a program is a good way for them to learn a more powerful compiled language while still maintaining the easy access and flexibility offered by an interpretive language.

BUGS AND GLITCHES

You will undoubtedly hear the terms **BUGS** and **GLITCHES** mentioned from time to time when you're around computers. These terms are used to describe something that has gone wrong. A **BUG** is generally an error that exists in the design of a software program—or the software contained in the ROM chips of hardware—and will persist until it is fixed. A **GLITCH** is usually temporary in nature; can be caused by electrical problems, malfunctioning circuitry, etc.; can be hard to find (as can a bug); and may occur only once. Problems generated by bugs and glitches can range from a minor and insignificant bother to a programmer's or technician's nightmare which might take many hours or even days to find and correct.

(In case you're wondering where the term *bug* came from, it's more literal than you might think. In the early days when computers used vacuum tubes, the glow they gave off proved irresistible to moths and other insects, which would sometimes get into the computer room. Attracted to the warmth and glow of the vacuum tubes they would often fly too close to them, get zapped, and fall into the circuitry—where the insects caused numerous shorts and other problems. Back in those days when someone said "We're still getting the bugs out of the system," they sometimes meant it!)

YOU'VE PROBABLY ALREADY WRITTEN A PROGRAM

It's very likely that you've already done some kind of programming. Programming is really just a matter of issuing a series of precise instructions on how to do a particular operation, whether it be an engineering calculation or something less complex. A modern microwave oven is a simple example: when you enter cooking instructions you are, in effect, writing a small program that will be **RUN** (that is, executed, or started), when you press the start or cook button. You might, for instance, place a frozen casserole in the oven when you're home at lunch time, and then enter something like this:

Turn on at 4:15 PM
Switch to the defrost cycle
Adjust the power level to low
Defrost for 30 minutes
Adjust the power level to medium
Defrost for 15 minutes
Switch to the cooking cycle
Keep the power level at medium
Cook for five minutes
Switch to the holding cycle
Keep warm until I get home

These instructions, along with those used for calculators, adding machines, VCRs, stereos, and many other devices, could be thought of as simple programming. Programming a computer is really no different; you must simply give it instructions it can understand and carry out. Following is a very simple program written in BASIC:

```
1000 REM ***** this small program prints *****

1050 REM ***** a greeting on the screen   *****

1100 CLS

1200 PRINT "HI"

1300 END
```

Unlike machine language, high-level languages such as BASIC tend to be much easier to understand and write in. High-level languages come closer to looking more like ordinary English, as in the above example which uses the BASIC language command **PRINT**. The line numbers are used by the interpreter—or compiler—to keep each set of instructions separate. **REM** is simply an instruction that tells the computer everything on that line is a remark (a note), and should not be executed along with the other instructions. **CLS** is a common BASIC command which tells the computer to clear the screen (**CLEAR SCREEN**). Compare this with the same program we did in machine language earlier: Quite a bit easier, right?

LEARNING TO PROGRAM

There are many reasons why people learn to program. Some think it might be a good career. Others feel that if they could write their own programs they would have more flexibility in what they could do with their computer systems. A lot of people just do it to learn more about computers. Whatever the reason, there can be a lot of satisfaction in watching a program run that you know you created. And programming can indeed be considered a "creative" function, for once you have learned the basics of any computer language you can build on them to design your own computer program. You might write a program that no one has ever written before. Or, you might see if you could write a program for your own use that is better than what's already available. It is probably this creative ingredient that appeals so much to people who decide to learn how to program.

The individual twists programmers give to their work are also what makes programs difficult to categorize. Two checkbook programs, for instance, might both perform the same functions but work entirely differently. For example, when allowing the user to write a check, one program might simply allow the person to enter the amount on a plain screen, while the other program actually draws a check on the screen and lets you fill it out the same way you would a check from your checkbook. The possibilities, the ways in which programs can be different or better, are limited only by the ability of the programmers who write them.

Programming is not only best learned by doing, but it can be learned *only* by doing. Only by actually putting into practice each new concept as you learn will you be able to clearly grasp the logic and capabilities of programming. If you have a computer of your own, so much the better. You will also find that programming can be very time-consuming—in the beginning because you are learning, later on because good programs take time, and, lastly, because if it should turn out you like it, programming has a way of becoming almost addictive to some people. It seems that for a programmer to spend every available moment working on his latest project is the rule rather than the exception. For the most part, this is just a matter of the programmer's trying to get something done while creative ideas are flowing. On the other hand, a marriage breaking up because a spouse was spending too much time working on a computer is not unheard of! Obviously, as with most things in life, there has to be a sensible balance.

PASCAL

What language is best for learning purposes? Probably one of the best languages for learning how to program is **Pascal**. It was originally designed as a teaching tool to make it easier to learn proper programming techniques, and, unlike some teaching languages, has features which force the learning of good programming habits. Pascal soon became so popular, however, that enhanced versions were developed which made it a useful language suitable for general-purpose and business use.

Pascal also uses and teaches structured-programming concepts (see below), and, as you will see, learning a language which allows you to build a good foundation would prove extremely valuable if you went on to career in programming. Another big benefit of learning Pascal is the ability to apply what has been learned to other languages and areas of computing. This is possible because Pascal instructions and commands are common to many other structured languages.

STRUCTURED PROGRAMMING

Good programming habits include a technique known as **STRUCTURED PRO-GRAMMING**, designed to bring increased order and efficiency, as well as accuracy, into programs. Structured programming came about primarily as a response to programming in the business world. Many businesses were finding a great deal of inefficiency in their programming departments. Programs often took too long to write, were not well designed, required too much time to debug, and were difficult to maintain. (**PROGRAM MAINTENANCE** refers to the process of periodically modifying and improving a program, as well as correcting any bugs that have been detected.) Good programming practices require not only that a program be fully documented when it is first written, but that the documentation is updated and maintained along with any changes made to the program. This fact was frequently neglected before structured programming became common.

Structured techniques encourage putting more thought into the planning and development of a program. When the program is finally written, it is done using what is referred to as the **TOP DOWN** approach. This simply means the program is logically organized so that the execution of instructions starts at the beginning, or top, of the source code, and continues down through the various instructions until the last lines of the code are executed. This discourages programmers from designing instructions that "jump" around indiscriminately from one section of code to another. Programs that do a great deal of jumping from place-to-place, and from instruction-to-instruction, are usually not well designed.

Source code can be written as just one long program. This is considered bad practice, however, because it makes the program overly large and awkward to work with. Debugging also becomes much more difficult because you have to search through the whole program in order to find even a single error. In structured programming, programs are written in many small sections, called **MODULES**.

Modular programs have many advantages. Large programs can often take many months to write. It would not be good to spend that long writing a program only to find out that something doesn't work the way it's supposed to. If the program is divided into modules, however, each module can be written and debugged separately. One module might handle all screen displays, while another might handle organizing information that needed to be sent to the printer, etc. Another big advantage is that different modules can be given to different programmers to write. With this **TEAM APPROACH,** often used by software houses as well as companies which have their own programming departments, a number of people working on the same program can finish a project in far less time than if it were written by one or just a few people as one long program. When all members of the programming team have finished writing, the modules are brought together to form the complete program, ready for final overall debugging.

ONE LANGUAGE FITS ALL?

In many instances, no single language is exactly suited to an application. In these cases, a frequent solution is to write the program using more than one programming language. For instance, the portions consisting of mostly straightforward business functions might be done in COBOL. Other areas which require more extensive mathematical and analytical functions might be done in FORTRAN, while the sections of the program which require extremely fast sorting and searching for stored information might be written directly in assembly language. The program is designed so that, when complete, all of the various modules function together as one. The fact that different languages were used will probably never be apparent to users.

BUT WHAT ABOUT BASIC?

Almost everyone has heard about BASIC at some time or another, yet it remains a source of confusion to many people. Why? Perhaps because BASIC first enjoyed widespread use, and became widely known, through the increased availability of home computers. Unlike previous languages, which could only run on mainframes and large computers, **BASIC** was one of the first that could be adapted to operate within the more restricted capabilities of home and small computers. This paved the way for small computer users to enjoy—many for the first time—the availability of a high-level language. In fact, as mentioned earlier, BASIC stands for **BEGINNER'S ALL-PURPOSE SYMBOLIC INSTRUCTION CODE**. It was designed to be easier to learn than other languages.

Over the many years since its introduction, all of the above reasons have combined to make BASIC popular with a great many people—so versatile and popular that it was actually built into many popular home computers and, even today, is often included with the purchase of business systems as well. There is more than one side to this story, though. Because BASIC has been so closely associated with home computers and beginners, programmers accustomed to using structured business-oriented languages which feature compilers often feel BASIC is not even worth considering for anything but the smallest applications. These two programming language "camps" take sides at times, with one side saying they use BASIC for everything, and it isn't necessary to program in another language, while the other says BASIC belongs on toy computers, and has little use or place on business systems. The question is, who's right? As is often the case, both sides are partly right.

Let's look at the home computer users first. They invested the time and money to buy something on which they could learn not only about computers, but also how to program. Many hours were probably spent learning what the system could do, and how to use it. Because BASIC in all likelihood came built right into the computer, naturally, this is the language they started to learn. Being their first experience with computers, they probably had little knowledge of the various other programming languages available—or the advantages they had to offer. In time, they eventually learned how to use and program their computer. Some programs they may have purchased at a store, while they proudly wrote other software themselves.

Both the computer and the programs they wrote proved more than adequate for anything a person might want to do at home. A lot of people used their computers for business, others actually installed their home computer at the office. For all practical purposes, these small computers, and the languages they were programmed in, seemed as if they could handle whatever was needed. Sure, larger systems ran many times faster, but the argument here was always: "For the small amount I have invested in this system, I can wait." Place yourself in their shoes: You are the proud owner of your own computer system, and it does everything you need it to do. For the uses mentioned above a home computer, as well as programs written in BASIC, would probably be all a person needed. But then along comes the programmer of a large business system, which dwarfs even the most sophisticated home computers by comparison. Even though BASIC is a highly versatile language, for the programs this business is running only a large computer and structured languages such as COBOL, FORTRAN, C, or Pascal will provide the convenience, speed, and reliability that is needed.

You can now see why both sides have valid points. But the question still is: should I use BASIC or not? As was just shown, the answer to that question will depend on what your needs and applications are. If, for instance, you own a small home computer, BASIC probably came with it, so, if you will not be using more powerful machines, you have little choice in the matter. On the other hand, if your system is a little larger, and it appears you might be writing more serious applications, it might not be a bad idea to see if one of the higher-level languages such as Pascal or C is available for your system. If almost all of your computer software needs will be in the form of serious applications, or involve business use, a structured language such as C or Pascal would no doubt be the only way to go.

There is nothing wrong with using BASIC as long as you make sure it is matched to an application suited for it—usually small, specialized, or limited applications. That leaves the remaining question of what to do if someone offers you a program written in BASIC. If it is for business use there may be a number of things you wish to know first. One of the greatest sources of confusion with BASIC, or any other language, for that matter, is the fact that different versions are likely to exist. Most are enhanced versions which have many more capabilities than the language did when it was first developed. As you may have guessed, the original version of BASIC was easily categorized as not being suitable for business. But because BASIC has been improved many times since then, this is not true of all versions. Some versions of BASIC have had many of the features of structured languages added—most notably the versions of Basic produced by Microsoft. Many versions of Basic are also now available in compiler versions. A number of the publishers of these enhanced versions have even chosen to call them **BUSINESS BASIC**. This would imply that they contain all of the features necessary to handle the more sophisticated applications of most business programs.

Unfortunately, because every publisher's idea of what a "business" version of BASIC should be capable of is different, the only way to be sure a program written in BASIC will be adequate is to see it run and find out how well it has worked for others. Arrange for a demonstration. Find out whether the program has the features you need. Does it run fast enough? Does it run on your system as presently configured? Do you think you will soon be using a different type of computer system? If so, is the program portable enough to run on that computer also? The questions above should be asked regardless of how a program was written. But, in this case, you will need to pay even closer attention to the answers. Only then can you determine if the version of BASIC being used will offer the capability your application needs. As far as having a custom program written for you in BASIC, since in this case you can still choose one of the more traditional business languages with known capabilities, it might be best to stick with a language that has already proven itself for applications like yours.

RESOURCE LIST

This book has been carefully written so that as much information as possible will be as meaningful tomorrow as it is today. Obviously, in the fast-changing world of computers, this could not have been the case if numerous references had been made throughout the text to specific software, hardware, or other services or products, that are likely to change. Therefore, the text concentrates on general information and concepts rather than specific brand names.

The information that follows is designed to provide a brief reference to products and services that the average reader is likely to need, or that may be hard-to-find or not immediately come to mind when needed. Naturally, any of the information below is subject to change. However, the companies listed—and their products and services—are well known, and many were the first to introduce such a product or service to the computer industry. At the time this book went to press all of the phone numbers and addresses were accurate.

Reading materials:

The Computer Glossary
By Alan Freedman

Webster's NewWorld Dictionary of Computer Terms

PC Magazine	800 289-0429
PC World Magazine	800 234-3498
Byte Magazine	800 257-9402

(An excellent resource, but primarily intended for experienced and technical readers.)

Backup software and equipment:

Fifth Generation Systems   800 873-4384, 504 291-7221
10049 N. Reiger Road
Baton Rouge, LA 70809
(Makers of "Fastback Plus" backup software.)

Peter Norton Group   800 365-1010 or 800 411-7234
Symantec Corporation
10201 Torre Avenue, 95014
P.O. Box 161690
Cupertino, CA 95016-1690
(Makers of "Norton Backup" backup software.)

Central Point Software   800 445-4073, 503 690-8090
15220 N.W. Greenbrier Pkwy., #200
Beaverton, OR 97006
(Makers of "PC Tools Deluxe," a combination disk-utility,
 disk-backup, and integrated software package.)

Colorado Memory Systems, Inc.   800 432-5858, 303 669-8000
800 S. Taft
Loveland, CO 80537
(Makers of tape backup systems.)

Mountain Network Solutions   800 458-0300, 408 379-4300
240 East Hacienda Avenue
Campbell, CA 95008
(Makers of tape backup systems.)

Data-recovery, disk- and file-management, and diagnostic software:

Peter Norton Group   800 365-1010 or 800 411-7234
Symantec Corporation
10201 Torre Avenue, 95014
P.O. Box 161690
Cupertino, CA 95016-1690
(Makers of "Norton Utilities.")

Paul Mace Software   800 523-0258, 503 488-2322
400 Williamson Way
Ashland, OR 97520
(Created the "Mace Utilities" software,
 and offers data-recovery services.)

Central Point Software   800 445-4073, 503 690-8090
15220 N.W. Greenbrier Pkwy., #200
Beaverton, OR 97006
(Makers of "PC Tools Deluxe.")

Data-recovery services:

Paul Mace Software   800 523-0258, 503 488-2322
400 Williamson Way
Ashland, OR 97520

ONTRACK Data Recovery   800 872-2599, 612 937-5161
6321 Bury Drive Suite 15-19
Eden Prairie, Minnesota 55346

Computer insurance:

SAFERWARE   800 848-3469, 614 262-0559
The Insurance Agency, Inc.
2929 N. High Street
P.O. Box 02211
Columbus, OH 43202

Stay-in-place-while-you-work keyboard protection:

SafeSkin Keyboard Protector   214 339-0753
Merrit Computer Products, Inc.
5565 Red Bird Center Drive, Suite 150
Dallas, TX 75237

On-line information services:

CompuServe Information Service   800 848-8199, 614 457-8600
5000 Arlington Center Blvd.
P.O. Box 20212
Columbus, Ohio 43220

Prodigy Services Company   800 776-3449
445 Hamilton Ave
White Plains, N.Y. 10601

The GEnie Information Services   800 638-9636
401 N. Washington
Rockville, MD 20850

Delphi   800 544-4005, 617 491-3393
3 Blackstone Street
Cambridge, MA 02139

Computer rental companies:

Micro-Rental USA   800 62-RENT-1 (627-3681)
24481 W. 10 Mile Road
Southfield, MI 48034-2931

General Electric Rent/Lease   800 GE-RENTS (437-3687)
3800 179th Street
Hammon, ID 46323

Used-computer brokerage and exchange houses:

National Computer Exchange   800 359-2468
118 E. 25th Street 10th Floor
New York, New York 10010

Boston Computer Exchange   617 542-4414
Box 1177
Boston, Massachusetts 02103

Index

Chips 13
        production methods 32

Circuit boards 151, 207, 208, 209

Clicking (with mouse) 55

Clock speed 33-34

Clock, internal 33

Clock-calendars 33

COBOL (Common Business-Oriented Language; a programming language) 260

Codes, embedded 28

Color graphics adapter (CGA) 64

Color monitors 64-65

Columns (horizontal characters) 61

Command-driven programs 91-92, 226

Commands 24

Common Business-Oriented Language (COBOL) 260

Communications channels 39

Communications bus 39

Communications pathways 39

Communications, external (for internal, see System communications) 173-186

Compaq Corporation 232

Compaq portable computer 232

Compatibility
        of hardware 147, 148, 245
        of software 85, 148, 245

Compatible, defined 85, 148

Compiled programming languages 262-263
        compared with interpretive languages 262-264

Compilers and compiling 262

Composite monitor 64

Computer brokers 276

Computer magazines 273

Computer on a chip 207-208

Computer programming 255-272
        appliance programming 265-266
        assembly language 260
        compiled languages 262-263
        high-level languages 261

Configuring hardware/software 174, 193-194, 244-246

Connect-time 178

Constant 25

Consultants 249-254
  advantages of 249
  allow ample time for 250
  finding 250-253
  preparing for using 253

Continuous forms paper 125

Control codes 28

Coprocessors (see also Math coprocessor) 34

Copy protection and piracy 106

CP/M (control program for micro-processors; an operating system) 83

CPS (characters per second) 120

CPU (central processing unit). See Microprocessors and CPUs.

Crash, head 72, 73

Cray Research Corporation 47

CRT (cathode ray tube) 60

Cursors 53-54

Custom programming. See Custom Software.

Custom software 112-115, 251-254
  cost 112
  finding a supplier 113-115
  indicators of need for 112-113

Customizable software 109-110

Cut and paste (a word processor feature) 93

D

Daisy-wheel printers 122

Data 24
  how stored in computer 35-36, 201-205
  mass storage devices 65-77
  transmission 174-176

Data bus 39

Data loss and its avoidance 66, 69, 71, 72, 73, 77-78, 146
  recovery software 274

Data recovery services 275

Database managers 94

Graphics drivers 62

GREATER THAN (a logical operator) 22

Green screens 62

GUI (graphical user interface) 225, 228-229

H

Hackers 106

Hard disks. See Hard-disk drives.

Hard-disk drives 71-74
    accidental erasures 77-78
    advantages over floppy disks 72
    capacity 74
    data loss and recovery 72, 73
    described 71-72
    determining requirements 74
    formatting needed 77
    handling 73

Hardware (see also individual devices, such as Computers, Keyboards, Monitors, Floppy-disk drives, etc.) 51-79

Hardware-dependent software 84-85, 263

Head crash 72

Help screens 88

Hex. See Hexadecimal numbering system.

Hexadecimal numbering system 26-27, 260
    compared to decimal system 27

High-level programming languages 261-263
    compiled languages 262-263
    interpretive languages 261-262

Home computers 49

Host computers 181

I

IBM (International Business Machines) 219

IBM AT computers 223

IBM PC computers (see also Personal computers)
    compared with Macintosh 220-221
    operating system 85

IBM PS/2 computers
    features 223
    market share 224

Inkjet printers 121-122

N

Networks 196-205
file sharing 196-197, 200
hardware and its configurations 196
local area networks (LANs) 196
nodes 198
sizes 196
wide area networks 196

Nonvolatile memory. See Read-only memory.

NOT (a logical operator) 22

NOT EQUAL TO (a logical operator) 22

Notebook computers 233

O

Off (a bit state) 22

Off-line (an operating status) 128

Off-the-shelf software 107-109

On (a bit state) 22

On-line (an operating status) 127

On-line information services 182-183, 276

Ones and zeros in computer logic 13

Operating systems (see also specific systems, as CP/M, MS-DOS, UNIX, OS/2, XENIX) 39, 82-86
DOS distinguished from OS 83-84
history 82-83
machine-language-programmed 258
ROM-based sometimes 86
software 82-86

Optical mouse 57

OR (a logical operator) 22

OS/2 (Operating System/2)
and MS-DOS 223
market share 223-224
Osborne 1 portable computer 231

Output 158

P

Page description language (PDL) 121

Page-white screens 65

Pages per minute (PPM) 121

Paper feeders 125-126

Paper, computer types 125

Parallel communications 40

Pascal (a programming language) 268

Software licensing and ownership 116-117

Source code 256, 263

Spelling checker (a word processor feature) 93

Spider legs 32

Spikes, electrical 134

Spills damaging computer or disks 133

Spreadsheets 102-104

State (of a binary bit) 16

Static electricity effects 136-137

Stop bit 28

String 25

Structured programming 268-269

Subtraction symbol (-) 20

Supercomputers 43, 47

Superminicomputers 46

Surge protectors 134, 235

Switching speed 135

Syntax 24

System communications 39-42
    parallel 40
    serial 40

Systems software. See Operating systems.

T

Tandy Corporation 46

Tandy Radio Shack-80 (TRS-80) computer 46

Tape cartridges 143

Tape drives 143

Tech support. See Technical assistance.

Technical assistance 152-155

Telephone lines and computers
    control and security of 185-186
    dedicated lines 181
    modem requirements 181

Television interference by computers 137

Temporary memory. See Random access memory.